Turn West, Turn East

MARK TWAIN AND HENRY JAMES

Turn West, Turn East

MARK TWAIN AND HENRY JAMES

BY HENRY SEIDEL CANBY

BIBLO and TANNEN
NEW YORK
1965

© Copyright 1951 by Houghton Mifflin Co.

Reprinted 1965 with the permission
of the publishers by
Biblo and Tannen Booksellers and Publishers, Inc.
63 Fourth Avenue   New York, N.Y. 10003

Library of Congress Catalog Card Number: 65-23485

Printed in U.S.A. by
NOBLE OFFSET PRINTERS, INC.
NEW YORK 3, N. Y.

Acknowledgments

I WISH TO ACKNOWLEDGE with thanks the generous permissions of the publishers of the books mentioned in this work from which brief extracts have been made. I refer especially to the trustee of the Mark Twain Estate and Harper and Brothers, Charles Scribner's Sons, the Oxford University Press, The Harvard University Press, Alfred A. Knopf, Inc., and Little, Brown and Company. These books are all listed in the brief bibliography at the end of the book.

I am indebted to the courtesy of both the Yale and Harvard Libraries. To Bernard DeVoto I owe particular thanks, not only for the use of his books but for his especial knowledge of the unpublished manuscripts of Mark Twain gained when he was Custodian of the Twain Papers. He has been kind enough to read and criticize my manuscript. His successor, the late Dixon Wecter, had completed before his death a book on Mark Twain's youth, and his widow by her knowledge of the contents has advised me on my own study. Especial indebtedness should be registered to the encyclopedic information contained in *The James Family* of the late F. O. Matthiessen, published by Alfred A. Knopf. I have been helped also by many talks with the late Henry James, Jr., Henry James' nephew, and with a number of friends and associates of both Henry James and Mark Twain. For the right to reproduce John La Farge's portrait of Henry James at eighteen, I am indebted to the Century Association of New York. I thank Yale University for the right to reproduce the photograph of the young Samuel Clemens, taken probably in his early twenties, and very possibly when he was a pilot on the Mississippi, and known as a "dandy."

To Dr. S. Marion Tucker I am grateful for his fruitful reading of my manuscript, and also to my wife, Marion S. Canby, for her helpful criticisms, and to Mr. Siegle Fleisher of Harvard for his laborious task of checking my quotations and references.

HENRY SEIDEL CANBY

Killingworth, Connecticut

Table of Contents

Introduction

PLUTARCH, that eminent Greek who, as Emerson said without meaning disrespect, prattled history, wrote his famous *Parallel Lives* of noble Greeks and Romans at the end of the first and the beginning of the second century A.D. He was the inheritor of the great Greek culture, a citizen of a Roman Empire which in his own day reached the peak of wealth and power and was consciously responsible for world leadership between the Atlantic and the deserts of central Asia. He was only one of many who asked the Roman equivalent of the current question, "What does it mean to be an American?" but, being happily ignorant of the economic interpretation of history, he was able to concentrate on an explanation which suited his genius as well as his education, and became, as Perrin, his translator, says, the greatest of ethical portrait painters. His consummate art was to make "deeds and words, whether authentic or not, portray a preconceived character — a more or less idealized character." In short, he was essentially what we call a historical novelist; and to make his style "denser," as Henry James would say, he constructed his greatest work in parallel lives of Greeks and Romans, born some centuries apart, but in the same stream of Mediterranean history, the same moral climate, and facing situations of great resemblance. His interest, like a first-rate novelist's today, was essentially in men and women in action and the results of such action. He wrote to please and instruct, and indeed his book has been one of the most successful of all time, and a notable influence upon later creative literature as well as upon history.

There is a parallel with the United States and the Roman empire of c. 100 A.D. too close to need overemphasis. Christianity and the Industrial Revolution between them, and with "assists" too numerous to mention, have made a new society, science has shrunk the planet and has increased power and liability in almost equal proportions, yet Julius Caesar would probably be more at home in the nineteen-fifties than Eleanor of Aquitaine or St. Thomas Aquinas. And once again, to give up generalizing for observable fact, a single nation has become the wealthiest and perhaps the most powerful on earth, and has been forced (reluctantly to be sure) into responsibility for world leadership. And the old questions that historians and philosophers and poets and dramatists and novelists have always asked are pertinent again. "Upon what meat doth this our Caesar feed?" — why, and how, and in what likeness, and to what end was our present conditioned by our past?

It is certain that the economists, the psychologists, the sociologists do not have all the answers: Plutarch was content to show the effect of character upon environment, and of environment upon character. If he treated his rather fluid sources freely and invented, or rather interpreted, when his imagination required it, his argument is always *ad hominem* and he has persuaded at least sixty generations of the essential truth and unquestionable interest of his men and women.

The task of Plutarch, even though one could give fifty years to it, as he seems to have done, is too great in this overgrown world for one man or one book. But we can borrow from the amiable and perspicacious Greek without attempting to rival him. If it is American men and women that interest us, and especially men and women morally, not economically, considered, and imaginatively projected in the great formative century of our present Republic, the nineteenth, then our best source is in fiction, which of all the literary arts we have created most abundantly, and on the whole best. And of the many possible choices of subject, there is one peculiarly American; indeed it is widely recognized as indigenous to our New World civilization. The American way of life is a European culture surprisingly altered by a turn to the West which continued across an ocean and a continent. And American culture ever since it became self-conscious has sent its favored sons and daughters back to the richer and older home for fresh intellectual stimulation. Also, it is characteristic of a mobile nation that every progressive American family has at some time or another, or in some of its members, turned either West or East. They have, especially in our earlier history, made themselves new men and women by Western experience. Or they have tried (many of them) to make themselves more civilized by going back for nourishment to the sources of our culture.

As it happens, there are no more excellent examples of this than the families of Mark Twain and of Henry James. And no more happy instances of the great contrast than Mark and Henry themselves, for both are highly articulate, both close observers, both creative to a high degree, and both are almost humorously exaggerated as representative of the Turn West and the Turn East American. Also, both were novelists of manners — not mere romanticists who belong really to no time or place. They came from the same moral climate, although Henry James was brought up in a hothouse and Mark at the back door of a Sunday School. They belong, actually, in the same stream of pioneer American history, although Mark plunged in more thirstily than any of his contemporaries in literature, and Henry fought the current until he could scramble out. And for a final return to Plutarch, the difference between Henry s old New York, Newport, and Cambridge, and Sam Clemens' life in printshops, on the Mississippi, or in the mines of Washoe and the newspaper offices of San Francisco soon after the gold rush, was sufficiently in contrast to offer some of Plutarch's advantages in comparing the Greece of earlier centuries with imperial Rome. And of course the men were violently in contrast in temperament, in their art, in their strengths, in their weaknesses, and in their excesses, of which both had plenty. Neither would or could read the other. Everybody else read Twain and only the élite have as yet read Henry James. Mark was often offensively American. Henry shocked even his family by his patina (it was only a patina) of Britishness. Yet both men will live in literature by best describing what each called American innocence for an increasingly curious world.

It is unwise to let a thesis hamper the full development of critical biography in a book like this, and I do not intend to do so. It is the men, their personalities, and their art, and for this somewhat specialized discussion, the American impulse behind both of them, that particularly interest me. The plan of parallel lives and parallel chapters is, however, more than a device. It is a good way in which to make more definite the virtues, the faults, and most of all the significance of both writers. Both are Americans of our most vigorous century — Henry James much more than has been supposed. Without the creative imagination of Mark Twain especially, but also without the perceptiveness of Henry James, we would know much less of the human background of twentieth-century America. And if the new Russian method of reducing man to a workable formula for a dominant state is worth intense study, certainly the U.S.A. and its recent past offers the most interesting view of human nature evolving with dynamic power and in reasonable freedom. The divergent views and still more divergent experience of Mark and Henry in the same half-century, seem to sharpen the significance and project the qualities of each writer.

Turn West, Turn East

MARK TWAIN AND HENRY JAMES

Chapter I

MARK TWAIN'S YOUTH

THE BEST brief biography of Samuel Langhorne Clemens was written by himself. It is to be found in a fragmentary copy of a letter sent to an unknown correspondent probably in 1890, and published in Albert Bigelow Paine's biography on pages 915–916. It is a fair guess that someone had been reading *A Connecticut Yankee in King Arthur's Court*, published the year before, and wanted to know why Mark did not stick to boy's-life on the Mississippi with which he was really familiar. If Mark replied what he had said elsewhere, that he had known all the heroes of King Arthur's Court on Mississippi steamboats, it was in the lost part of the letter. But the word "familiar" evidently stung him. He had familiarity enough with all kinds of life to equip a novelist:

> I confine myself to life with which I am familiar when pretending to portray life. But I confined myself to the *boy*-life out on the Mississippi because that had a peculiar charm for me, and not because I was not familiar with other phases of life. I was a *soldier* for two weeks once in the beginning of the war, and was hunted like a rat the whole time. Familiar? My splendid Kipling himself hasn't a more burnt-in, hard-baked, and unforgettable familiarity with that death-on-the-pale-horse-with-hell-following-after, which is a raw soldier's first fortnight in the field — and which, without any doubt, is the most tremendous fortnight and the vividest he is ever going to see.
>
> Yes, and I have shoveled silver tailings in a quartz-mill a couple of weeks, and acquired the last possibilities of culture in *that* direction. And I've done "pocket-mining" during three months in the one little patch of ground in the whole globe where Nature conceals gold in pockets — or *did* before we robbed all of those pockets

1

and exhausted, obliterated, annihilated the most curious freak Nature ever indulged in. There are not thirty men left alive who, being told there was a pocket hidden on the broad slope of a mountain, would know how to go and find it, or have even the faintest idea of how to set about it; but I am one of the possible 20 or 30 who possess the secret, and I could go and put my hand on that hidden treasure with a most deadly precision.

And I've been a prospector, and know pay rock from poor when I find it — just with a touch of the tongue. And I've been a *silver* miner and know how to dig and shovel and drill and put in a blast. And so I know the mines and the miners interiorly as well as Bret Harte knows them exteriorly.

And I was a newspaper reporter four years in cities, and so saw the inside of many things; and was reporter in a legislature two sessions and the same in Congress one session, and thus learned to know personally three sample bodies of the smallest minds and the selfishest souls and the cowardliest hearts that God makes.

And I was some years a Mississippi pilot, and familiarly knew all the different kinds of steamboatmen — a race apart, and not like other folk.

And I was for some years a traveling "Jour" printer, and wandered from city to city — and so I know *that* sect familiarly.

And I was a lecturer on the public platform a number of seasons and was a responder to toasts at all the different kinds of banquets — and so I know a great many secrets about audiences — secrets not to be got out of books, but only acquirable by experience.

And I watched over one dear project of mine for years, spent a fortune on it, and failed to make it go — and the history of that would make a large book in which a million men would see themselves as in a mirror; and they would testify and say, Verily, this is not imagination; this fellow has been there — and after would cast dust upon their heads, cursing and blaspheming.

And I am a publisher, and did pay to one author's widow (General Grant's) the largest copyright checks this world has seen — aggregating more than £80,000 in the first year.

And I have been an author for 20 years and an ass for 55.

Now then; as the most valuable capital or culture or education usable in the building of novels is personal experience I ought to be well equipped for that trade.

I surely have the equipment, a wide culture, and all of it real, none of it artificial, for I don't know anything about books.

This scrap of autobiography is like most autobiographies. It tells only what the author most happily, or most unhappily, remembered. Yet for a picture of Sam Clemens, later Mark Twain, it has two advantages. In its occasional boasting and frequent exaggeration (Sam for example was only an amateur at pocket-mining) it is highly characteristic of the writer, and even more so in its tone and style, which for lovers of Mark are unmistakable. And the reader will note that Sam's adventures and misadventures are described only as potential material for Mark Twain the writer. Like Tennyson's Ulysses, he had been familiar with

> Cities of men
> And manners, climates, councils, governments.

And surely "I am a part of all that I have met" would very well describe Mark the reporter. When he came to write, he had that stock of familiar information upon which a novelist's imagination has to play if his work is not to be mere fantasy.

This book of mine, like Mark's letter, is an attempted answer to those who wish to read and estimate his writings justly and with penetration. It will emphasize what made him a writer, leaving general biography to others. Plutarch lets his narrative flow toward a battle or political or moral crisis in the life of his heroes. With Mark Twain, or Henry James, or any creative writer, his achievements are his books. No one writes of such a man unless he has published something memorable. The mute, inglorious Milton, like the unpublished great poet in Captain Stormfield's heaven, has no recognition or biography in this world. Tom Sawyer and Huck Finn are from our point of view more important than the author himself.

The limitation of this first chapter to youth is somewhat misleading. Psychologically in some important aspects, Mark's youth never ended until the day of his death. Olivia Langdon, that flower (and vine) of New York State womanhood, knew him as wife, mother, and censor of his literary conscience, knew

him more intimately than anyone else. She called him through
all their long life together by the pet name of "Youth." Yet
when he married her and settled back to exploit his first real
success with *The Innocents Abroad,* what might fairly be called
an extended adolescence came sharply to an end. For thirty-
four years he had not only wandered (he would always do that
but usually in her company), he had been a professional vagabond living by his wits, whose purpose had been to make
money, but still more "for to admire an' for to see" — "admire"
in its old sense, as Kipling used the word, of "wonder" at the
infinite varieties of the by no means always admirable creature
man. This adolescence of thirty-four years is the subject of
this chapter.

2. A BOY IN THE BACKWOODS
AND ON THE RIVER

Sam Clemens was born in the struggling log village of Florida,
Missouri, on November 30, 1835. Until he was four years old,
and was taken to live on the great river at Hannibal, his childhood was normal for thousands upon thousands of children
whose parents or grandparents had crossed the Alleghenies before the Civil War and were settling the great central land
which stretched to the Indian country beyond the Mississippi.
This central land, the Middle West, was of the same general pattern from the western slopes of the mountains through
Ohio and Kentucky and Tennessee on to the prairies and the
plains. It had been the greatest hardwood forest in the world,
and still enclosed among settled farms and hacked-out clearings
great tracts of wilderness. Even near the villages it was wild,
but not savage, not dangerous. It was conquered land, con-

quered from the Indians, the French, the British, but more
importantly, conquered from nature. Back from the village
settlements and the country and river towns, life and its human
abodes were still crude and raw. If these backwoods settlers
were not still pioneers, they lived like them, and on slight excuse would move on West again. But this frontier life was
hearty in spite of malaria and typhoid, agreeably free, and
rough, if sometimes disagreeably tough. Sam's father's family
had brought a tradition of literate, courteous Virginia with
them into Tennessee. His mother had been a lively Kentucky
girl, famous for her dancing, at home in the new frontier culture as her husband never became. Both, like at least half of
their neighbors wherever they settled, were still mobile; seeking
some western star of prosperity. The family barouche, a relic
of Virginia grandeur, was soon left behind on the way. At last,
on the great river, they came, not to prosperity, but to rest.
Mobility was in the blood of this Westward-turning strain.
Mobility was in the stories Sam heard as a child. For a while
in this early mid-century, the tempo of change in the middle
land was rapid beyond precedent in American history. A single
generation passed from trader with the Indians, to pioneer
hunter, to frontier clearings, and then to the log villages and
rough farm houses where Sam Clemens' family birthed their
children, and finally to the little towns which were already
"civilized" in what was to be an American pattern for a century.
And each stage had left its survivors who kept the morals and
the manners of the past in a changed environment. When the
boy Sam went back for the summer to Uncle John Quarles'
farm at Florida, fifty miles from the river, he lived in much
the same backwoods culture across which his father and family
and a slave had moved from log village to log village in the
great forest.

The past was present even for a boy. Drunken Pap Finn,
Huck's father, complained with entire justice that the so-called

march of civilization had reduced a free hunter and fisher living in a land of plenty to poverty and drink — made a poor-white of him. Injun Joe, the half-breed, Tom Sawyer's boyhood terror, recalled the fur traders and their squaws of a generation earlier. It was river pirates preying upon immigrants who hid the treasure that made Tom and Huck rich.

Mingled with the flotsam and jetsam of pioneer life, and backwoodsmen now become comfortable farmers or poor-whites, were representatives — so they might have called them-selves — of the culture and sophistication of the East. These came or drifted to the towns, particularly on the great river. There were pre-bankers, like Judge Thatcher, the financial anchor of St. Petersburg, as Mark called Hannibal in his book; lawyers or would-be lawyers, like "Judge" Clemens, Sam's father, who kept store when there was no law to practise; homely but well-read philosophers, like Puddin'head Wilson, who amazed his village by what seemed to them asinine ideas. There were cultivated drifters from Europe, like the famous twins; and smart rascals like the King and the Duke of *Huckle-berry Finn,* who worked upon the innocence of the river towns in all affairs but their own. And ministers, professionals from the too competitive East, or amateurs, like Tom's Uncle Silas, who supplied a moral code without theology.

Also the Negroes. The Clemenses had brought one slave with them through the backwoods, and Missouri where they ceased roaming was a slave state. But in this part of the center land, the slave was not the exploited machine he had become among the cotton capitalists of the South. Slavery was a do-mestic affair, as it had once been in the upper East, and was still in all the border states. The slaves, at least in the Clemens family, were part of the home circle, helpers and companions, with their human rights limited only by a little physical disci-pline, and the painful necessity of occasional buying and selling. On the long vacations at Uncle Quarles' farm, they were Sam's close companions. His first imaginative education was in the obligatory ethics, poetry, and folklore of the Bible; and also in the voluntary and absorbing folklore of his Negro friends. It is the undercurrent of the tragedy of slavery for both white and black that gives *Huckleberry Finn* its moral depth; but that book was written thirty years after the legendary voyage. The pure folklore of Miss Watson's Jim, the runaway slave, is from Sam's own memory and belongs with the best of *Uncle Remus*. Thanks to their social status, these Negroes had remained adult children, who talked to little Sam on their own level. Yet even though Sam and his friends believed that slavery was God-ordained and abolition the work of the devil, conscience gnawed like a worm in the subconscious. Slavery among the easygoing Missourians was morally insecure.

Behind all frontier mobility of the center land were two dynamic motives. The first was a desire for freedom from castes and classes, from cramped land and forbidden opportunity — freedom (the Negroes always excepted) to be self-willed, to rise in the social scale, and almost equally to degenerate. Now that we are emerging from the false absolutes of the economic interpretation of history, the craving for freedom in this broad sense is seen to be a fundamental shaper of American society. Whitman understood its power, and based much of his romantically optimistic but psychologically sound poetry upon an idealization of the shiploads of immigrants he watched disembarking in the harbor of New York on their way to the West. *Tom Sawyer* and *Huckleberry Finn* are boys' epics of freedom.

Yet, for both the imaginative and the greedy, there was an economic motive grosser than, and quite as strong as freedom. It was speculation. A few hundred miles from Hannibal in the eighteen-forties and -fifties when Sam was a boy there, the Far West began, of illimitable extent and possibilities. A thousand miles away in the East across country as yet only partly settled, wealth and energy were piling up eager to spill over the moun-

tains. The steamboat had come. The railroads were coming.
Land was cheap to buy, if hard to conquer. "Judge" Clemens
had bought a vast tract of wilderness in Tennessee at probably
less than a cent an acre. Anything could happen to property
in such a country — and eventually, very eventually sometimes,
it usually did. Every man with a little free cash, or a chance
to borrow, was a speculator, and the greatest speculators, in
dreams, if not in money, were in the Mississippi Valley. It
was the Promised Land at the foot of the rainbow, where
present fact was forgotten in the glare of hope. William Allen
White believed that when Mark wrote *Huckleberry Finn* he
was stimulated by the great real estate boom of the eighteen-
eighties which populated farms and towns from the Alleghenies
to the Pacific. It would be truer to say that Mark's youth had
been spent among earlier dreamers, who had visions of what
was to come forty years later which at the time were as illusory
as the warmth from Colonel Sellers' stove with a tallow candle
inside. The boy Sam was of their stock, his imagination was
conditioned, unhappily, by theirs. He was "familiar" enough
with the speculators to create from them some of the most
typical Americans in literature — including himself. For he
was a lifelong speculator, who made millions, but only out, of
his books.

The Clemens family moved in 1839 from the cleared farm
and tall-timber country to Hannibal on the Mississippi — age
four for the boy. Hannibal was a town and a port on a river
that was already a stream of history, with a well-developed culture of its own. Except for the diverse humanity of the river
and the felt proximity of the backwoods, Hannibal might have
been duplicated in the more rural parts of New York State or
Virginia. But the great river had no real parallel in the mid-
land forests or in the East. Already the flatboat had yielded
pre-eminence to the steamer, and by the time Sam was twenty-
two and a pilot's assistant, there would be a mile of steamboats

lying side by side at the sloping wharves of St. Louis, only a hundred miles below Hannibal. That absorptive period which comes at an indefinite age in the youth of every writer seems to have begun for Sam when he was old enough to be conscious of the contrast between the backwoods and the river — "a whole mile broad, and awful still and grand," as Huck was to say. Watching the as-good-as-a-circus-parade of the steamboats coming in, staring at strange figures from the outer world as they came ashore, swimming to the passing rafts, exploring the islands, he had that first expansion of the imagination which with every great writer seems to determine not the extent but the quality of his success. One remembers how the hero of *Locksley Hall*

> . . . *at night along the dusky highway near and nearer drawn,*
> *Sees in heaven the light of London flaring like a dreary dawn;*
> *And his spirit leaps within him to be gone before him then,*
> *Underneath the light he looks at, in among the throngs of men.*

For the Mississippi not only looked big in the American colloquial sense of extensive, important, unsurpassed, it was big. It ran from northern wilderness to the sea and the outer world, and from the Rockies to the coastal swamps, although Sam did not know much about the Missouri branch. He was more conscious of the pineries of the North — for from there came the rafts, "an acre or so of white, sweet-smelling boards in each raft," which floated past their shores — and of New Orleans and the deep South, from which came upstream the molasses in hogsheads. The islands, long and narrow, like Indian spears pointing southward, were the South Sea atolls and Timbuctoo for the boys, wild, unsettled except for a squatter, or a vagabond like themselves. Indeed, the Mississippi was not like any other of the great rivers of the world. It lay athwart the progress of a country westward; yet it was not a barrier, but a vast road with feeders that caught the settlers moving westward and ran them down by trail or current to the main stream that turned them either north or south, or passed them across to the Wild West beyond. And in Sam's time it was flowing, not from savagery or barbarism as did the Nile, or the great Chinese rivers, but through all the variants of American sub-cultures — lumber and trapping life in the great northern forests; ex-New England and ex-backwoods Middle West in its upper ranges, just tinged with French ex-voyageur; then the same mingled with Virginia and Kentucky, down through an ex-Carolina and ex-Georgia plantation culture, to a Latin-American Colonial civilization plus the overlay of a great port in New Orleans. And still mobile on the long river were the ever-moving settlers in search of more land, mingled with a froth of money-hungry speculators, scamps in search of safety, and the rivermen themselves, "a race," as Mark wrote, "apart, and not like other folks."

Nor, thanks to Mark's own books, can we ever forget the steamboats themselves; so much more gregarious than railroad trains, where the young pilot sat down to eat with an exhibit of world types and frontier society, usually all in shirt sleeves. The river gave life a flavor that it was Mark's genius to record.

These showy steamboats, "floating palaces" (and brothels), chugged past, or with a noisy ritual brought their gay decks above the wharves of little river towns like Hannibal. Here the population was no longer mobile. It was made up of descendants of the long trek across the hardwood forests mingled with Southern whites driven West and North by the monopolies of slave labor. And everywhere north of cosmopolitan New Orleans, and the vast cotton and sugar plantations of the deep South, they had become home folks, and more like each other (as Bernard DeVoto shrewdly says) than the people of the old North or the old South of the Atlantic Coast whence they had come. They were "folks," intending to stay where they were and whatever they were, whoever might get off the steamboats. Sometimes they saw real dukes and eminent travelers with

manners and elegant clothes on their streets, but they kept
their own way of life and were solidly skeptical of any accents,
customs, or codes but their own. Even when Huck Finn on his
famous voyage got far South, "a mighty long ways from home,"
where Spanish moss hung like long, gray beards from the trees,
Tom's Uncle Silas and his friends proved to be just like the
folks behind, even though small-lot slavery was the fabric of
their society. And so it is not surprising that along a river
where more varied types of humanity traveled familiarly together than since the days of the Roman Mediterranean, there
was also an isolationism almost as complete as in an English
village or in a Chinese provincial town.

3 . TOM AND HUCK

I am writing in this section a literary biography of Mark Twain
the writer, not a complete study of Samuel Langhorne Clemens.
For Sam Clemens' boyhood in Hannibal, I do not propose to
compete with Mark himself. The substantial accuracy of the
background of *The Adventures of Tom Sawyer* and *Adventures of Huckleberry Finn* has never been questioned. They
are full of "stretchers," which was what Huck called the exaggeration and romanticizing of Tom. And it is not surprising to
learn that Becky Thatcher was not too much like her original
in the village, and that the major events of the stories were a
reminiscent dream of what might very well have happened.
The important question seems to be the relation of Tom and
Huck in the books written about them to the highly personal
imagination of Mark Twain. What will become clearer as we
go on is that vital aspects of Sam Clemens and his boyhood are
lifted into symbolism and then made brilliantly concrete in

these books. If you wish to find out what Sam was like and
what he did or wished to do you must read them. They are
much the best history of his actual life in Hannibal, even if
they are full of "stretchers." And you must read them if you
are to understand the later Sam who, as Mark Twain, turned
this "boy-life" into an art which has deeply influenced the
imagination of millions of readers.

I must assume, in carrying this discussion back to Mark
himself, a familiarity with the books themselves. No one indeed should read these chapters of mine who has not read, or
who does not read, at least the key books which make Mark
Twain and James worthy of a Plutarchian study. It should be
an easy assumption with Twain; this is by no means so with
Henry James, although I hope in the course of this book to
make it easier.

To begin with, *Tom Sawyer* is a small-town book and
Huckleberry Finn is a great-river book — a difference by no
means so noticeable but almost as considerable as between
Cranford and *Vanity Fair*. The focus of *Tom Sawyer* is school,
home, and the adventures of two boys exploring the night life
of St. Petersburg and the romantic freedom of the islands. Its
emphasis is upon freedom as the Westward-turning American
experienced it in youth. The focus of *Huckleberry Finn* is
always the river, and its theme also is freedom, but in a dramatic
counterpoint where Huck, who has run away himself to be free,
encounters a runaway slave for whom freedom is a crime against
the morals of Hannibal. *Tom Sawyer* is a miniature, sharp and
vivid; *Huckleberry Finn* is a mural with an epic rhythm.

Tom Sawyer is of course Sam Clemens, but only one aspect of
a self-conflicting personality, which was dual throughout his
life. Tom's adventures are the stretched wish-fulfillments of a
romantic boy. He dreamed of robbers and pirates and made
his companions believe in them. When the wish, as often with
a boy, tangled with reality, Sam gave to Tom the adventures

that such a boy would like to have experienced himself, yet kept them real and familiar. Injun Joe belongs to the dream world of a boy, but he came true in Hannibal, and the Tom in Sam knew how to handle him. All his life, as we shall see, Mark Twain was Tom when he was not someone else; particularly in his books, but often in his own life. It was the insatiable ego of Tom, always craving a show-off, that invented the Yankee and sent him back into the Age of Chivalry to overthrow the knights by lasso and six-shooter. Sam was the tender-minded Tom who left his pirate friends on the island to steal across the river and kiss Aunt Polly in her sleep. It was the romantic Tom in Mark who discovered with such a shock that the God in whom Aunt Polly believed was not a humanitarian, nor even moral. It was the Tom in Mark who turned romantic pessimist in the end, thinking that he was hard as nails. William James saw Twain only when in 1892 they lived near each other in Italy, but it was enough for that great psychologist to see that he did not belong among the tough-minded in his famous categories.

"A fine soft-fibered little fellow," so he described him in a letter to Josiah Royce, "with the perversest twang and drawl, but very human and good. I should think one might get **very** fond of him."

Most of all, Tom Sawyer had the quality which was to make Mark Twain's easier success, and, carried to an extreme, some of his worst failures. He was immensely inventive, whether in plots, like the murder story of Injun Joe, or in such absurdities as the rescue of the Negro Jim after he was known to be free already. It was the flow of invented exaggeration which made Mark's really very informational lectures a triumph of splendid clowning, and got him his first pseudo-literary reputation in the East. Invention is the indispensable gift of a triumphant story-teller. Henry James had his fair share of it; but if Fanny Kemble passed on to him a rich anecdote, he would be off like a mole grubbing the roots of the story until he had found every last ramification that drew nourishment. Mark invented or experienced his own stories, and told them on a springboard — from which sooner or later he was sure to turn a double somersault in the air, to the delight of the vulgar and the dismay of the judicious.

Twain's beloved daughter Susy remarks that "the difference between papa and mama is, that mama loves morals and papa loves cats." Susy's intuitions were more accurate than her childish vocabulary. Substitute "romance" for "cats" and you get a very good definition of the Tom in Sam Clemens. Tom's morality consisted of a fear of Aunt Polly's vindictive God until he came to distrust him, and an uncritical respect for the ethics of Hannibal. In spite of Susy, this was not entirely true of the adult Mark, and except in the Sawyer corner of his soul, it was not true of Sam Clemens either. For Tom indeed was too limited, too romantic, and too specialized in egoism, to hold all the inner life and outer experiences of Sam Clemens. He dominates the book that bears his name, in which Huck is little more than comic relief, yet it is significant that it is Huck at the end, not Tom, who speaks last in a passage of ideas, ideals, and realistic common sense of which Tom was incapable. Mark, in the epilogue to his story, promises, if it seems worth while, to describe in another book the boys after they become men. But when he came to write it, he found that there was much more left to say about the boy Huck, and made him the hero of what proved to be his greatest book.

For Huck proved to be quite as much Sam Clemens as was the show-off Tom, and the better and the deeper part. His dense ignorance of everything except the real essentials of life kept the fun going, but while cats, or at least dead ones, were his specialty, conscience and freedom were his two chief concerns. He hated the one and was a fanatic for the other. Shoes, stiff clothes, and school he knew how to escape from, but dad-rat it! he could never get away from a question of morals, which Tom slid round so easily. Huck, the son of a disreputable drunken failure, as Sam was the son of a frustrated lawyer, was a congenital product first of Westward-turning America, next of the backwoods, and most of all of the Mississippi. He was a tolerant cynic like the later Mark, suspicious of mankind, and he had the common sense which Tom lacked, and which Mark could use when he was not Tom. Huck was a river rat, a tough offspring of decadence like the London cockney, shrewd like a rat, kind like most vagabonds, a realist by necessity. He was an ideal storyteller of the saga of the Mississippi, where Tom's romantic egoism would have been too childish for a great theme. He was a born actor, like Mark, loved honest lying as did Mark, and used it as a protection of his thoughts, but hated it when it was pretentious or mean. And Huck was a sharp observer also (he had to be), in this respect unlike Tom who looked through his own iridescent haze, but very like Mark at his best — and also Henry James. It is this Huck who records (from a boy's point of view) the sordid, cruel, terrible incidents in the river towns, which, though often rich in sentiment, needed only to be described in order to become powerful satire, and would have been ruined by romance. It was only Huck's personal freedom that was romantic to him.

And his imagination was central to the region. The poverty, the sickness, the hardships of the women were as natural to him as they had been to little Sam Clemens, and also the kindliness of the "folks." Seen by Mark through Huck's eye they get youthful reporting. And the deep emotion stirred in the river rat by the conflict in his mind between his hatred of "the dirty low-down business" of abolition, and his love for the Negro Jim, his best friend, was to be the disrupting theme of the next American decade. If freeing Jim was a crime, "all right then," he decided like many a humane Southerner, "I'll go to hell" — for Huck was afraid of witches, but not of "ornery sermons by pro-slavery pastors." Huck was tough, as Mark was also except about speculation and women. He was easygoing but just so far, as with his Pap until Pap tried to murder him. Then he ran away, or rebelled as when the Widow got him too clean and taught him manners at table. "I can't *stand* it," he would say, as would Mark when, having reformed everything else to New York State standards, Olivia tried to make him stop cursing and smoking. In fact if Tom was the speculator in Mark that kept him from ever missing a trick, and led him to take many that should have been left on the table, Huck was the fascinated student of manners, the hidden skeptic, the persistent democrat, the sensitive conscience.

We may, therefore, and for the purposes of this book, accept these two reminiscent stories as a literary biography of Mark Twain's boy-years in the valley, not less true for being idyllic and idealized in both, but never to the damage of a realism which is outstanding in *Huckleberry Finn*. To them must be added *Life on the Mississippi,* for it was on or from a steamboat that a still youthful, but not boyish, Sam saw those lower river towns — beyond the boys' actual voyaging — which with skill and subtlety he resaw through Huck's eyes and wove into Huck's story. It was Sam, either in reality or in his fertile imagination, who cornered the Bible market, bossed the whitewashing of the fence, saw Injun Joe do murder, and was lost with Becky in the great cave. It was Sam, looking back to his early youth, who found that Huck in his rags and his sugar hogshead could make articulate his own moral puzzles, his wide tolerance, and the sad wisdoms which a frontier boy so easily acquired. And it was Huck with his passion for freedom who was allowed to see what Sam with the careful accuracy of a pilot had stored in his memory. It is the Huck in him, not the Tom, that made Mark not just a wisecracker or an inventor of tall tales, but a great humorist when he dropped the pose of funny man and wrote to please himself. "I don't give a

dern," says Huck, "for a thing 'thout it's tollable hard to get.
. . . No, Tom. . . . I won't live in them cussed smothery houses, I
like the woods, and the river, and hogsheads, and I'll stick to 'em
too." And it is the Huck in Mark who made him a novelist
who could draw the sentimental Emmeline's picture gallery as
sharp and clear as a shoal in Sam the pilot's memory. And
Huck, not Tom, who added the King and the Duke and Uncle
Silas and Pap Finn to the classic human portraits of literature.
(Pap Finn — who has never been properly appreciated — is my
favorite character next to the boys and Colonel Sellers in all of
Mark Twain. He is as good as the best of Dickens, and, of the
humorous kind, as the best of Shakespeare — a backwoods
Pistol, a poor-white Falstaff.)

4. "JOUR" PRINTER

The next stretch in Sam's life was important for him but not
for his imagination. When he was twelve, in 1847, his father
died and, to his delight, he was taken out of school and appren-
ticed in the printing shop of a Hannibal newspaper editor. The
idyll of Hannibal in its golden glow ends sharply at about age
twelve or thirteen. There was little freedom, less variety, if not
much hard work, in Sam's new life. Pet McMurry, the journeyman printer of the establishment, leaves a portrait of Sam the
apprentice written much later and quoted by Paine. He describes a sandy-haired boy in the printing rooms over a drug-
store, mounted on a little box at the case of type, and pulling
away on a huge cigar or a diminutive pipe. He sang as he
worked and played jokes on the other apprentice, a huge boy
named Wales. Mr. Ament's printery was also an editor's establishment. In the early nineteenth century a poor boy with a

sense for words was very likely to be put into the printing trade. It happened to Walt Whitman when he was about Sam's age, and Walt, like Sam, soon drifted into editing also, which was natural when the trade and the profession mingled as they did in Sam's next job on a little newspaper which Sam's fantastic brother Orion had bought on mortgage. An articulate boy (like Tom Sawyer) was the best kind of apprentice in printing and editing, provided his fingers were nimble, for he could spell and correct copy, and write at a pinch. He knew the wrong word when he saw it, even if he did not know the right one, and he had that sense of living grammar and rhetoric which a far longer education than Sam's seldom gives to the ungifted. Walt Whitman became a real editor, and what he learned in a profession which was essentially a branch of politics deeply influenced the *Leaves of Grass*. Sam at least learned language, began his mastery of words which in his maturity was, in my opinion, greater, if less extensive, than Henry James'. He had a chance at journalism too when Orion was out of town. If Orion had possessed even the rudiments of common sense, the boy might have short-circuited his next adventurous years and become in Hannibal the journalist he was predestined to be, but that would have been unfortunate for American literature. Orion was a strange fellow, a visionary like Sam, but slow, honest, and earnest like his father. He was more self-centered than Sam, so oblivious to outer reality that he left his bride standing on the street side when he set off for his honeymoon. He was a dreamer on low levels, always sloping toward disaster, as Sam was a dreamer on high ones which usually ended on a precipice. The paper was a failure, of course, but Sam had not gone into printing with the idea of learning the language, or of making "literature" which when written to please the general public he described, just before his first great success, as "bosh." He wanted a trade which would save him, and eventually, he hoped, his family from the poverty they had so nearly reached in the downward career of his unfortunate father. Sam was a mother's boy. From her he got his drawl, his obsession with old-time religion, his restless energy. He respected his father if he never loved him. What his father did for him was to grind into him a resolve to make money, and to share it with his family — a resolve he kept. It was his father's death that made him a printer.

Of that trade I need say little more, because it never got into his books. It was his years at a type case which undoubtedly, made him, when his success as a writer was secured, a "sucker," as the American colloquial puts it, for a typesetting machine that would do away with millions of hours of such labor as his had been, and bring in millions. Mark was a lazy man physically and a speculator, so his printer's imagination was easily stirred. Unfortunately it was the wrong machine, and cost him a fortune. And it was presumably the ink in his blood stream that set up a fatal fascination for publishing books which reduced him at last to bankruptcy. But the trade clearly bored him. At eighteen he left Hannibal, ostensibly for a job in St. Louis, but did not stop until he got to New York, and never came back to stay.

And here is a curious contrast with the youth of both Walt Whitman and Henry James. Printing took Walt from a Long Island farm to Brooklyn and to New York, whose celebrant he became. Henry, in his school days abroad and later, lived in a golden haze of the great past, and its great cities. It is quite possible that when Sam ran away to New York and Philadelphia, he was following the back track of an urban civilization such as he had seen flaunted on steamboat decks — but if so he gave no sign of liking it, or big cities ever. Paine's guess is that he hoped to wander as a journeyman printer did, and come back full of stories like those that Pet McMurry, the journeyman at his first job, told the apprentices. Certainly there was little glamour, though plenty of hard work for him in the great Eastern cities. He lived in New York at a workman's boarding-house, neither drank nor "threw cards" because he promised

his mother not to, worked long hours and read at a printers'
library at night — read certainly history as well as romantic
yarns. Turning East meant little to him. He was more impressed by the solid marble columns he saw in Philadelphia
"larger than a hogshead at the base" than by anything in the
great array of art and invention at the Crystal Palace World's
Fair which was then open in New York. It was at this fair that
Whitman spent so many hours, expanding his imagination with
a first view of the great world outside of America, and storing
images for the *Leaves of Grass*. Sam was not the Turn East
kind — unless, as later, he was paid to be so. He wanted adventure, not culture, and got neither in the East, although
later in Cincinnati he encountered Macfarlane, a philosophic
Scotchman with a type of free thinking foreign to Sam's experience in what even then could have been called the Bible Belt.
These were Sam's dull years. Big cities were not his métier,
never would be more than places to sell his goods. Huck, it
will be remembered, was never allowed to get so far as New
Orleans, although Sam's life there had been really glamorous.
Sam was clearly too restless to stick to a trade, too inventive
for the proletarian life.

Tom Sawyer's romantic imagination was cramped. Huck
Finn had lost his freedom, or rather had learned that wandering from job to job was not freedom. It was Tom that broke
away first. At the library Sam had been reading Lieutenant
Herndon's book on the Amazon. Sam resolved to go down to
that other great river and pay his way by collecting coca, and
writing back letters for publication. Travel letters for home
consumption was almost a profession in the America of that day.
Bayard Taylor had made a fortune by travel books, Emerson
was lecturing on English traits, the young Henry James paid
part of the expenses of his first excursions on his own to Europe
by travel letters and descriptions of scenes abroad. Sam had
already tried his hand, though unsuccessfully, for he had not
been a sub-editor without learning how to be paid for wander-

ing. At last a fifty-dollar bill flew past his face and stuck on
an opposite wall. After another printing interval, he got as far
as New Orleans on that, but the Tom in him, as so often happened with Tom himself, had a better idea than the Amazon
on the way down. (Believe all this or not, as you please.) Sailing from Cincinnati, in April of 1857, he entered as in a dream
into the old river life, which had seemed to the boys the height
of unattainable excitement and grandeur. But now he was a
passenger who could visit the pilothouse and watch the direct-
ing brain of the *Tom Jones* at work. Horace Bixby was the
pilot's name. I quote from Paine's interview with Bixby, who
recalled Sam's great moment:

> Bixby was looking over the bow at the head of Island Number 35,
> when he heard a slow, pleasant voice say: . . . "How would you like
> a young man to learn the river?" . . . The pilot glanced over his
> shoulder and saw a rather slender, loose-limbed young fellow with a
> fair, girlish complexion and a great tangle of auburn hair. "I wouldn't
> like it. Cub pilots are more trouble than they are worth."

But Bixby was persuaded by a promise of five hundred dollars
on installments, and learned that Sam knew the Bowen Boys
who had taken to the river, that he didn't drink, didn't gamble,
swore only under pressure, "but I *must smoke.*"

That was the end of both printing and the Amazon.

5 . MISSISSIPPI PILOT

CONFEDERATE GUERRILLA

Mark's best books are all accounts of a picaro — a young or
youngish fellow zestful for life and living by his wits. In his
first attempt to learn a trade, Sam had been merely industrious.
The best he could do was to boast that he was never down-
hearted, which would have been a much chastened remark for

Tom Sawyer. Sam's second trade engrossed far more of his total mind, for it was both a trade and an art. His job was first to learn and then to practise the navigation of over two thousand miles of a great river. He had to know by heart every shifting shoal, every woodpile on the banks, every snag, every shallowing channel where when the leadsman called "mark twain" it was time to slow down and creep. And if he did not know, to guess what might have happened since he passed before. For the great river was a living thing that had to be felt as well as understood. Those cheap, gaudy packets that arrived twice a day at Hannibal, black smoke pouring, funnels glaring, upper decks crowded, were now his concern instead of a type case or a proof sheet. And it was not in order to write about it that he took on this trade. It offered probably the best-paid job anywhere for a youth with no backing but a good capacity. It was the most rewarding job for a sensitive youth who would always enjoy a show-off or an adventure as much as cash. You can see how Sam felt about it by reading how his Captain Stormfield enjoyed steering his dirigible among the planets, and racing the comets. But even though for Sam the river was romance in its early sense of mind-expanding, his chief purpose was to learn a profitable trade, not only in order to sport fancy clothes, and fling his money about a bit on shore, but to get that solid sustenance under his feet which his family had always lacked. Sam Clemens always wished for money. Though he liked fame, take the cash and let the credit go was his motto as well as Huck's. There was no money in writing for him yet. He had promised to send Orion some letters to publish, but "when one is learning the river, he is not allowed to do or think about anything else." He had the name among the other pilots of a witty, bookish young fellow, and wrote at least one burlesque of a sententious retired pilot who pontificated in New Orleans under the pseudonym of Mark Twain, the pseudonym Sam adopted later when the old man was dead and forgotten. But he was not allowed to think about other things than piloting, which may be the reason why when Mark began to write his *Life on the Mississippi* in 1874, he wrote a history of a trade, as well as the story of a picaro, probably the best history of a trade.

For biography in these years we must go elsewhere, and find little. There are a few Tom Sawyerish episodes in that famous book, but in general it is as unrevealing of Sam as it is definitive for life on the river. Everything of importance happens in the pilothouse. It is as focused as *Tom Brown at Rugby*. Even the trial chapter from the manuscript of *Huckleberry Finn* which Twain inserted in the final book, and unfortunately left there, is part of the river saga, if not of piloting, and not personal to Sam. This was the story of how the "iron-jawed, brass-mouthed, copper-bellied corpse maker from the wilds of Arkansaw" challenged the "Pet child of Calamity" to a fight.

It is not true as has been asserted that Mark never drew upon his river experiences except for this book. Where, as suggested above, does the observation of feuding river families and decadent river towns so different from Hannibal come from if not from Mark's experiences as a pilot out of hours? Or Roxana of *Puddin'head Wilson* who was stewardess on a river boat. *Life on the Mississippi* really tells very little of what happened to Sam in four years of what should have been the most impressionable years of his life. Compared with the lively panoramas of mining camps, old gold fields, and corrupt San Francisco in *Roughing It,* with everything picturesque reported, and Sam in the midst of it all, *Life on the Mississippi* is singularly concentrated. As *Moby-Dick* is a whale-and-sea story, so it is a river pilot's story exclusively, though vivid enough with its boats in the fog and dark, tricks in the pilothouse, and a race between two rival steamers that makes Currier and Ives seem tame.

I raise this question only biographically, for it would seem to be obvious that a youth of twenty-two to twenty-five lived far more than he tells of these voyages. A voyager in these crudely

magnificent boats would find himself in a kind of night club
on Main Street, in which gamblers, prostitutes, confidence men,
speculators, plied their trades on the same decks with immigrants, farmers transporting their produce, slaves in chains,
and travelers everywhere. If Sam shared this life he does not
say so. His one amorous adventure was an attempt to show off
before a pretty and obviously innocent girl. And yet he did
dance till midnight and shock his mother when once she went
along, by embracing and kissing the girls. My guess is that Sam
was young for his age emotionally, though old for his years in
thought and experience. He was certainly fastidious, and probably shy. Off his job, he took more joy from watching life than
grossly experiencing it. "How to Take Life," he copied down
in his notebook from some writer. "Take it as though you
were born to perform a merry part in it." He was as tolerant
of all kinds of life, including his own, as was Huck, and though
he kept a notebook, probably felt as Huck did about writing,
"If I'd 'a' knowed what a trouble it was to make a book I
wouldn't 'a' tackled it." As for the social conscience which
burnt in him later in life, he probably felt about conscience as
Huck did: it was a nuisance that made simple things tediously
complex. Certainly he must have been aware that the Mississippi steamboats were, as DeVoto says, examples of shameless
profiteering. Built all gimcrack on top, they were fitted with
cheap boilers, and raced to capture the traffic. When they blew
up, which was often, with sudden death for most on board, no
one complained except the bereaved. Mark risked his life
daily for someone's pocketbook, but never thought back to the
cause. At this stage he was a reporter with no need to think or
write about what he saw. "For to admire an' for to see" and to
make sound money while doing it was still his life plan. What
happened next is a perfect instance of how a great moral
humorist, in his youth could be apparently unconcerned about
moral and economic principles.

He left his job of piloting in 1861 because he was afraid of being shot. He had surprised his family by learning and sticking to a most difficult trade, and came through with a pocket full of money. Even at this time Sam had begun to spread the story that he was incorrigibly lazy, and this he kept up and made it prevail even through the years when he was working harder than any nineteenth-century author except Balzac at another specialized and difficult job — writing. He had fulfilled one boyhood dream, to be the captain of a steamboat standing "by the big bell, calm, imposing, the envy of all," or better still a pilot. The outbreak of the Civil War in 1861 ended all that. The river was quickly closed to long-distance commercial travel. A pilothouse of glass at the top of a steamboat was, as Sam pointed out, a perfect target for a rifle ball from either army. He quit. In 1860, while still on the job although the war was impending, he called himself a Union man, but admitted sympathy for the problems of a small slaveholder, as his father had been, who did not like slavery but could not afford to free his slaves. If he had been deeply concerned with what historians call "vital issues," his course was clear. He should have offered his extremely valuable services to the Northern army or navy as a river expert, as did a friend and fellow pilot who hesitated only until they tried to argue with him at New Orleans. But Sam was from a border state, and if he had his mind on the question, which from what happened afterward seems not probable, it was a mind confused, pushed one way or another by fanatics on both sides. This was true of millions of our population, although it has been convenient for their descendants to forget. I could give chapter and verse for it from my own native border state of Delaware. What he did was to drift back to Hannibal, where he joined fifteen "boys," some of them out for a lark, to form what they called the Marion Rangers, who were to defend the state of Missouri against any invader. Since both Governor and Commanding

General were avowed Confederates, the trouble was not likely
to come from the South. The Rangers set up camp where food
and girls were accessible and went into training. There were
alarums almost nightly and Sam on one occasion fired with others
on a friend approaching in the dark, and killed him. But
even in the account Mark wrote of it in 1885, "The Private
History of a Campaign That Failed," it was all very unlike
his remark in the letter quoted at the beginning of this chapter.
There he hints at familiarity with that death-on-the-pale-horse-
with-hell-following-after which is the raw soldier's experience in
his first fortnight in the field. Nonsense! The Rangers spent
a good deal of time trying to mount unmanageable horses and
mules, still more in practising retreats through rocky night
woods, and very little on discipline or hell-following-after.
When it was reported that a real Union Colonel (U. S. Grant,
as it happened) was marching in their direction with real soldiers, Mark left hurriedly, pleading a confused mind.

Mark was never a convinced pacifist, although he did believe
that in war you merely learned to call your fellow man your
enemy, and then shoot him. He was not a coward or he would
never have stayed a pilot for four years. He was not, I think,
an escapist. He was just not interested in the War Between the
States. Southern in manners and Northern in mind, though
not too much of either, it was not the Union, but the continent,
that excited and persuaded him. He was a perfect type of the
mobile Turn-always-West American of the period, who had
not struck deep roots since his family's trek ended, and had
always regarded government as a meddlesome, impersonal,
though advisable restraint. If Thoreau had not at last been
aroused by the evils of slavery and disunion (and it took a long
time to do it), Thoreau would have felt very much like Sam
Clemens. But Mark was a prize specimen of the type because
of his intense interest in men, and his small concern with "vital
issues." For look what happened. As soon as practicable after
his final "retreat," and leaving a dubious reputation behind

him, he pulled out for the Far West as assistant to his brother Orion, who had been made Secretary of the Union-made state of Nevada. And through all of the dark and bloody years that followed 1861, most of all in the darkest and bloodiest toward the end of the War, it is difficult to find more than mere references in his letters to the fearful tensions, the disasters, the burning issues in all the land east of the Rockies. "If the war will let us alone," he wrote as early as October of 1861, Orion and he can make their friends as well as themselves rich from the mines. To Mark, at least, and his mining and journalist associates, that great war, whose influences are yet strong upon us, was a nuisance, an interruption of business, and an irritant in politics. It was not again "morals" but "cats" that he loved, "cats" in this instance being "feet" of mining lodes; and also playing his humor like a firehose over the raucous life of the new West, and sharing a scene as lively, if not as impressive, as the Mississippi. The Far West indeed was making a new country of its own.

The contrast is sharp with Henry James, eighteen years old in 1861, incapable because of an injured back, but wracked and depressed because he could not take part in some way in what all his family felt had become a great moral conflict. His patriotism was abstract, for Cambridge (and Boston and New York) meant very little to him. Mark's feeling for the West as another New World was burningly concrete.

6. WASHOE

Nine years after Sam came to Nevada, he began a book called *Roughing It*, which told in the first person of his experiences in the great silver mines, the country called by the "pet name" of Washoe, also in the worn-out gold fields of California and

in San Francisco. It is a travel book of a very high rank, but
as biography, like *Life on the Mississippi,* it leaves out probably as much as its author put in. We can supplement it from
numerous contemporary letters of Sam's and in any case our
first concern is with the youth of twenty-six, who had not yet
become Mark the professional writer.

Sam was running away. He took the Overland Stage with
its six horses (or sometimes galloping mules) for its non-stop
rush (except for meals) across thirteen hundred miles of continent, over the Plains, up through the Rockies, and the desert
and the jagged Nevada mountains beyond. With his brother
Orion, as full of fantasies as he, but devoid of either humor
or common sense, he rolled and bumped through the country
of bad-men bandits, and into Mormondom, passing the Pony
Express on the way, passing Indians which he saw with scorn-
ful Missourian eyes. The narrative in his book is so vivid that
we might take it for literal if he had not asked Orion, in preparation, to give him the names of the routes and the stations,
having forgotten everything but his impressions. He was not
a journalist when he went, but a picaro running away with
his pockets full of money (he paid Orion's $170 fare as well as
his own) from his last adventure, looking for a way to keep out
of the War, and get rich. "Even at this day it thrills me through
and through to think of the life, the gladness and the wild sense
of freedom that used to make the blood dance in my veins on
those fine overland mornings!" But it was not for thrill or
escape chiefly that this curiously duplex youth, who was to
make more money probably and certainly lose more than any
writer of his time, was crossing the Plains. In his letters after
his arrival it is all money, money, money — to be rich in five
or six months (he believed it) and then back home again,
down the Missouri after that. "I have been a slave several times
in my life, but I'll never be one again. I always intend to be
so situated (*unless* I marry) that I can pull up stakes and clear

out whenever I feel like it." Here is the picaro in three moods.

No sooner in Virginia City than he began to expand his imagination. First it was a timber claim on Lake Tahoe which would have been very valuable someday if he had not burnt up most of it by careless camping, and lost the rest. Then mining — or rather speculation. Sam was never a real miner, though he did take a pick-and-shovel job for a while to get money in his purse. His knowledge of "hard rock" and of "placer" was elementary. The sight of a bit of gold quartz or silver ore in a piece of stone threw him off his balance instantly. From that moment he thought only in terms of the sample, which usually (invariably with him) was only a rich streak from an otherwise sterile hillside. He was not even a good prospector. You can tell that from his boasting, for his stories are usually of how he quit just too soon. In his later book, which was the only successful prospect he made, his talk is often of mining, but in his letters it is "feet," usually in someone else's lode, being bought or sold that has excited him.

If there was a crisis in his career at this time, and I think there was, it came when it was apparent even to his Tom Sawyerish imagination that he had to choose between manual labor of an elementary kind (very different from piloting) and going bust. At approximately that moment in 1862 he was offered, as a result of some burlesque letters, a job at twenty-five dollars a week on the *Territorial Enterprise* of Virginia City. It took some time for the common-sense Huck in Sam to persuade the Tom Sawyer in his imagination to give up the golden dreams of a mountain full of ore, but when the decision was made, it was Tom who discovered a formula for changing one golden dream into another. Journalism as a career appealed to him then as little as pick and shovel in a pit. What the *Enterprise* could give him in exchange for easy write-ups of a sensationally picturesque scene was an inside seat in the speculators' ring. He knew, of course, that the price of shares

in new veins was sensitive to newspaper talk. It was customary
to give inside information on "feet" in return for such publicity. Sam refers to many such gifts. About a year later he is
writing to his mother that he already has the widest reputation
as a local editor of any man on the Pacific Coast, and could get
a situation in San Francisco at any time he asked for one. "But
I don't want it. No paper in the United States could afford to
pay me what my place on the *Enterprise* is worth. If I were
not naturally a lazy, idle, good-for-nothing vagabond [he
should have added, "and indifferent honest"], I could make it
pay me $20,000 a year."

Here we have the two Marks running side by side. (By February 2, 1863, when Sam was on the *Enterprise,* Captain Isaiah
Sellers of New Orleans, the first "Mark Twain," had died and
Sam had taken over the pseudonym, and henceforth I shall call
him Mark, as all his friends and family, so I am informed by a
constant visitor to the household, did in the Hartford days and
presumably much earlier.) It is true that the Tomish Mark
still expected to make his fortune quickly out of speculating.
But the emerging writer had in a year made a reputation as a
humorist of new scenes, which was not dependent upon speculation. Whether he knew it or not, he had committed himself
to journalism for life — whence his only departure would be
occasionally to lift journalism into pure literature. Speculation
continued as an avocation for thirty-odd years when Mark at
last discovered that whatever it might be for other people, it
spelt only ruin for him.

Again I shall not try to compete with Mark's uproarious, and
often delightful and reasonably true, account of all these experiences he wrote in *Roughing It* some years later, of his life in
Virginia City, Carson City, and California. Virginia City, a
movie director's dream, "roosted royally midway up the steep
slope of Mount Davidson. . . . It claimed a population of fifteen
thousand or eighteen thousand, and all day long half of this little

army swarmed the busy streets like bees and the other half
swarmed among the drifts and tunnels of the 'Comstock' [fabu-
lous lode] hundreds of feet down in the earth directly under those
same streets." Each street was a terrace and from each to the next
street below the descent was forty or fifty feet. Along the roofs
next below them, Mark and Artemus Ward, happily drunk,
walked arm in arm one night until a policeman threatened to
shoot them down. No wonder that he wrote his mother, "I am
not so old as I was when I was eighteen." He was twenty-seven
and had quickly become the humorist, the columnist, though
the word was not yet invented, to the explosive town and the
whole Washoe, and his wit and also his news of "strikes" carried
his reputation down to San Francisco. What he wrote is lost,
but it could have had no more permanent value than a
columnist's gossip, wit, and burlesque today. See how he in-
structs his family on the importance of using personal names.
Only the threat of libel stops a columnist, only the threat of a
duel slowed up Mark. He did get a challenge, variously described, and probably less creditable to him than he admits.
Whatever the case, he left for San Francisco in a hurry, and
this was the end of the most boisterous and possibly the happiest years of his life.

I do not believe Mark Twain had either time or inclination
to reflect while he was in Nevada. The "heavy-headed revel
east and west" which disgusted the young Hamlet never seems
to have troubled him. The flocks of opulent prostitutes never
get into his later pages, yet he must have been tolerant both
of their civilizing charm and their constant greed and frequent
bestiality. It is said that his accounts as a correspondent of the
Nevada legislature (one of the most corrupt in history) showed
signs of a reforming tendency. If so, it may have been because,
as in San Francisco later, corruption made a good story. It is
hard to find any interest in "vital issues" in Mark at this time.
If we had all this lost journalism, it would probably prove to

be horse-and-mule-play, salted with wit and excessive exaggeration. That was the style of Southwestern frontier humor, which
he had learned by ear on the Mississippi.

His reputation at home got him a writer's job in San Francisco, and he kept a well-paid connection with the *Enterprise*.
He was on the *Call* with Bret Harte, whose sentimental gold-
field stories ran to the phony, as Mark's more realistic humor
runs to the burlesque. And in the *Call* but more emphatically
in the *Enterprise,* he lashed at the hideous political corruption
of San Francisco. For San Francisco in the sixties was rotten
from the decadence of the gold fields and the immorality of
easily acquired wealth. After a while the city ring, by a skillful
bit of framing, got him out of town.

The congenital vagabond was ready to go. City life seemed
always "tiresome" to Mark, as to James it was the height of
civilized living. He had found San Francisco a little dull. Its
epic days were past, it had already its pack of famous writers;
his experiences in the Washoe had been of an absolute novelty,
but that could not be true in a city already become (as now) a
metropolis. Or perhaps Mark's zest had carried him too high
in Virginia City. He seems tired, a little stale. The reporter's
life was "fearful drudgery — soulless drudgery — and almost
destitute of interest." "My life is so uneventful," he wrote his
mother in 1866. After all, he was no longer eighteen, and his
sensitive imagination was suffering perhaps from a hangover.
It was luck but no accident that took him for a winter to the
deserted placer fields of Tuolumne County. There lived Jim
Gillis, elderly, philosophical, well read, companioned by his cat
named Tom Quartz, and Dick Stoker upon whom Jim fathered
his best yarns. It was a retreat and company more suited to
Thoreau than Mark, but just what he needed. When he was
restless, he could always take to the hills with Dick Stoker and
try to trace down (or rather up) a pocket of gold overlooked
in the rush. But this was more like trout fishing from a Maine
camp than mining.

DeVoto, for whose opinions on what Mark actually did in comparison with what he said he did, I have great respect, believes that Mark matured in a literary sense in these months on Jackass Hill. Perhaps, but I doubt it. His pattern for a successful book — narrative, description, yarn, burlesque, with an underlying theme — was not set until *The Innocents Abroad* in 1869. He had always been a good storyteller and the yarn that made him famous when it was published in a New York paper and copied everywhere, "The Celebrated Jumping Frog of Calaveras County," was folklore or rather saloon lore of Calaveras County which in retelling he made superb, unquestionably one of the best humorous stories in any time or language. But this evidently was a spark of genius, by no means the sign of a matured writer who knows what he wants to do, as Henry James did at the age of Mark on Jackass Hill. In the same letter to his mother from which I have just quoted, he says —

"To think that, after writing many an article a man might be excused for thinking tolerably good, those New York people should single out a villainous backwoods sketch to compliment me on! . . . a squib that would never have been written but to please Artemus Ward."

This is false modesty, and an apology in advance to his mother, who had forgotten her Kentucky girlhood and wanted her clever son to write respectable, high-class literature. But it is not the word of a matured writer who had come to recognize his own real talents. It took Howells to persuade him later that *Huckleberry Finn* was not too much of a "villainous backwoods sketch."

The truth is that Mark was restless again, and it was not any "literary" urge that made him so. The picaro had "hot feet" once more. San Francisco when he went back pleased him no more than before — or at least his job there. It is safe to say that the picaro was tired of describing other people's wit or lack of it. He wanted, as he wrote Orion in 1868, to write to please "himself" — "not literature and all other bosh," written to please the general public. What he meant I doubt if he knew himself. Certainly everything that could be called litera-ture (but not bosh) was all through his life written by him for the general public — or at least the best writing in it. What he wanted was clearly a change, and he got it in 1866 by taking on a series of letters from Hawaii, then in the final stage of transition from the greatest of Polynesian cultures into a do-main of pineapples, sugar, and missionaries, who "came to do good and did well." With a news beat on a dramatic ship-wreck to help him, he returned to San Francisco to capitalize somehow on the success of his Sandwich Island letters which had been published in Sacramento. "In prison again and all the wide sense of freedom gone. . . . God help me, I wish I were at sea again!" he wrote in his notebook in August of 1866.

7. LECTURER

The letters themselves are historically interesting yet only mild newspaper narrative; but there was more juice to be squeezed out of them. Bored, needing money, Mark was urged, and finally propelled, into giving a lecture on the Islands. Lecturing in the United States was in the second stage of its incredibly successful history. It had burst the bonds of the pre-Civil-War – New-England-Lyceum system, which was chiefly educational, ethical, and informative. There Emerson had made his repu-tation, and Thoreau got his first and very limited hearing. Now the preachers, like Henry Ward Beecher, and humorists like Artemus Ward (who made Lincoln laugh) joined in with hundreds of the fluent and articulate to add an eloquence with which the Lyceum was not often familiar, and raise mirth which would have perhaps shocked the progenitors of this form of adult education. By Mark's time it had become the resource of editors whose magazines had failed, journalists weary of their trade, ministers needing more income, writers with a reputation to support them, and indeed anyone capable of getting and holding a large audience. Many (as Mark soon noted) could do the first, but not the second. It was a certain success if well conducted (as commercial agents soon noted) with the now vast middle class of the North and the West seeking culture, information, and amusement of a "refined variety." No one has described it better than Henry James in his too little read *The Bostonians,* published twenty years after Mark's frightened beginning.

He had spoken to crowds in Carson City and Virginia City, was a top-flight storyteller, had already (his chief literary asset so far) a mastery of humorous dialogue, and knew his audience wanted chiefly to laugh. They hired the largest hall in San Francisco for him and he supplied the text for the advertising posters: "Doors open at 7 o'clock. The trouble to begin at 8 o'clock."

He had a resounding and hilarious success, for in San Francisco he had already a columnist's reputation, quite enough to draw an audience, and a subject of great topical interest. His biographer, Mr. Paine, thinks his success was a result of his eloquence in literary description of Hawaiian scenes, and gives a surviving fragment to prove his thesis that, when he let himself go in a literary way, Mark was always a man-of-letters. It is true that Mark had a weakness for purple patches, but read in cold print they usually turn out to be mauve. There was no pausing place for him between wit, real humor, and Victorian description of the Landseer variety. He lacked now — and always — that taste with which Henry James was endowed

from childhood. I much prefer Mark's description of a Turner
as a cat in a fit in a platter of tomatoes, to his often quoted set-
piece, "Sunrise from the Rigi."

Yet all accounts agree that from this first experiment to the
end Mark was a magnificent lecturer. His own accounts of his
"effects" give the reason why. On the stage (and off it) he was
a superb actor. He had early learned that American, but particularly South Western, trait of delivering his most outrageous
exaggerations, his most absurd burlesques, and especially his
most brilliant wisecracks, with a poker face. One of his tricks
was to sit quietly at the side of the stage until the audience
grew restless, and then surprise them into laughter. Mark
always had interesting things to tell, witty things to say, but it
was his quiet histrionics that got them listened to. Intentness
is the first requisite for successful lecturing. This was the
secret of how to hold an audience of which he boasted in his
autobiographical letter. And something whimsical in him, the
drawl he got from his mother, a power of projecting his personality into words which all good actors have (and which
Mark carried over to the printed page), all helped greatly.
I saw him in old age enter, late and dramatically, with Dr.
Twichell, his close friend, on the arena of a great campus celebration at the two hundredth anniversary of Yale. His white
suit, his shock of hair, brought instant recognition. But it was
when with an engaging vanity he swirled his hat with a gesture
of "here I am at last," that the applause rose into a roar of
laughter.

A series of successful lectures followed in his old Western
haunts, including a triumphant return to Hannibal, which
must have made Tom Sawyer glow and probably strut a bit.
His triumph, however, was an invasion of the East, where reputations still had to be perfected. In New York, in danger of a
half-empty Cooper Institute, the house was "papered" with
schoolteachers who craved information, and needed a release in

laughter. It was a great success. After that night he had a new and profitable career, signed, sealed, and delivered. Nast, the great cartoonist, wanted to make a joint tour with him. But something better suited to his still restless spirit intervened.

I have dwelt upon Mark Twain's unexpected burst into the lecture field because it seems of really first importance in his literary biography. It made him known East and West as a voice, or, to put it more accurately, a "character" speaking not always *of,* but always *as,* a representative of the new human attitudes developed in the Mississippi Valley, and given emphasis in the Rockies and California. Henceforth everything he said, and everything he wrote, at least until his biography of *Joan of Arc,* was, for America and soon for Europe, the great West speaking through a personality that became symbolic.

Even more important was the effect on the man himself. Mark's art, such as it was, and at its best it is a great art, is essentially oral. He was not only a born storyteller and wisecracker, but he early learned how to transfer to the written word the overtones, the color (to mix my figure) of conversation, how to select the words which lift narrative, no matter how rapid, above a mere record of events. Few novelists achieve this excessively difficult transubstantiation. Mark's simple statement that in *Huckleberry Finn* he represents seven different local dialects with accuracy may run a little below one hundred per cent truth, but it is a true description of one of the most sensitive ears among craftsmen in language. Henry James, in the Preface to *The Golden Bowl,* has a word to say here. Any literature whose highest bid is addressed to the imagination must lend itself to *viva-voce* treatment. Such writing will give out its finest secrets when articulately sounded. "It then infallibly, and not less beautifully, most responds." It is not accurate to say that Mark wrote as he talked; he learned to write so that his words sounded as if he were talking. His written dialogue speaks itself, and presents a flesh-and-blood,

personally seen-and-heard speaker to the imagination of the
reader. I am not sure whether Henry James learned to write
as he spoke, or to speak as he wrote. Finally, it seems to have
been the latter.

Not so with Mark. The style is subtly his own, the "tune
of it," and you could pick out a speech of Huck's from a Dictionary of Quotations and write his name after it. Well adapted
to the lecture platform, where the prime necessity was an immediate response in applause or laughter, this great talent of
his was subject to corruption. On the stage he had to exaggerate to get his effects, and include a little acting. There, as
Dickens added the effects of excellent acting to a text already
written for print, and stirred his audience to tears and shouts
so Mark preparing his lectures added his props, his overempha-
ses, his wisecracks and exaggerations, and acquired habits which
he carried over into writing and from which he never escaped.
To appreciate Mark's genius in his great books you must think
of them as oral. To understand his rhetorical weaknesses, you
must note the lecturer's tricks. The last pages of *Huckleberry
Finn* are rather distressing to anyone of literary taste. Read
aloud by Mark to an audience they probably "rolled them
over." Nor is it surprising that Mark's style should have been
so much influenced by these lectures. The newspaper serio-
humorous column on which up to the late sixties his reputation had been based might slay its thousands with laughter, but
the lecture often repeated would slay its ten or hundreds of
thousands, who paid cash down on delivery for the privilege.

8. ASSIGNMENT IN THE HOLY LAND

Mark was restless again, and depressed. In June of 1867, just
before he sailed away for a new adventure, he wrote to his

family, "I haven't anything to write, except that I am tired of
staying in one place — that I am in a fever to get away. . . . My
mind is stored full of unworthy conduct toward Orion and
towards you all. . . . I have got a spirit that is angry with me
and gives me freely its contempt." "There is no satisfaction in
the world's praise anyhow . . . save in the way of business." This
is one of the earlier examples of neuroticism which will prove
to be of final and disastrous importance.

Relief was near. In St. Louis he had heard of the proposed
excursion of the steamer *Quaker City*, with a load of ministers,
tourists, intellectuals, and Americans seeking culture abroad,
which was to sail for the Mediterranean and the Holy Land.
In general, it was to be an ecclesiastical pilgrimage to biblical
sites, though there were plenty aboard whose interests were
much more worldly. Anson Burlingame, our Minister to
China, whom Mark had met in Honolulu, had advised the
rather crude young columnist of Virginia City to seek companionship among men of superior intellect and character —
to refine himself by association. Mark, who was always humble
when the question of frontier manners came up (though he
did very little about them), was impressed. It was the same
advice which about this time young Henry James, in a review,
gave to Walt Whitman. Dubious advice to a creative writer in
any case, especially bad, I should say, for Mark, whose faults in
refinement were inextricably entwined with his peculiar genius.
But it may well have influenced him in choosing the trip on
the *Quaker City* for his next enterprise. General Sherman and
Henry Ward Beecher were both supposed to be coming along.
And his accounts of the missionaries in Hawaii had given his
name a pleasant odor among the clerics in general. So he
applied to the *Alta-California*, of San Francisco, for which he
had been corresponding, to be sent on the voyage as a correspondent with passage paid at $1250, and letters ordered at $20
a letter. The "Reverend Hutchinson" was to be his supervisor,

presumably of manners and morals. When he stepped on board, the Westerner had definitely turned East at last.

The result was to be the exact contrary of Henry James' experience in expatriating himself. Mark was to return more American than when he started. While Henry became famous later as an "internationalist," Mark was to make his first great success with an attack on Europe and the Near East, which backfired into an unwitting satire on his fellow countrymen. It is clear that he was engaged to write as a Westerner, to describe his supposedly distinguished cargo of more or less Easterners, and to ask them and all foreigners such questions as a Californian would want answered. He was to be a roving reporter, a job they knew he could do.

Mark, in 1868, had written to Orion, a phantom chaser if there ever was one, "We chase phantoms. . . . I must go chasing them until I marry." This was prophetic. What he had chased had been the vagabond dream of the picaro, seeking wealth around every corner. "I cannot rest from travel," he could have said with Ulysses. "I wish I never had to stop anywhere for a month," he wrote just before he sailed in 1867. The great success of *The Innocents Abroad* which came out of the *Quaker City* trip calmed if it did not cure this obvious nervous tension; his marriage in 1870 supplied a point of return which gave at least a direction home to all his later wanderings. This biographical sketch of Mark's picaro phase can therefore conveniently end here, and the account of *The Innocents Abroad,* one of the most interesting and significant, but certainly not one of the greatest, of American books, be left to a later chapter where it belongs with Mark's achievements.

He is thirty-two years old when he returns from the ecclesiastical voyage, but already his career as a writer — if he were to be a writer, which is not yet in his own mind certain — is conditioned. His memory and imagination are deeply charged, his forms of self-expression are definable, his style, at least in dialogue and storytelling in general, is shaped if not perfected, his attitudes toward life, with the exception of his deep plunge into cynical pessimism at the end, are determinable, even if he had certainly not determined them for himself. The extraordinary fact is that after *The Innocents Abroad* which belongs in this first period, *all* his great books, and most of his good ones, are directly or indirectly reminiscent of his youth in the West which had ended in 1866. This youth it should be noted is not normal, it is supernormal for the life of the Westward-turning American. Henry James, it will be seen, is abnormal, even for the Eastward-turning men and women of our nation.

Chapter II

THE YOUTH OF HENRY JAMES

WHEN WE THINK of Mark Twain in his formative years it has to be in terms of action, and of changing environments as diverse as scenes in a moving picture of travel. Into these scenes he projects himself, driven by an itching curiosity and zest for experience and, after childhood, by a resolve, often renewed, not to be driven back into small-town frustration like his father. He chooses his environments and they push him into action, but he has no real control over them, or himself, except in his imagination. A consuming interest in human nature keeps him moving, and he hopes always to get back sometime, with a bag full of loot, and be king in Ithaca — which meant in Hannibal, or Hartford, or rural Connecticut.

Henry James' early environment was, as his older brother William James very justly said, the James family. It was an isolated culture of chosen intellectuals, of whom two younger brothers were of an extrovertish quality and his sister a nervous invalid of great intellectual force. Henry was a born artist, and William and his father students and speculators in human welfare and God. There was no necessity for young Henry to seek for an education in morals, in history, in philosophy, or in religion outside the James circle, for he could not escape it at home. Mark was like a wind- and oar-driven Viking, pushed on from coast to coast, poetic perhaps and certainly in love with action, but never forgetting that his job was portable wealth. Henry resembled an inmate of some fortunate monastery, where ideas were discussed, the arts at least approved, and only restless minds left its pleasant cloisters for the spiritual adventures of Rome. The comparison is a little rhetorical, but it is sound.

2. THE JAMES FAMILY

William James Senior, the founder of the American family, was a Scotch-Irishman who turned Westward from Europe, arriving in this country about 1789. He got as far as Albany; but good fortune, multiplied by Albany's excellent position on the Hudson and later at the mouth of the Erie Canal, enabled him to leave a fortune estimated at three million dollars. It was distributed by a will which was curiously influential upon the career of his grandson, Henry James. In order not to dissipate his estate and for the "true interests of all," William Senior trusteed his fortune with provision for incomes for his heirs, but no final distribution to be made until the youngest grandchild at the time of his death should be twenty-one. And both incomes and the size of each heir's final portion should be determined by an avoidance of a "grossly immoral, idle, or dishonorable life." The court finally ruled this provision unworkable, yet it is clear what this Scotch-Irishman *par excellence* had in mind. He proposed that his descendants should have the opportunity to belong to the privileged class, but share the responsibilities, including morality, which should accompany privilege. What became of the bulk of this fortune Henry the grandson could never make out, unless it was lost in the notorious high-stepping of some of his own generation. But his father, Henry Senior, in spite of a quarrel with his progenitor, received at least a generous interest and final share.

The result was an interesting instance of the influence of economics upon activity. The elder James was a city planner, a financial power, a speculator, and a salesman. The two Henrys, the father and son who followed, were not only ignorant of, but utterly uninterested in, business. Money for them was not dynamic power but a dependable income which released very different energies from the typical American struggle for financial independence. In a very true sense neither ever understood or practised what was called in America "competition." When Henry Junior became a novelist, he liked particularly to write about very rich American men, but frankly dodged any attempt to explain how they got their money. He could not even guess, though he was very likely to intimate that it was in some demeaning trade like washtubs for Californians.

Henry James Senior, our Henry's father, was also indifferent to the source of his income, and could not be bothered even to look over with care the real estate in which most of it seems to have been invested. He was a student and thinker from his youth, a thorough-going philosopher who found his friend Emerson insufficiently metaphysical; and all the Transcendentalists too optimistic. His strongly held belief was that evil came from the injection of selfhood into that part of the universal which he called the individual soul. Hobbling on one leg, for he had lost the other in an accident, he found getting about difficult, and was happiest in his own chair at home with his family about him. There he talked incessantly when he was not writing books and pamphlets which he could afford to publish, even though almost literally no one ever read them. But this was a remarkable man, with elements of greatness, and one of the kindest hearts that ever beat. The trouble was that his far-ranging mind dealt usually in abstractions of scope and magnitude, of which his own modified Swedenborgianism was one of the easiest to grasp. He was what might be called a spiritual collectivist, and in this respect ahead of his times; but his demands on the reader's attention were too great for the relaxed minds of Unitarians and Transcendentalists. His son, Henry, was to complain of the same lack of attention for a very different subject matter in his novels.

As has been noted by others, nothing could be more dangerous for a novelist than to neglect selfhood. But the influence of Henry James Senior on his most brilliant children was not in dogma. His far-flung speculations, and later the more persuasive arguments of young William, slid easily over the mind of Henry Junior, engrossed from early years in the infinite complexities of the concrete. And yet Henry never escaped from the effect of living in what he called afterward "a domestic moral affectionate realm," where discussions went on even at mealtime, so eager that someone was usually on his feet. The effect was as strong (and far more rational) as the doses of old-time religion forced down into Sam Clemens' imagination.

The universe was first presented to young Henry as a moral order, and when he began to think of fiction he was quick to see that only in some kind of moral order did the characters that interested him make sense, and what was even more important, dramatize themselves.

But this was an order of true morals, not moralism, which Henry Senior detested. It was the subject of these interminable discussions which flowed around the father's chair. When a consciousness of what the world called morals, and a sense of virtue, entered the conscience, he felt that both became pedantry and priggishness and seriously affected character. This also was good doctrine for a youthful pre-novelist. Henry Senior, indeed, entirely agreed with Huck Finn, who felt that what everyone in Hannibal called conscience merely kept you from doing what you ought to do, and that good conduct was superior to what Henry Senior called "flagrant morality," and

what Huck called "ornery sermons." The necessity of an unconscious morality, accepted not argued about, was the basis of
Henry James' writing all his life. Virtue becomes in his novels
a social grace. Resentful at the attitudes of the English upper
classes in the beginning of our Civil War, Henry James Senior
exploded in a speech as he must often have done at home:

"Conventional routine, an entirely artificial morality, has so
bitten itself into the life of the [English] people . . . that the
kindly human heart within is never allowed to come to the surface. . . . Its hideous class distinctions . . . and [the] abject snobbery or inbred servility of the lower classes . . . gives to a log-cabin
in Oregon the charm of comparative dignity and peace." But
this is the theme of *The Wings of the Dove,* and of all Henry
Junior's dramatizations of the American "innocent" abroad.
To be sure, Henry Senior was speaking of manners, but neither
he nor his son made much distinction between manners and
morals. This is all of the philosophy that an artist-minded boy
carried away from the James family, which was indeed a little
world within a world, but this moral scheme was as fundamental for him as it was usually unconscious.

3 . HENRY JAMES' CHILDHOOD

AND EDUCATION

Henry James Junior was born April 15, 1843, at Number 5 (not
Number 2, as he said later), Washington Place, the second in a
row between the New York University buildings and Broadway,
New York, a house with a portico in the older New York
manner. Henry James Senior records the number in the year
before his son's birth. Young Henry was whisked away to
Europe with his parents in his second year, and his first remem-

bered "impression" (he became a specialist in impressions) was of the Place Vendôme in Paris. His childhood was spent at another New York house, on the south side of Fourteenth Street, near to Sixth Avenue, where they lived for ten years until 1855, and young Henry amused himself by walking the streets of mid-New York as later he was passionately to walk and walk through London. In 1855 all of them went to Europe for three years, and again, after an interlude in Newport, the least American of native cities, to Geneva for 1859–61. Only the Civil War concluded the experiments in mobility of the family.

They were not random. The father, who was philosophically an internationalist, had determined that his children should not settle-in domestically or educationally until they were able intellectually to resist the localism which he felt was responsible for so many of the world's evils. Henry Junior remembers in his first twelve years a series of schools, most of them described by him as "sordid," in no one of which was he allowed to stay long enough for a shaping influence. This experiment of taste-and-go was continued in Europe. It was a planned education, which, as is usually the case, got unexpected results. When Henry was six and William eight, Henry Senior wrote to his friend Emerson:

"Looking upon our four stout boys, who have no play-room within doors, and import shocking bad manners from the street, with much pity, we gravely ponder whether it would not be better to go abroad for a few years with them, allowing them to absorb French and German and get a better sensuous education than they are likely to get here. To be sure, this is but a glimpse of our ground of proceeding."

The bad manners from the streets were what Aunt Polly objected to in Tom's friendship with Huck Finn, but by "sensuous," the key word in this letter, it might be supposed that Mr. James would have regarded Sam Clemens' educational

experiences as quite perfect. Henry James Senior's idea was
rather different. He wanted his boys to be free to shape
their own souls. They must never stagnate in the care of the
self-contained or the complacent, whether of a nation, a culture,
or a school. But what to do with them afterward was not clear
to him, and the later careers of his two geniuses were a constant
series of surprises. His boys were not to be trained to make
a living, they were to be educated to live in a society which was
to be, naturally, the best to be found anywhere. He told them
to answer if anyone asked them what *his* business was, "Say I'm
a philosopher, say I'm a seeker for truth, say I'm a lover of my
kind, say I'm an author of books if you like; or, best of all, just
say I'm a Student." What they *did* say is not recorded.

Henry Junior himself in his later autobiographies is aware of
the value of his "sensuous" experiences. It released, he says, by
a process of "waste," talents that were congenital by providing
a mobile environment in which dedication to high intellectual
or artistic endeavor seemed inevitable to those susceptible to it.
The most "formative, fertilising . . . intellectual experience"
of his youth was in the great rooms of the Louvre. "I had
looked at pictures [there] . . . but I had also looked at France
and looked at Europe . . . looked at history, as a still-felt past
and complacently personal future, manners, types, characters,
possibilities, and prodigies and mysteries of fifty sorts." You
can scarcely get a better definition of the desires of the Eastward-turning Americans of the period, going back in search of
culture — nor a more "sensuous" one. It was in its own way
as "sensuous" as Mark's life on the Mississippi.

And yet it is quite clear from Henry's autobiographies, as
well as from easily deducible facts, that Henry's ideas of good
and bad, his dedication to the "difficult" as he admits himself,
his selection of those who were to become his close friends, are
most of all to be credited to the immediate Jamesian environment. For this center of his affections became a portable hearth,

which went with the boys, the father in his chair, the mother, upon whose devotion they so much depended, going with them, a hearth always at least accessible until Henry's full maturity. They had traveled and resided, particularly with Henry, in the scholastic period abroad. They were in Newport when in 1862 Henry went (most unwillingly) to the Harvard Law School, William being at work in science in Harvard College. It was Henry who kept closest touch with the parents. In 1864 they followed to Boston, and in 1866 set up what was to be a permanent home in Cambridge. Not until 1871 did Henry escape, escape as will be seen is the right word, from this brilliant, affectionate home where nothing was ever taken for granted, no sally of the intellect discouraged, no thought taken for money except the responsibilities of a privileged group. By comparison with what happened in this little circle, not only school experiences in America and abroad, but even Henry's childhood life in New York, and in Albany, and his associates there and among his relatives, are unimportant until his Newport and Boston days. If Mark's early youth was supernormal for America, Henry's was abnormal to a high degree. Few educational experiences anywhere have ever distilled a more stimulating atmosphere for minds and temperaments able to take it, sweetened as it was by affection, conducted by persuasion, and enlivened by a constant humor shared by all. The two ablest Jameses broke away of course from their father's dominance, and Alice, much younger, was, it would seem, frustrated by her experience. It was dangerous for the two boys, but when they escaped, it was with an extraordinary absence of lesions. Psychiatrists should take note.

But if Henry Junior's early youth was abnormal, it was not un-American, no more so than the rather specialized boy-life of Sam Clemens on the great river. The two decades before the Civil War were, at least in the upper East and nearer mid-West, an age of coteries, and coteries are notoriously the hotbeds of literature and religion. The James family, gathered about their father, was no less a coterie for being only a domestic circle. There were hundreds of such eddies of "seekers" in these remarkable decades in this God-smitten region, although most of them were religious or mystical or economic rather than cultural and philosophic. Henry James Senior can best be defined as one of the most ardent (and fortunate) of the "seekers." Sometimes these eddies were of true Communists, like Brook Farm, and the later Communist experiments in the new Middle West. Sometimes they were tempestuous swirls bearing a new religion and its folklore with them, like Mormonism, or the Millerites. In one rare instance, at Concord, a local whirlpool, both intellectual and mystic, sent its words across the world. There Thoreau was part of the Emerson coterie, and his abnormality was not in Transcendentalism, but in the excess of his sincerity and the tenacity of his direction toward a life in nature which sent him to Walden Pond.

The James coterie was not only more limited than Concord, it was more worldly (with a possible exception for Concord's Hawthorne), and more mobile. It was also less spiritual, and more vigorously intellectual. It was, of course, far more civilized than the religious and economic experiments which spread from New England into the West. A contrast and a comparison would be with the Alcott family in Concord. The deeply spiritual, radically social, but naïve and moony-minded Alcott was very different from Henry James Senior, with his sharp intellectual instrument. Yet the Alcott family, like the James, was a hothouse for talent and noble intentions. The men were equally impractical: Alcott because he attempted to reform the world every morning, Henry Senior because he was always tilting at the gross stupidities of human living, without ever trying to correct them except by changes in philosophy so fundamental as to be utterly unworkable and therefore inoffensive. His idea of preventing the Civil War was to reor-

ganize immediately the iniquitous social systems of both the
North and the South!

Henry Junior in his *Notes of a Son and Brother* quotes the
letters which this courageous, high-spirited man wrote to Mrs.
Tappan, or to Jane Norton (for Henry Senior like his son had
a taste for attractive intellectual women), or to Harry and
Willie. They are among the most delightful ever written by an
American intellectual. They are better letters, more unforced,
more natural, more witty than his famous novelist son was
capable of writing. The influence of such a father as the center
of a coterie is incalculable, even though his philosophic ideas
got little more real attention in the home circle than when published. A writer, indeed, as Henry was to be, needs both
shelter and protection in a coterie. Yet a purely literary coterie
may, and often does, produce only an ingrown closet art. Henry
shared the high aims, the stimulating atmosphere, the intellectual confidence, without the dangerous shaping of a dogmatic
mind. His father believed in perfect freedom.

New England never captured the James coterie, although
Harvard gave William his science and a platform for broad-
casting. Both Henry Senior and William were too tough-minded
for Concord Transcendentalism, and young Henry found
Boston too professionally intellectual for his artist's mind. He
never disliked Boston, he said later, nor liked it either. The
James family was a Middle States, specifically a Hudson Valley,
family, with no Brahmin traditions nor Puritan fanaticisms in
their ancestral memories. Only recently have we begun to appreciate the importance of such a difference in our literary
history. There is a shadowy margin running somewhere
through the borders of Connecticut and the Hudson Valley
which was as significant intellectually and socially as the Mason
and Dixon Line in politics. This margin the Jameses finally
crossed to make New England their nearest approach to a permanent home, but in a spiritual sense they never became resi-

dents. Newport, cosmopolitan, artistic, wealthy, was, Henry says, his first introduction to New England, and this was in his eighteenth year; but it was as James knew it the least New England of towns. There is more affection for Newport in his reminiscences than in all he has to say of either Boston or Cambridge. It was in Newport, as we shall see, that the direction of his talents first began to reveal itself, but not because of New Englanders chiefly. Pragmatism, as William worked it out (and Henry said he had been practising it all his life), is an American, not at all a New England, phenomenon. The American women in Henry's later novels who stirred his emotions are from New York or the Middle States. These Americans from west of the marginal line often both repel and fascinate him because they seem to indicate a possible future civilization in microcosm. But they never "chill" him, as did Cambridge. His novel, *The Bostonians,* which dealt with a fanatic fervor which he regarded as the essence of Boston, is a satire. His Milly and his Maggie, those creatures of infinite wealth and acute suffering, have lived in a vital, if not agreeable society; his two elderly New Englanders in *The Ambassadors* have not, and that is the moral of the story.

Yet to return once more to the James family — who, I am sure, exotic as they seemed, helped to keep Henry fundamentally American all of his expatriate life. Even more than in Emerson's household, the James coterie was a place where ideas floated in freedom tempered by humor and restricted by good sense. It was an atmosphere where speculation of some kind came as easy as breathing. It was an environment in which writing something was as natural as planting corn in Iowa; where all the cultures were regarded as the natural expression of man, so that a budding writer could scarcely tell in which direction he wished to begin. But for a budding novelist it was clearly not enough. In his Notebook for December 26, 1881, Henry records his earliest memories of his "untried years."

While abstract philosophical discussions billowed about his head at home, "Never did a poor fellow have more; never was an ingenuous youth more passionately and yet more patiently eager for what life might bring. . . . It is touching enough to look back. I knew at least what I wanted then — to see something of the world." Which meant for him turn Eastward, to get impressions. "My impressions!" he says sarcastically in a moment of depression. To put it briefly, he wished to experience life in the act, beyond this happy circle, and make it articulate. He craved, as he said later, "persons."

And indeed, there was one obvious lack in this happy family group, how much, or how little, it is one of the purposes of this book to consider. There was no easy outlet from it to the coarse world outside, although plenty of access to the parlors of the literati and even to the salons of the rich. In this world men and women acted, but did not speculate except in material things. At home and in the abstract the speculation was in the welfare of mankind, the nature of evil, the origin of motives, the nature of values. These were always reverberating among the family and its friends, and the father (unlike Alcott) would forage into the outer world and come back laden with selective evidence which no one would read. Yet I fear that Henry Senior on the deck of a Mississippi steamboat would have found some traveling parson to converse with and been quite oblivious (not merely, as with Mark, silent) to Old Adam and his brood roistering, cheating, whoring, and full of corn liquor in the cabins. But the important resemblance between Mark and James in youth is that both wanted most of all to see something of the world, and did, one West, one East. Was it in any respects the same world, or was it the men themselves not the skies that truly differed? In any case, both had their idyllic days, the one at Hannibal, the other in the personalized seminar of the James coterie. The James family corresponded to Mark's Hannibal and the Mississippi.

4. HENRY HIMSELF

"Harry," wrote his father to his mother in 1857, when the boy was fourteen, and the boys for reasons of economy were at Boulogne instead of in Paris with the family, and studying at the college there, "Harry is a devourer of libraries, and an immense writer of novels and dramas. He has considerable talent as a writer, but I am at a loss to know whether he will ever accomplish much." Henry was writing these dramas of a few pages each, illustrated by his pen. His novels seem to have been weird romances, with villains and sophisticated heroines. He was a dreamy boy, quite charming, to judge from a daguerreotype of him taken a few years earlier in his little "American" coat which made Thackeray, when he saw him, call him "Buttons." Outside the family he did not mix well, had never played with other boys, admitted later in New York that he could not cope with the street boys whose shocking manners it was William who brought home. He read much and as naturally as eating. But it is questionable whether he ever devoured a book as Sam Clemens did Cervantes between watches on the Mississippi — except in later years, Balzac. In maturity James was never an excessive reader except for professional reasons, and then of fiction, not history or poetry. He was to all appearances a passive youngster, content to let the others do the talking. He was like a fine-fibered sponge, quietly absorbing all that interested him, especially the most delicate essences of his environment. The strong flavor of his life then, he said later, was his spiritual independence of the winds of doctrine blowing through the New York household. He was left "alone" and "master of my short steps" to wander through

54

the beguiling streets of New York. If Tom Sawyer had met such a shy and exotic creature on the sidewalks of Hannibal, I fear he would have bloodied his nose, as in Tom's encounter with the too well-dressed boy. But each youth was out to see the world with certainty that he would find something to fit his imagination. Harry in his boyhood even was clearly seeking "persons," as he said himself, to fit the representations of art with which he was already so familiar. Sam's fascination was with the persons themselves — the human race as art and history see it, he took for granted. It is a vital difference between two potentially creative imaginations, one of which was to work with personalities, created whole and self-explanatory, as God's touch in Michelangelo's fresco created Adam; the other with characters that did not yield their significance except by minute analysis. At about the age of Mark when he was storing his memory with rugged and primitive individuals who were to become prototypes of the Wild West American, Henry was visiting Ruskin (whom he did not like). A little bored even by Ruskin's lively nieces, Henry drifted away from the group to study the painting of an old doge by Titian, which gave him a new sense of the meaning of art.

But to return to the boy in earlier scenes. In 1858 the family returned unexpectedly to America via Newport. Their stay was not long, but after the winter of 1859 when Henry studied at Geneva they returned again to Newport where William, who had suddenly decided to become a painter, was put in the studio of William Morris Hunt, then very influential. Henry tagged along until William's enthusiasm was spent. But there were other reasons for the repatriation, soon to become final for the elders of the Jamesians. Henry Senior had begun to worry over his finances, something new in his experience, probably as a result of the panic of 1857, and from this time on, the note of financial concern is constant. The boys first try to spare their father by traveling alternately. Then Henry sets

out to earn some of his expenses abroad, and William, his education finished, soon becomes self-supporting. The details are
not important. Yet it was from this time that Henry Junior,
the supposedly fortunate man of letters who never had to worry
about his income, begins to worry at least as much as the young
picaro Sam Clemens, until eventually how to be secure
materially affects his career. More of this later. Their return
to Newport in 1860 was quite certainly determined by the desperate conflict so obviously ready to break somehow in America.
Henry Senior loved his country and must have felt that in the
rising storm he would be better informed as well as more comfortable in mind if he should return. Later he was to become
strong for Lincoln and the Union. In 1858–60, he and his
family were philosophical observers rather than partisans.

But before the clouds broke suddenly in 1861, Newport was
an interlude, and remained an influence in Henry's life, at
least until he went to Harvard in 1862, of much more importance (I should say) than the Civil War.

For the quaint and charming seaport, with its aristocratic,
almost separatist traditions, had gathered to itself not only an
art center, but a fringe of residences in which lived the traveled
and the cultured who were wealthy enough to pursue the
leisured life. The rich friends of the Jameses, who belonged
both to intellectual and social Newport, had all lived abroad,
and there was plenty of money with no visible signs of money-
making, exactly as in the society of Henry's novels. We see this
society in *An International Episode,* yet one would scarcely guess
from this book how powerfully the imagination of young Henry
from age fifteen to his early twenties was formed in the society
of Newport. The mature James remembered it as a "basis of
reconciliation" to America, when the habit, the taking for
granted, of America had been broken or intermitted. It might
be unfairly said that after childhood, Newport, Cambridge,
and Boston were as near to America as the youth ever got, and

not very near. But that is radically untrue. There were American men and women in the James circle quite as American as Mark Twain's Mississippi Valley or Carson City friends, though, like them, special cases, not common elsewhere. There were friends of his father, like Alleyne Otis, a man who "did" nothing — he only *was* — and returned expatriates as cultivated in good living as the Jameses in good thinking; indeed, there were many such sophisticates of the social life — Eastward-turners come home — whose European stay-behinds the young Henry, when settled abroad, met with a shock of recognition. And in Newport were the Temples, Albany cousins, and more or less relatives, who married with the Emmets, lifelong friends and painters of ability — the "Emmetry," as James came to call them. It was the death of Minnie Temple which drew from Henry his most appealing, most human letter. If it had not been for Minnie Temple, the catalogue of Henry's women emotionally realized, either in life or in his novels, would be very short.

In Newport also was John La Farge, a great painter, recently returned from a European life, not much older than Henry, "an artistic, an aesthetic nature of wondrous homogeneity," Henry wrote of him later. Not only did he introduce the youth to important French reading, but was the first creator of art to become intimate with a youth whose most vivid education had come from looking at pictures. He introduced him to Browning and Balzac, who blew away very quickly the false romance of the stories he was writing in the sixties. He painted Henry most probably in 1861, when the youth was eighteen. I shall recur to this remarkable portrait, which is now the property of The Century Association in New York, a little later. It is, I think, one of the great portraits of men of letters, essentially much finer than Sargent's well-known picture of Henry in his age. No one can study it without new conceptions of what underlay H.J.'s reticent, deeply emotional character. There is fortunately a good verbal portrait also of Henry in his Newport period in a note from young Thomas Sergeant Perry — "Super-excellent and all-reading, all-engulfing friend of those days," Henry calls him. Perry was his companion on long walks, ever Henry's only form of athletic recreation until the bicycle extended his range. Perry wrote to Lubbock, the editor of James' letters:

"Mr. James the father was getting out a somewhat abstruse book called *Substance and Shadow, or Morality and Religion in Their Relation to Life.* W.J. amused himself and all the family by designing a small cut to be put on the title page, representing a man beating a dead horse. This will illustrate the joyous chaff that filled the James' house. There was no limit to it. There were always books to tell about and laugh over, or to admire, and there was an abundance of good talk with no shadow of pedantry or priggishness. H.J.'s spirits were never so high as those of the others. If they had been, he still would have had but little chance in a conflict of wits with them, on account of his slow speech, his halting choice of words and phrases; but as a companion in our walks he was delightful. . . . He had a certain air of aloofness, but . . . to his friends he was most tenderly devoted."

This description would have held good at any time of his life, except that, if he never overcame his hesitation in speech — sometimes almost a stammer — he learned to use it for the sounding of incomparably rotund clauses, and the insertion of his innumerable qualifications. His charm in youth glows out from the farewell of a letter from his intensely expressive father in 1873:

"Good-bye, my lovely Harry. Words can't tell how dear you are to my heart; how proud I am of your goodness and truth; of what Mr. Arnold calls your 'sweet reasonableness.'"

It was a broad and diverse America that could present two types as genuine and as convincing as Pap Finn and Henry

James Senior. And I must call attention to James' unusual out-pouring of words to his children, unusual in America, unusual in any English-speaking country. Was it the Irish in him? Certainly the atmosphere of his home, however intellectual, was warm. Was it possibly of him the ethereal Emerson was speaking when he said that *he* could never be a stove?

There are a few items more to add to this sketch of relevant youthful biography. The Civil War put a period to the age of what might be called spiritual speculation in eastern America, especially to metaphysical and transcendental experiments. They went on but lost the color of confident universality. And it set a semicolon at least after the prevailing moral concern of New England intellectuals. You can see the confusion of a transition period in Horace Greeley and his *Tribune,* where abolition, temperance, practical politics, and expansions to the undeveloped West not so much mix as alternate. Those who, like the Charles Francis Adams family, came back from Europe after the war's end found the country changed almost beyond recognition. Only the young extroverts of the turbulent Far West, drunk with excited action which they called progress, discovered that the post-war industrializing East was by no means alien or difficult. The success of Mark Twain's noisy onslaught upon the capitals of culture in the Old World was a sign of the times. But what soon made him at home in the East of the raucous Reconstruction period was soon to drive Henry James away from Cambridge and New York.

The reactions of the James family to the War Between the States were as characteristic as Sam Clemens' advance and rapid retreat. Seated in Newport, then Boston and Cambridge, they shared the local belief in rightness for the North, but with no passion of enthusiasm. The trouble with abolition, the father thought, was that it was directed at an institution instead of the general triumph of social justice. Our evils are all fossil, he wrote — there are no new evils. What the family felt was a

solemn duty to defend their country in a war which, like so
many other Americans, South and North, they watched at first
with some indifference as an unhappy interruption of the good
life. Judging from William's letters written at Harvard, it did
not even interrupt it except for the two younger boys, in danger
at the front. The difference from Mark's attitude was in a sense
of duty, and was perhaps as much geographical as moral.
Henry's comments in his memoirs are intense, but very
Jamesian. What he called at the "risk of fatuity . . . my relation
to the war" was a sore and troubled, a mixed and oppressive
thing. It was "the general pang of participation." And he
walked rather "ruefully" before those who went and suffered,
as not having at the time shared "more happily their risk." Yet
there is a far livelier sense of what war means to a country in
later reflections in letters on the battles abroad of Sadowa and
Sedan. Europe and its civilization was more vivid to him in its
dangers than the union of the United States. There seems little
ground for the attempt of recent psychological critics to assign
deep mental maladjustments to Henry's failure to take part in
the great American war.

For one thing, it was not his fault. The two younger brothers
enlisted when they were boys, and were shattered by their
experiences. William, who was then physically infirm, and on
the verge of hypochondria, could not go, although it is certain
that he would have enlisted. So would Henry, though not by
any desire. He was supremely unfitted for the military life.
But he was also at the time physically incapable from an accident which had far more serious and lasting effects upon him
than keeping him out of a conflict where at eighteen or any
other age he would have been worse than useless in active
combat. Nor did he have an iota of those gifts which enabled
Whitman, in his forties when the war broke, to do great service
to his countrymen as a friend and consoler of thousands of the
sick and wounded. Henry's reserved and hesitant unfitness for

such a mission is evident even in his age when he visited Belgian and British wounded in the First World War. He had suffered in 1862, when he was nineteen, what seemed to be a slight accident. Falling over a fence (so the story was told me by his nephew) he strained his back, perhaps misplaced a vertebra or injured the sacroiliac. Through "crazy juvenility" no competent attention was given to the lesion at the time, and afterwards there was recurring pain, and "years really of recumbency" which made him uncertain of any participation in physical exertion. If he had got even as far as the front he would have been invalided home at the first upset.

At the very time therefore when, the war apart, a boy must depend upon activity for the normal social contacts of youth, when he should have been off to the woods and mountains, like his brother William, or "sparking" the girls, as they said in those days, he would be prone and suffering. As late as 1870, so he wrote in *The Middle Years,* he had been "so long gravely ill." And as late as 1899 he is still writing Howard Sturgis "with it" still harassing him, and had written *The Awkward Age* with the pain in addition to his mental labors. (Perhaps some of the tortuosities of that overintricate novel may reflect physical as well as mental tensity!) All this happened to a youth already too much retracted from a world, especially from a youthful world, which fascinated him but which he had approached chiefly by walking the streets. His father was troubled by his recessive habits even before the accident. He wrote from Bonn in 1860, that "Harry and Wilky are getting to an age when they want friends among their own sex, and sweethearts in the other; and my hope is . . . that they may 'go it strong' when they get home." Early marriage was, he thought, the cure. But when they did get home, Henry was soon flung into a retirement by necessity which must have confirmed his earlier habit of letting the expansive and adaptive William make his contacts for him. And it is hinted in many passing remarks that he then gave up the hope of active participation in much that to youth of his age is as natural as breathing — including love. It was then that he must have assumed the role of observer, which was so well adapted to a boy who by necessity if not by choice formed so many of his associations among a society much older, and less normally active than he should have been himself. This role was his for all of his life as a novelist, where he describes his usually semi-detached functions in the story itself and his limitations so often that it is a surprise to the reader when once (in *The Sacred Fount*) he admits that he (as narrator) has done more than question and analyze, but perhaps has been himself in love!

That I do not exaggerate the effect of this long recurrent invalidism of a kind as devastating in the long run as a toothache in the short, two quotations will indicate. It is 1881 in Cambridge. Henry, called home by the death of the beloved mother upon whom all the temperamental family relied for quiet devotion, is sitting writing in his notebook "in the old back sitting room which William and I used to occupy," when both were at Harvard. "The feeling of that younger time comes back to me in which I sat here scribbling, dreaming, planning, gazing out upon the world in which my fortune was to seek, and suffering tortures from my damnable state of health. It was a time of suffering so keen that that fact might [claim?] to give its dark colour to the whole period." What he thought about when he wrote was "the freshness of impression and desire, the hope, the curiosity, the vivacity" that came "when the burthen of pain was lifted." "Some of my doses of pain were very heavy; very weary some of my months and years," when indeed he was often bedridden with no calculable time of recovery.

What must have been a frequent conviction, that he must make his disability a condition of his life, is woven into *The Wings of the Dove*, as was his practice with all his experiences. The book presents, as he says in his Preface, a "very young motive." It is built upon the situation of "a young person conscious of a great capacity for life, but early stricken and doomed, condemned to die under short respite, while also enamoured of the world; aware moreover of the condemnation and passionately determined to 'put in' before extinction as many of the finer vibrations as possible, and so achieve, however briefly and brokenly, the sense of having lived. Long had I turned it over."

Milly Theale, the heroine of *The Wings of the Dove*, was not Henry James. She more clearly resembles Ralph Touchett in *The Portrait of a Lady*, who, however, had achieved the sense of having lived. And in her desire to "put in" before extinction as much life as possible she was very like Henry's beloved cousin, Minnie Temple, who died unachieved if not of a broken heart. Henry spent hours in talk with her, bringing his news from the outer world, and concealing his own physical distress. And both Henry and Minnie put to themselves the same question, which in the terms of the Preface is, "Why should a figure be disqualified for a central position by the particular circumstance that might most quicken, that might crown with a fine intensity" what was permitted of life? Minnie Temple was frustrated by tuberculosis before she had her desires fulfilled. Henry James escaped with "weary" pain, but not without deprivations in his youth which I feel sure conditioned much in his future. The extensive activity of a long adolescence which so enriched Mark Twain's reservoir of memory was denied to Henry James, whose youthful emotions, except for art, grew prematurely middle-aged. Both men failed of intimate experience with young women of their own age, for reasons not entirely clear with Mark, but with Henry in part at least from lack of opportunity.

Certainly the cost of all this thwarting, at least in early youth, was heavy, in spite of his courageous reactions to sacrifice. It was a restriction in life and love that sharpened his efforts but

narrowed his scope. His father's only objection to his choice of
writing as a career was that the literary profession was "narrow-
ing." So was everything else in his opinion but being a Student
and a lover of his fellow men. Henry in his turn was to complain of Kipling, after a first enthusiasm, that the life experiences in his stories were too limited in variety — a complaint
which many critics have made of James himself.

Of course, there may well have been something physiological
or psychological in the boy and man. He was presumably of
the median sexual type, like Thoreau, the kind of man who
gets along most easily with men, or — as with James, and his
father — with attractive older women, usually married. I am
told by one of the James circle, whose mother was close to James,
that Henry always had one woman friend of whom he was especially fond at a given period. Yet he found it difficult, as with
many such men, to marry, by which I mean no nonsense about
congenital or accidental impotence. He felt, he wrote William,
that he believed in marriage — for other people. More cogently he wrote Grace Norton, in 1881, that he thought himself
unlikely to marry — because he did not estimate himself highly
enough. Yet there are several remarks of the *if* and *perhaps*
type. With so many close female friends, there is no known
record of Henry having been ever passionately in love, no indication in his books. He expressly denied it of Minnie Temple.
The sensitive face, the sensuous mouth in La Farge's portrait
at eighteen are of a boy one would have said was destined to
passion both high and intense. What he got afterward were
rare and even exciting affections, unclouded by sexual desire.
Pain, according to my thinking, had deprived him in youth,
certainly till twenty-nine, of the first steps toward a normal
sexual life; and later the urge was not strong enough, the deep
involvements in art, intensely emotional as we shall see, satisfied a nature always most responsive to the esthetic and the in-

tellectual. For good or for ill? I do not apologize for this long, and very important, interlude on the frustrations of ill health.

Readers of Henry James have too much neglected his three autobiographies, the last unfinished: *A Small Boy and Others* (1913), *Notes of a Son and Brother* (1914), and *The Middle Years* (published in 1917). They leave many questions unanswered, but for charm and nostalgia and for quiet humor no biography will ever equal them. *A Small Boy and Others,* for example, is the record of a budding novelist made articulate as a boy never could do, yet faithful to what belongs in representational art. It has the glow of Twain's reminiscent stories, without the drama, which James reserved, with very few exceptions, for adult sophistication. What might be called a genius for places was already in his power. The material is rich. The little vignette of the shop where his extraordinary uncles came for their handkerchiefs and collars; the account of young Vernon King, that brilliant youth educated by an expatriate and violently unpatriotic mother, who flung his life away in the Civil War, and was buried upon a Newport hill with no mention made that he died in a war for his country; most of all the accounts of his father — these make you long for stories such as Mark Twain made from his youth. Although it must be admitted that Henry's elaborations of English style would in a story have buried even Tom Sawyer fathoms deep! A warmth breathes, nevertheless, from these books that never blows from the notebooks of the novelist who almost passionately sets down the technique of a situation where people stir him less than their complications. The stories of his early years are far less personally emotional than these scattered memoirs of himself when young. Have we here a rare phenomenon — a great artist in the making, whose ego (overawed perhaps by the family) modestly gave way to a brain which preferred to analyze others rather than to express, however indirectly, himself?

5. HENRY THE WRITER

In 1869 Henry set off again for Europe, after delaying his dearest wish because William was using the family surplus for a stay abroad (William feared he was using up Henry's birthright), but also and more particularly on account of his own health. Henry had written to William in 1867, "It is plain that I shall have a very long row to hoe before I am fit for anything, for either work or play." Indeed, one of his objectives in his trip was the hydropathic cure at Malvern in England, which he later revisited. Returning again in 1870, he went over once more as a tourist with his sister and aunt in 1872, with a commission from *The Nation* to do a series of travel sketches (the same year in which Mark was writing his travel sketches of the Wild West). There in Europe, he made a momentous decision to stay longer for his own improvement. It was as decisive as Mark's resolve in 1870 to live in the East. James came home only in 1874, partly to relieve the family of his burden of expense, partly to be "on the premises" where he could place his writings with friends to help him. These Eastward turnings were toward the Continent where he had spent so much of his boyhood. Now he drank deep. So far his writing had been criticism, description, and only poorish fiction. He craved the "picturesque," a strong word in those days, and his search was for art, both of which were best found in the romantic decadence of Papal Rome, which became the city of his fantasies; as London later was the city of his mind. It was the starry-eyed habitants of the galleries and cathedrals who roused the philistine laughter of Mark Twain; it was the vulgar, ignorant scoffers at an Old World which they could not understand who became the comic relief of Henry James.

Yet it was more than the picturesque which drew him also to England. In his memoirs, and especially the earliest, it is well to note an obsession with English characteristics which belongs to all English-speaking peoples (even the Irish as was James by blood) and to no others. At first he was a little afraid of the English, and was often suspicious of the French and Italians as persons who seemed to belong to a different moral kind. Even when he became a familiar of the great French writers themselves, Flaubert, Turgenev, Daudet, Zola, morally they troubled him. But the English were and always had been on the outskirts at least of the James family. There was an inner urge and prophetic necessity for a young writer to see through their "coating of comely varnish and colour," into the reality with which literature had made him at home.

Rather silly remarks have been made upon James' determined, if not uncritical, Anglomania in his youth. The English bookshop in New York where he lived inside of *Punch* and English novels, his awe of Thackeray, visiting in his father's house, so much greater than of Emerson, are instances, but most of all the furnishing of his boyish mind with English scenes and characters that seemed to him so much richer and more various than those of Albany or New York. Yet this is to view the nineteenth century as if it were the twentieth. Henry belonged to a day when, at least in the East and the South, the English literary tradition was almost as immediate as our own, and certainly more articulate (except in New England). One must remember that the Old World came to young Americans nearly everywhere, both in type and picture, chiefly through England, or borrowed from England. No other impression not an actual experience was so strong, except possibly the Wild West (this was Twain's specialty), as from Dickens, Scott, Shakespeare *par*

excellence. This Eastward turning of the sensitive boy Henry
James was the result of an intense and natural curiosity, plus
sheer romance. My own first experience as a young adult in
England came thirty-odd years later than James' 1869 visit,
yet I could use his words to describe my own excitement and
desires nourished by youthful reading. Henry's decision to live
as an expatriate came later, and was most realistic, most painful — and I think most wise.

The record of James' state of mind at this moment is to be
found in literature, indeed in the only piece of fiction worth
reading of his apprentice period. It is "The Passionate Pil-
grim," a short story, written in 1870. The plot is ridiculous,
the characters faintly absurd — although Henry is twenty-seven
he does not know yet how to make a convincing story about a
situation. But it is hot with passion — the kind of passion
which, to my mind, was always to surpass with Henry the love
of women. The story is of the almost lunatic obsession of a
young American for the evidences of a rich-lived life in an
English manorial house that he has been told may have been his
by inheritance. The mistress of the house understands and
sympathizes until her romance (quite bloodless) falls in love
with his, while her cold brother quite rightly treats him as
either a fool or a crook. Meanwhile, the Observer of the story,
as Henry was later to call him, watches the show with an excited
scrutiny which misses no value for representational art. It is
the engaging tale of a dilettante in culture by a dilettante in
storytelling, more interested in his own emotions in a place of
pervasive beauty than in the story of its people.

Yet dilettante is not the word to apply to the young James
either at home or abroad, except in its original Italian sense of
a fine mind absorbed in the perception of the beautiful and the
wise, with no fixed purpose as to what it proposes to do with
the results. Henry was by no means aimless in his devotion to
a literary career, but if asked at any time before the early

seventies probably would have (like many a young fellow) said nothing more specific than that he wanted to write. And certainly his strongest talent, so far, was for criticism and description, rather than fiction. What he could write and publish, and thus establish a little freedom even though a financially dependent youth, were reviews, travel articles, and — by the grace and help of one friend — a few shaky and usually imitative stories. He assuredly knew — as his emphatic discarding of most of his stories showed later — that he had not mastered his technique for storytelling, did not quite obviously yet know what kind of story he wished to write. There is a letter to his friend, the arbiter of taste at Harvard, Charles Eliot Norton, a letter often quoted but not enough of it, that should be read by talented youngsters with enough discrimination to decide what they cannot do before they plunge into productivity. It is of 1871, written in Cambridge — clearly, James at twenty-eight is thinking hard of his career:

"We have over here," he says finely of his country, "the high natural light of chance and space and prosperity." America is "a very sufficient literary field. But it will yield its secrets only to a really *grasping* imagination. This I think Howells lacks. (Of course I don't!) To write well and worthily of American things one need [s] even more than elsewhere to be a *master*. But unfortunately one is less!" This is shrewdly put. He has the imagination, but it does not grasp America, even familiar America. Only a master could grasp this country with its "maniac contempt of the refined idea," and see it in relation to "richer and fairer things." (He might have been, but certainly was not, writing of a real master, Mark Twain.) "I myself have been scribbling some little tales [some of which were American]. . . . To write a series of good little tales I deem ample work for a life-time. I dream that my life-time shall have done it. It's at least a relief to have arranged one's life-time."

This letter, with its mixture of self-depreciation and cockiness is not dilettantish. Nothing is more obvious than that, at this moment, James feels he needs a lifetime of devotion to his art — and did feel so, for though his father offered to get his little tales published, he did not push the idea. At least he knew what he could not do, and apparently what he never would be able, or wish, to do, "the high national light of chance and space and prosperity."

What made the young Henry change from the dreamer, the absorbent sponge of finest texture, into the self-estimating man of twenty-eight who has broken into the literary world, and knows it at least for what it is worth? After the Newport period, he has settled down for a long stay (and a long exile) from Europe. For reasons that puzzle his biographers he has entered the Harvard Law School, emerging, so far as I can see, without rag or tag of a legal education or even memory to trouble his later works. There is a key in the Preface to *The Reverberator*, if I translate it properly into direct statement. His parent, he says, had advised Henry in this "languishing American interval" to partake of "the fruit of the tree of knowledge." This left a bitter taste which only the practice of one's own attempt to make art could assuage. Perhaps the father remembered the long English tradition of the English Inns of Court, and Henry had reflected that these had been a nourishing home for so many English writers with only the dimmest interest in the law, yet needing an occupation while they were learning to write. I assume also that Harvard was a place then, as later, where a reasonably intelligent man who behaved himself could stay as long as he pleased, if he paid for his tuition and did not ask for a degree.

Henry, of course, was engaged in far different affairs. The study and practice of law in most of its immediate aspects is a job of untangling the financial and social difficulties of mankind while ignoring so far as possible the psychology involved. In such matters Henry was as little interested as his father in the real estate upon which he lived. That Cambridge was a seat of a university did not interest him at all. But as the home (with Boston) of writers, critics, and editors, all easily accessible through family connection, it might be an answer to prayer. He could find company, guidance, and, what a young writer always feels is of supreme importance, opportunities for publishing through those who possessed them. The family of Charles Eliot Norton, that scholar, historian, and biographer, who was as much a professional friend of the great as a dominant critic of art, were closely associated with the Jameses. Norton became editor of *The North American Review* in 1864, published Henry's first review there, and what proved to be more important was one of the founders of *The Nation,* which proposed to establish, and did establish, new standards of literary criticism in America at the moment of post-war demoralization. It was Norton also who was leader of the New England Turn-East School, of which the historian Ticknor had been the informal founder. Norton believed that cultural salvation for an American was to be found only abroad, although his influence in this respect has been much exaggerated. Both Henry and William, so Henry's nephew, Henry James, Jr., told me, used to laugh in private at Norton's fanaticism. Yet Henry believed him halfway at least, and his influence in launching the youth as a professional critic in the newly established *Nation* of 1865, was most helpful. This was the career which his patrons in Boston and Cambridge seemed to expect for him. They and their magazines, including *The Atlantic Monthly,* made up that New England school by which Mark Twain was so awed, and which was still dominant in American literature.

The young James reviewed Walt Whitman's *Drum Taps* in the very first volume of *The Nation.* It is a searching, caustic, somewhat condescending review, in which everything is reasonably true except the young Henry's idea of America in 1865, and his estimate of Whitman's poetry, which represented "the effort of an essentially prosaic mind to lift itself by a prolonged muscular strain, into poetry." "This stern and war-tired people," James remarked, "is devoted to refinement," and Walt was clearly unrefined. Mark, turning West, had found (and sought) nothing of the kind. And indeed, "refinement" for him meant little more than to stop "cussing" in public, and to eliminate every possible sexual reference from his published works, in which he became far more priggish than James who resented Howells' expurgations. All said, in spite of a bias for refinement, this review is the work of a superior critical intellect. Even at twenty-two the young man showed promise of becoming one of the pillars of Boston's silver age. But the pull Eastward was too strong. America, as he soon learned, was not to become "a great civilizer among the nations," at least not in his sense of civilization. He learned later deeply to appreciate and to read aloud from Whitman; yet America, even after he had come home to write about it, remained a *terra incognita* with some pleasant bowers but more frightening animals drawn upon the map.

There were indeed many resources in Boston, particularly for a negligent law student. Mrs. James T. Fields, famous hostess and wife of the owner of *The Atlantic Monthly,* had a salon which was in effect more like a modern literary cocktail party than anything French. The presiding female genius of the *Atlantic,* still the slightly frigid queen of American letters, entertained every literary celebrity, especially if foreign. They could be met by a youth whose membership in an intellectual family gave him entrée. *The Atlantic,* he says, somehow, while the good season lasted, seemed to live with us. "The light of literature . . . seemed to beat with an intensity which was a challenge to dreaming ambitions."

Most of all, although here the relationship went far beyond

the salon and literary homes, was William Dean Howells. Standing in age between the two men, Henry and Mark, and enduring friend to both, he was an expert in what was being written and could be published in the magazine world, a friend worth having. He took to Henry immediately — "a very earnest fellow . . . gifted enough to do better than anyone has yet done toward making a real American novel." This at the time was an absurdly optimistic forecast of fictional futures, far less justified than would have been a prophecy of critical eminence. James did not know how to write a novel yet, and never did feel competent to write a purely American novel. I can only guess that Howells who called himself a Westerner (though Mark called him an Easterner) was unduly impressed by Henry's obvious polish of culture, and of style, and also believed that the need of American literature was refinement. It did more credit to his heart than to his head, for he admitted to others that while Boston liked James, it did not like his fiction, either in his youth or afterward.

Unquestionably the introduction to Boston literary society was a cardinal fact in Henry's career. For he was not merely welcomed, he was published in short stories, and even a bad novel, *Watch and Ward,* in 1871, which it is most improbable that anyone but the hopeful Howells would have put in print. This gave him early confidence in seeking, I do not say in finding, an audience. The young writer needs more than critical praise. He quickly learns that the first task is to find a form to give to his ideas; but his second task, and almost as important, is to get the chance to communicate.

Henry himself in later years gave his thanks to Howells in a letter of public recognition of Howells' seventy-fifth birthday, which was as generous as it was perceptive:

My debt to you began well-nigh half a century ago, in the most personal way possible, and then kept growing and growing with your own admirable growth — but always rooted in the early intimate

benefit. This benefit was that you held out your open editorial hand
to me at the time I began to write — and I allude especially to the
summer of 1866 — with a frankness and sweetness of hospitality that
was really the making of me, the making of the confidence that required help and sympathy and that I should otherwise, I think, have
strayed and stumbled. about a long time without acquiring. You
showed me the way and opened me the door; you wrote to me, and
confessed yourself struck with me — I have never forgotten the beautiful thrill of *that*. You published me at once — and paid me, above
all, with a dazzling promptitude; magnificently, I felt, and so that
nothing since has ever quite come up to it. . . . You talked to me and
listened to me — ever so patiently and genially and suggestively
conversed and consorted with me. This won me to you irresistibly
and made you the most interesting person I knew — lost as I was in the
charming sense that my best friend was an editor, and an almost insatiable editor, and that such a delicious being as that was a kind of
property of my own.

It is difficult to say whether this letter is more notable as a
classic tribute to the almost perfect editor, or as a rare instance
of a great and generous author eager to give thanks to a friend
whose talent he has long since excelled.

And it is true that Henry might have stayed at home and
under Howells' expert guidance become not *the*, but *an*, American novelist so much hoped for. In spite of his passion for
Europe, the final decision to expatriate himself was much
harder, and so he felt more dangerous, than is usually realized.
It becomes articulate again and again in later years. In 1912,
in the letter just quoted from above, he says to Howells, "For
you have had the advantage, after all, of breathing an air that
has suited and nourished you; of sitting up to your neck, as I
may say — or at least up to your waist — amid the sources of
your inspiration." There will be many a sterile section in
Henry's later novels, praised by the literati for its brilliant technique, but almost unreadable by the mere good reader, where
the fault chased home turns out to be in the too shallow
sources of his purely English inspiration.

And yet he had to go, and not, I feel sure, only to absorb a culture richer than his own. To acquire the art of comparative manners which already absorbed him, it was people that he sought, and as with many a young American writer since, he found his own creative kind more accessible, granted the right introductions, more assembled in Paris, or in England with London as its center, than at home. Read, for example, in *The Middle Years,* the really extraordinary account of his early meeting with Tennyson (who proved to be not at all Tennysonian) as an instance of the youth's capacity for breaking down (or up) into an extraordinary complex his youthful concept of a great poet. Or his other story of the laureated Tennyson glaring at Lowell across the table and never speaking because unintroduced. The fresh eye of an American eagerly absorbed persons and scenes so exactly suited to his kind of imagination which had been starved in the (after all) aridities of Cambridge.

Nor did he fail to savor another experience of a society exactly suited to his tastes in the high social air of Newport — a society not to be matured until much later in America in general, if then. His specialty for the general reader was to be the delineation of sophisticated, usually beautiful, women of wealth and position. And here in Newport, though rather artificial and unstable, was a *fusion,* as he called it, between his Jamesian circle of intellectuals and the cultivated *mondain* or gentleman of leisure. Here was the returned expatriate reflecting a society as old as the great eighteenth century. Here he recognized a deep and easy culture, tainted with the "poison" of the Old World, yet attracting and repelling, and essentially dramatic. It was here that young Henry was introduced to Society, not as a caste, or a plutocracy (though he liked the evidences of functioning money), but as a medium of communication and self-expression. One feels his drag from these contacts alone toward the source in Europe. There were too few women to be found, for example, of the type he had come to prefer among the rather frigid academic girls of Cambridge.

Young Henry completed, for himself, this fusion. He did so, most importantly, without losing his fundamental moral philosophy or his equally important faith in that American trait of unsophisticated "innocence" which he felt was the best thing in America. A youthful circle, which when he was able he joined, including the young Temples, assembled in North Conway woods and mountains for their vacations. They "shine," in his memory "with the light of 'innocence.'" It was this "innocence" which was to make the drama of his best novels when it was caught and often crushed in that *mondaine* society which it was his business to understand — its fascinations first, its perils, its "poison" afterward. He mingled in Newport with its representatives who were like great ladies from Rome exiled or invalided to the Provinces; he watched these gay habitués of European spas and drawing rooms, mingling with the wives of profiteers, and parading in their carriages along the Newport shore while Grant and Lee were in a death struggle. This was a world to which, immoral or amoral, a novelist had to get a passport in order to know it on its own terms. That he did so is again beautifully illustrated in his Memoirs, by one of his early friendships with Lady Waterford, a great beauty of the recent past, who was a pre-view of some of his best efforts in fiction.

Yet it must be remembered also that these years of the sixties and early seventies, when the strain of war at last was over, were, for the North and West, a time of tremendous energy, when as even Henry said "things happened"; when there were gleams everywhere of a bright future; when the houses were filled with young veterans bringing new realisms of experience with them. The still young Mark Twain felt this excitement when he grasped success in 1869, and set about, like all the Reconstruction men, to make his fortune. And Henry, who was uneasy with veterans, and was repelled by the gross overturning of even such societies as America had produced, also felt the electric tension. The coiled spring of a new era beginning brought Mark, a type of the West, to the East to sell his wares, and propelled James into a broader world from an America that less than ever he was able to admire or even understand. "Europe," he says, in *Notes of a Son and Brother*, was the standard remedy with all Jameses, for every "wrong stress."

It would have been more accurate, I think, if Henry had written, every "wrong stress" for this particular James. Henry in 1875, after a final year at home in America with the family, finally left for good. He had various reasons, as I have tried to show, but there was one reason more and a compelling one. He says to his mother, in 1874, that although he can make the most money at home near the literary markets for an American, yet an "overwhelming desire" he knows will urge him to Europe. By 1875 in the autumn it is all settled, but in Paris, not in London, which still is strange, though attractive to him. What does not come out, except by deduction and frequent indicative references, is that he was definitely running away, and in part from his own beloved family. Unfortunately his brilliant sister Alice did not escape in time, and freely admits it in her Journal. Consider the quiet, hesitant youth, brought up so lovingly, brought up in the intense pressures of this most articulate and self-expressive family. These loving pressures, because they were usually irrelevant to his own emotions and interests, were bound to be difficult for an intensely egotistic boy, whose inner life was creative among a swarm of ethical interruptions. Even his shyness was clearly an escape from family responsibility. When Alice finally resumed companionship with him in London, she found him mildly intoxicated by his social success but shrinking from much personal conversation with her. He must never, she said, be asked Questions. Such questions, one guesses, as had filled the air when the James family was going full speed and Henry Senior, like a benign Jehovah, discoursing upon the moral complexities of human nature as

applied to the individual. Such questions as what he proposed
to do in a disrupted American society. Or what responsibility
he should assume in the family circle, which he notoriously
dodged. Or probably about the state of his ego. In Europe
he could look about him without answering except for his own
art. He could turn inward — hours at a time — without re-
proach; and the dangerous excitement of his impetuously brilliant family, which seems to have made a psychosomatic out of
his sister, was far away. That the great Questions his father
was always asking were charged with care and affection, when
turned upon him, did not make escape less necessary. It was a
wonderful family to live in, but enough was enough. Afterward, letters and occasional visits were better.

It would, however, be truthful to add that Henry ran away to
a Europe whose every scene and perception charged his imagination without interruption. America was too "thin" for him,
the opposite to that "density" of culture which in Preface after
Preface he states to be the necessity for a literary subject. And
"culture" for him had to be selected for him to assimilate it.
How could the two philosophers in the family adumbrating
universals fail to oppress his sensitive instrument? Indeed
James, although a cosmopolitan, was dependent upon a small
and carefully ordered and traditionally familiar, and intensely
"civilized" environment. There is a famous passage written in
his sensitive *Hawthorne* published in 1879, which almost burlesques his tastes. America, he said, lacks everything that makes
life dense, a king, a court, a standing army, an established
church (he wanted everything in America that we had tried so
hard to get rid of!) — leaving only a sense of humor, which
was presumably an escape from dullness. With what satisfaction he describes in a later novel the delightful approach to
the great English country house wide open for the week-end,
each couple followed by their personal maid and valet with
bags. Even nature, an American specialty from Audubon to
Emerson, was no solace to this packed and ordered mind. In

familiar proximity to every American home, to please him it needed to be mellowed into harmony with an English manor or an Italian villa. For Henry was entirely urban, as he was congenitally urbane. The rest of the family might climb Adirondacks, the only wildish New England he had ever experienced was in Swampscott, one of those summer refuges which was at least not one of the "silly" Newport fringes of American nature.

He complains of a nature in America so "thin" that it compelled even the perceptive Hawthorne to make flat remarks in his notebook about the smell of peat smoke, and he condemns Thoreau for his native parochialism, excusing him only because of some "natural charm," which places him at best in the rear of such really original writers as Longfellow, Lowell, and Motley! This graduate of a "sensuous" education in sophisticated art was bound to escape sooner or later from not only metaphysics and ethical sociology but also from untrimmed lawns and runaway forests; and from a middle class in the rough childhood of our civilization into something nearer his ideal desires. The surprise is only that he found the decision to stay away so hard to make, and took with him far more of America than he or anyone else suspected.

6. THOSE VULGAR, VULGAR, VULGAR AMERICANS

A good moment for finishing this chapter is 1875, the year of his departure. In 1874 he had planned, and it had been accepted for *The Atlantic*, his first real novel, *Roderick Hudson*, and had finished the writing mostly in America in 1874–75, publishing it as a book in 1876. In 1875 he still felt his education incomplete, but actually, after a brief unhappy obsession with the

French well-made play, it was places and people that he was
determined to study. As for the people, there was plenty to
learn, although by 1875 he had progressed a good way from
the Jamesian hothouse in an ivory tower with a lacquer of
snobbism which had been his habitat too long. Read Henry
in 1869, the year of *The Innocents Abroad* with its celebration
of the bourgeois Americans, and regard what the young writer
could write to his mother from Florence:

> The Englishmen I have met not only kill, but bury in unfathom-
> able depths, the Americans I have met. A set of people less framed
> to promote national self-complacency than the latter it would be
> hard to imagine. There is but one word to use in regard to them —
> vulgar, vulgar, vulgar. Their ignorance — their stingy, defiant, grudg-
> ing attitude toward everything European — their perpetual reference
> of all things to some American standard of precedent which exists
> only in their own unscrupulous wind-bags — and then our unhappy
> poverty of voice, of speech and of physiognomy — these things glare
> at you hideously. On the other hand, we seem a people of *character,*
> we seem to have energy, capacity and intellectual stuff in ample
> measure. What I have pointed at as our vices are the elements of the
> modern man with *culture* quite left out. It's the absolute and in-
> credible lack of *culture* that strikes you in common travelling Ameri-
> cans. . . . [The English] have manners and a language. We lack both,
> but particularly the latter.

But this youthful outburst which preludes Henry's lifelong
career as an "international novelist" is not all cultivated snobbery, nor without penetration. The "species of feverish highly-
developed invalids," as he described the traveling American
woman in the same letter, was often accompanied by young
girls who were "delightfully beautiful and sweet" (also intelligent) and there he will return later for heroines in his
novels. Nor should one miss the rather puzzled reference to
character as an offset to vulgarity. American character in a
deeply moral sense was to be the dramatic motive of his greatest
novels.

Chapter III

MARK TWAIN ARRIVES

IT WOULD BE a mistake to say that Mark Twain escaped from the Wild West in the same sense that Henry James escaped into the Old World in the East. He escaped to become a salesman of journalism because he needed money and he went where money was plentiful for his kind of work; also because obscure talents were working in his imagination that needed more self-expression than the lecture platform, and a more respectable environment. My guess is that he wanted to be someone like Bayard Taylor, whom he knew very well later. Bayard Taylor was ten years older but he had been young enough to see the great gold rush in its prime of 1850, not in its decadence as Mark did. He had written a book called *El Dorado,* which set the adventurous hurrying toward the Pacific. He had adventured into Africa, into Japan, into the Moslem world (as Mark adventured in the West), wrote home letters for the *Tribune,* and made them into books that sold famously. Also he wrote poetry, was an intimate of all the New York writers, was the kind of man of letters who would build a big house and become a celebrity. He could not explode his hearers or readers into laughter as did Mark, but he wrote more elegantly. Taylor, however, was born respectable, and stayed so in spite of his very agreeable ramblings in highly unrespectable countries. His poetry, which he valued most, is a tragedy of respectability. I do not say that Mark ever became respectable. But he certainly tried as hard as any man.

We can explain Mark's turn Eastward (carrying the West

with him) by a search for new markets. But it is difficult to
explain entirely the story of his falling in love and his marriage
except by an intense craving for respectability. Of course, this
is an oversimplified statement, but it is also true and important
— underneath the writer who wished to be respectable, is the
sensitive genius, neurotic and an exhibitionist; underneath
again the youth trying to make up to his family for their failure,
is the romantic needing some dream woman who will nourish
and protect the idyll of a friendly and tremendously exciting
universe he has made for himself. He had met no such woman,
though by 1854 he was dreaming of her. It seems possible to
the men who know his unpublished papers best that he had
known no woman in love until he married. It is quite certain
that he would never have been satisfied with the kind of women
he saw frequently enough on tough steamboats or the streets of
Virginia City; or with the sugar-and-cream women he wrote
into his stories: he needed a woman both morally and emotionally strong. Otherwise, she could not gain and hold the
respect of a man who still saw women with his mother's eyes.
He had known too many disreputable females; and too many
"nice" women, like Sandy in his novel of the Yankee, who were
dumb. His choice was between a respectable paragon, or a
heroine out of this world such as he made of Joan of Arc.

How he got Olivia Langdon is the best story that Mark lived
and never wrote. The years from 1867, when Henry James
was nibbling ever more hungrily at the European bait, include
Mark's first adventure abroad on the *Quaker City* to Europe
and the Near East. The letters he wrote became a book, which
made him famous, although it has taken half a century to discover just what he deserved to be famous for. They also made
him moderately rich. But with perhaps equal importance, at
least biographically, here are the years in which he courted
and married Olivia Langdon. Triumphantly he won to an
engagement a "lovely" invalid, a "simple" nature, a daughter

of a rich and established man, a woman who made up for a weakness in "nerves" by strength of character. She subdued the picaro, tired of mere wandering, into conformance with respectability. It was not difficult to make her fall in love with him — it can never have been too difficult for Mark to make people love him. But to capture her New York State conscience was a feat that required all his invention; the more so since her father stood like a lion in the path. Conscience, to quote Huck Finn again, was a nuisance that kept people from doing what they ought to do. But that this unequal match between an angel of propriety and the wisecracker of the Wild West was successful, that it broke through Mark's secret inhibitions and first stirred him and then finally possessed him spiritually and physically for life, is more surprising than his most fantastic stories.

Mark won her by a trick, which was no less a trick because it was his only chance to get what he most wanted in the world, and fair enough at that. A congenital skeptic as he freely admitted, he gave her every opportunity to make him into a full and free believer in her kind of Christianity. She failed, but in failing (as the rascal said himself), she dug a pit for herself into which she tumbled into matrimony. Perhaps a Puritan conscience was tricked, not Olivia. Mr. Langdon, a prohibitionist, and the shining example of Congregational morality and good business ethics in Elmira, New York, blustered but yielded rather easily. He was a self-made man, and a very human fellow too, with plenty of common sense. He proposed two tests for his prospective son-in-law when his daughter admitted that she was in love. Mark must reform his bar-side Western manners, stop "cussing," stop drinking "spirituous liquors." This was readily agreed to, although Mark by no means always or often knew what was meant by Congregational good manners. And he would *not* stop smoking.. Yet once he had charmed the family by his affection and his humor, he easily won their confidence for the future. Even so, he must prove by witnesses from this far-off West, which was presumably boisterous and immoral, that there was nothing in his picaresque past that might emerge and make a respectable marriage impossible of continuance. Mark drew up a list of witnesses, all respectable men, if not all ministers, with his beloved companions of streets and newspaper offices omitted with scrupulous care. He did not forewarn them, and got what might be expected. Dixon Wecter in his *The Love Letters of Mark Twain,* published in 1949, quotes the defendant:

"I think all my references can say I never did anything mean, false or criminal . . . that *all* the friends I made in seven years, are still my friends . . . that I never deceived or defrauded anybody, and don't owe a cent. . . . All the rest they can say about me will be *bad.*"

One of his character witnesses called him a humbug, another said that he might be destined for a drunkard's grave. Had he no friends? asked Mr. Langdon, and then like a sensible man, "burst forth, 'I'll be your friend myself! Take the girl. I know you better than they do.'"

There was another test, which if less dramatic was perhaps more relevant to Mark's literary career. Mr. Langdon's chief objection, after all, was that Mark was a roamer. "I have been a roamer," Mark replied, "for necessity three-fourths of my time — a wanderer from choice only one-fourth." Wandering, he justly says, had been part of his profession, a roving reporter and lecturer. Was this, the father asks, the kind of profession for a husband, who presumably does not want to live on his wife's money? The answer was to *own* something. He might be earning a hundred dollars a night lecturing all over the country with an occasional jackpot in a friendly town — his new book might be a jackpot, but did he offer security for a delicately nourished and home-reared wife? Mark agreed to a first project, to buy with his profits from the book an interest in the Buffalo *Express*. Journalists should own something. Like many practical men, Mr. Langdon made no distinction in his mind between good journalists, and good editors and proprietors. It was a bad speculation, as could have been prophesied in advance. But if Mark was to become respectable he must not only make but hold on to money. Thus, one of the reasons Mark at age thirty-four began to make a writer of himself instead of just the Wild Humorist of the West, such as Artemus Ward and the rest of that harum-scarum brood, was that he had a compelling reason to make respectable money. What he needed was the kind of income that becomes property, which means, or meant then, books.

2. THE JACKPOT

His first book began as a series of letters intended to be better than the Sandwich Island letters because the unique voyage of the *Quaker City* to Europe and the Holy Land was a far better subject. Revised, part of it with Olivia's help, it became a reverberating success, obviously because, except for the information (mostly secondhand) and the purple patches of description in the taste of the day, it was funny in almost every paragraph, and sometimes in every line. At least, this was obvious to Mark and to most of his readers. Humor made it sell, but actually *The Innocents Abroad* was better than its humor, which reads nowadays too much like nineteenth-century vaudeville. This fresh mind from the West, with plenty of wit and a trained observation, had caught without any pretentions to philosophy the Americans' attitude toward the Old World they had left behind them, and the Biblical East, an attitude characteristic of America. If there is a parallel it is not to be found in travel books, but in the great English novels of the eighteenth century in which the insular Englishman becomes a humorous type.

I do not know whether this once famous book is much read now — although it can be easily found in the reprints. If so, probably by readers past middle age who remember Europe well before the First World War, a Europe which was still vividly reminiscent of *The Innocents Abroad*. It was an Old World to which a new middle class, enriched by our war industry, their horizons broadened, were eager to travel or read about, as it would never have occurred to them to do before the Civil War. To these readers and travelers must be added for this special occasion the pulpiteers of the Protestant churches now reaching new heights of popularity, who proposed to bring back firsthand sights of the Holy Land to give zest to their sermons and titillate the stay-at-homes who could not afford so magnificent an excursion. James describes the more vulgar of these new middle-class travelers, but his was the rather supercilious view of a headwaiter in a fashionable restaurant looking over the patrons from the Provinces who are beginning to crowd the tables. The Innocents went in general, of course, even to the Holy Land, to have a good time, to see the sights, to acquire a veneer of "culture." Their predecessors before the War were intellectuals or rich Southerners seeking an education. The Irvings, the Coopers, the Emersons, wrote for them, and they were distinctly not middle class, and knew perfectly well what they were seeking. The later group, if they were not merely tourists like the Innocents, went definitely to "buy" culture in the "bring-it-home-with-me" form of pictures (mostly copies), furniture, tapestries, new clothes, jewelry in trunkfuls, that soon was to make the passage of the customs a battle. Or, more ambitiously (and this for the very wealthy), to raid the "aristocracy" for titles, or take part in a more sophisticated and freer moral life than they could practise openly at home.

Yet all, or almost all, of this post-Civil War middle class came back boasting and (except for rich and beautiful girls left as hostages) usually as ignorant of the real Europe as when they sailed away. It was such Americans and their relatives and children and grandchildren, for whom "I have been abroad" was a social lift, who made the great and surprising market for Mark Twain's first great success. The effect of this book was still visible to the third generation. At the end of the century fresh travelers still seeking the *cachet* of having been abroad, continued to cross the same Alpine passes which Mark then or later described, still saw the same famous sights, still crowded about the same famous pictures, though Ruskin had drawn off the intellectuals to others, the same pictures which Mark had described as inferior to the copyists' fresher colors.

One attitude, point of view, preconception — call it what you like — was common to ninety per cent of these newly rich, or rather well-to-do, American pilgrims abroad. They took no responsibility for Europe — or Asia either — and never did until after the First World War. It was a never-never land for many, it was faintly and delightfully absurd — quaint was the word — for more; it seemed to most, for all its beauty and interest, the remains of a way of life from which America had forever escaped. The beer gardens full of saluting officers were a Wild West show for them, which our own recent Civil War made to seem antiquarian. The servility, even the politeness, of waiters and chambermaids was a survival of an outdated class system; the arrogance, or the pompous poverty, of the aristocracy, in the midst of a show of luxury still unexampled at home — this was what they talked about. They were all innocents for three generations beginning with Mark, and much that they noted as quaint was actually a portent of a new social upheaval and a revived militarism which was to overturn the twentieth century. Yet the American Way of Life — they did not yet call it that in the sixties — was not altogether innocent.

It was the criterion for all our judgments and often a very vulgar one; yet it was the raw beginning of a way of living for uncounted Americans of a new middle class, which was to conduct the Industrial Revolution in an untrammeled continent. It was not so good as Twain thought it then; not so bad as James believed it to be and without much hope of salvation.

As for the book, Mark Twain's jackpot, it is like many a very popular book, much easier to criticize than to estimate at its true value. Easy transportation has dimmed the humors of provincialism. Mark's realistic account of his experiences in the Holy Land, which made his book a rather daring answer to long-suppressed desires of millions of children dully educated in Sunday Schools, has suffered with the loss of knowledge of an incomparably greater book, the Bible. And while *Huckleberry Finn* is as rich in laughter as ever, the conscious humor of *The Innocents* is definitely strained. It is the burlesque humor of the Southwest, built up to a climax, and delivered dead-pan. You can see Mark in an art gallery or on donkey-back in Syria, watching his audience as he builds up his exaggerations, until he releases the tension with a wisecrack. It worked then, but it does not now except on the radio. The book can no more qualify merely as a work of humor than the second part of *Don Quixote* — or as a travel book either. But as a more-or-less novel of manners — that is a different question.

Historians of literature describe *The Innocents Abroad* as the first debunking travel book — the first book to make fun of the rapt clergyman following what he thinks are the steps of Jesus, or the bemused spinster sucking culture from galleries like a fly in molasses. That there was a whole literature of such travel books should be well known for they are still being published, and many a skillful sentimentalist made his living thereby in the great days of the American illustrated magazine. In this mood, Ruskin wrote his *Stones of Venice*; and the young James was saved from it only by his finer grain and his novelist's sense of the proper use of environment.

I do not believe that Mark had the slightest idea of writing anything so unpopular as a book meant to make fun of other books. He was a debunker only in the sense that he was more honest (and often more ignorant) than other writers of travel books, and said so, and his readers agreed with him. In this sense Thoreau and Melville were both debunkers of social superstitions and emotional strains. What he wished was to be eloquent, informational, and get a laugh, which he usually did by opposing his own frank observation, not to a travel book, but to the patter of a professional guide. It is spirited and often deeply serious writing, especially when the history Mark did know (and it was considerable) is white-heated by his innate humanitarianism, which was another trait common to all his American kind. Mark spoke with such honesty that he reveals more of himself than he could possibly realize.. Like most Americans of his time, he was rather well read in political history and in the sacred history of Palestine. He was almost totally deficient — as they were, outside of Boston — in cultural history. The nature and history of composition in art, either in painting, sculpture, architecture, or music, meant nothing to him. Pictures to him were stories; and he was repelled by many of the great paintings he was supposed to admire because he did not like the story. An artist himself, though often a bad one, he had an instinctive feeling for some esthetics, but was merely disgusted by tourists who venerated a Murillo, each for different and conflicting reasons. What he would like to write about in Italy, he said, was the railroad stations, for he knew all about railroad stations. Of its art he would say what he thought. And so he called Venice dark and dirty, and San Marco not worth describing except to compare it to Memphis in a Mississippi flood. There have been better, and also worse, descriptions.

Of course, Mark burlesqued his comments, partly to escape from offense. And the book as narrative is really the story of a "clique" of male tourists, irreverent, a little out of hand, who did the high spots with him, and all the adventurous trips on the margins of the Holy Land. They even got the ugly women of the African East to lift their veils and send Bayard Talor's romance slithering. These good-natured, like-minded Americans act like the chorus of a minstrel show with Mark as Mr. Bones. They leave behind them a trail of lying donkey-boys, obsequious couriers, swindling waiters, and paid panegyrists of the beautiful, their professions ruined by this poker-face humor of invaders from Missouri. For all of the "clique," like Mark, had to be shown; and if they were cheerfully ignorant, they spoke from a new world where all the social values were being retested, with no prejudice to the old if they could prove themselves to be values. And when Mark knew what he was talking about, he was fair even to the heights of rhetoric.

The novelty in Mark's book is that it is a kind of picaresque novel of American adventure. The picaro is part of a group, and the fun they make is of travelers, which is as old as history, and of history, art, and social customs, which is somewhat new. Yet the picaro is the same old unconventional realist living by his wits, and a sharp fellow too, since by making up his ship-load of such respectable Americans (with a religious service at least once a day), he never shocked the equally respectable Olivia or her kind. Actually, he was more honest than those he made fools of.

I must write more warmly about this clown of a book, since it is clear that I have not yet revealed its most significant value. There were sixty-five passengers aboard the new paddle-wheel steamer when she sailed from New York, of whom nineteen were women, mostly middle-aged, and a few young folks. They were a rather dull lot, and Mark makes them so. He soon found his own "clique" and let the rest alone except for a versifier, an orator, and one or two other serio-comic characters whose skin was thick enough to stand burlesquing in print. Mark was

either afraid of the women, or bored, probably both. Only
Mrs. Fairbanks, a middle-aged woman journalist, became his
companion on board (she was also a professional!) and censored
his letters home, which in their first drafts evidently needed it
— not for decency, of course, but for taste. He let the women
of the voyage alone, and wrote a man's book, and about foreign
women but as a man sees them. Not one of the characters on
board is of the slightest importance, including his gang of fellow
burlesquers. All he claims for them and himself is that the
reader will learn to look at Europe and the East as he would
see them if he looked at them with his own eyes instead of the
eyes of those who traveled in those countries before him. These
eyes, of course, are the eyes of Mark himself, a Western American, who, better than the respectable Easterners aboard, was
less blinded by convention, more familiar with freedom of
opportunity, and more impudent in his honesty. Walt
Whitman had described him a decade earlier:

> *I speak the pass-word primeval, I give the sign of democracy,*
> *By God! I will accept nothing which all cannot have their*
> *counterpart of on the same terms.*

And again:

> *I celebrate myself, and sing myself,*
> *And what I assume you shall assume,*
> *For every atom belonging to me as good belongs to you.*

And for a summary:

> *I was looking a long while for Intentions,*
> *For a clew to the history of the past . . .*
> *It is not in those paged fables in the libraries . . .*
> *It is in the life of . . . the average man of today,*
> *It is in the languages, social customs, literatures, arts,*
> *It is in the broad show of artificial things, ships,*
> *   machinery, politics, creeds, modern improvements . . .*
> *All for the modern — all for the average man of today.*

Now it would be fantastic to say that Mark on the *Quaker City* was seeking for Intentions, or was himself an average man. But he *was* in essence the man Whitman describes, believing in the modern for the average man and assuming only what he assumed. He would accept nothing else of Europe, and especially its products of inequality and privilege (by God!), no matter what intellectuals and esthetes had said about the Old World. Hence he writes what is in effect an adventure novel of these average Americans. You get their hospitable nationalism; you get their apparently absurd habit of judging everything by their experience of a free and really classless if often vulgar society; and you get their really absurd conviction that this proves everything. You get their contempt for refinements of manners (Mrs. Fairbanks probably took out a good deal of this — one letter he had to throw overboard entire). You get their hatred of "stuck-ups," of dudes, of stick-in-the-muds incapable of the modern; of copy-cats of culture; of the servile; of the petty corruptionist; of stupid lying; and also of their extraordinary ignorance of another way of life that was preferred across the seas. And Mark speaks for them, sees part way round them, but not all the way, for otherwise he would not be so good a reporter. He believes what they assume is true, because even if what they say is sometimes funny it *is* true, at least for Americans as he has known them from the Mississippi to the Pacific.

There are few spiritual values, if any, in this book. The pilgrims on their way to the Holy Land were not the Americans who created new religions by dozens, or lived in the fear of an angry God. They were all for humanitarianism and the modern, but not much further. The churches of the Faith in Italy did not impress them. If you fell out of a third-story room in Rome, Mark said, you would fall on a soldier or a priest. His idea of what a modern Roman *ought* to like is almost the exact opposite of an established church, etc., a standing army, etc., that James thought we ought to have in America. His ideal for civilization was social justice, humanitarianism, and a fair deal for all including the Jews (he did not mention the Negro). In Rome, decadent Papal Rome, as Henry James and he saw it at about the same time, Mark was not the least impressed by the evidences of the long history of the human spirit, and the beauty of decay. The need for a city of the soul was not so obvious to him as the greater need for modern improvements. Neither could have understood the other. Both were Americans, but of the Turn West, Turn East varieties. It was silly to call Mark's variety vulgar, though it gave off vulgarity like steam from early central heating. Henry had all the comforts already; the average man was just beginning to reach for them. Mark was to live long enough to suffer from spiritual deficiencies, but not to see the possible danger of a new decadence in a brute materialism. He would have fought against it as hard as anyone, and with more immediately effective weapons. It is questionable whether Henry's traditions of a humanist culture were strong enough to put up a fight. But we are not discussing ultimates — only, as throughout this study, parallel lives.

It is only right to add that the Russian Communist propaganda which is much like Mark's, boasts, it is true, a new way of life for the common man and belittles the old, but lacks the honesty, the love of the individual, and most of all the saving wisdom of Mark Twain.

3. ESTABLISHED WRITER

Already Mark had lost some of his *Quaker City* jackpot, in escaping from his one-third interest in the Buffalo *Express* and the sale of his house in Buffalo. Now he took what free-lance writing was in sight, but chiefly went back to lecturing, with a good agent who dragged him all over the East. He liked performing, but his taste for this kind of travel was ended. He was trying to play, and wanted to play, the devoted husband, with less roaming — yet he needed the money. From Buffalo he took the family to Quarry Hill, a hilltop by Elmira which for years proved to be his best summer writing place, and soon to Hartford where he settled on Nook Hill near Charles Dudley Warner, Harriet Beecher Stowe, and other writers, near also the preacher Twichell, who was to become his closest friend. His agent was in Boston, and by 1872 the Hartford friendships were extended to the Bostonian Howells, who had given his blessing to young James now intending definitely to be a novelist. Hartford, for a writer not very fond of the real Brahmins of Boston, was an almost ideal and convenient respectability. It was intelligent, literary, but not too intellectual.

Nearly every writer repeats, or tries to repeat, his first success. There was no new trip of Innocents, nor is there the slightest indication that Mark, like the younger Henry James, had caught the virus of Europe in his blood. For him, Europe was to become a cure for stress and strain as with the James family, but there is no other slightest resemblance between Mark's years of later expatriation and Henry James'. It is more interesting that he had not any desire to return to the West, except for passing engagements. The reason for this I think is clear. He was crammed with experiences in a western region which already in a decade had become legendary. What he needed he found in his memory, and this was the obvious successor in subject to *The Innocents Abroad* — a different kind of innocent, a much younger innocent in the Wild West.

Roughing It, which I have already described, was a better-written book than *The Innocents,* — an American classic of the travel-book kind, and in no danger of going out of fashion, if only because the scenes it describes have become the mingled myth and history of the American nation. Yet however powerful upon the imagination, the book is less significant for American character because it is written as from a young and unformed mind. Mark describes a vanished era, but his creative power has not yet found the formula for lifting it into art. Nor are his Western Americans as yet more than sensational special cases. *Roughing It* remains vivid autobiography, anecdotal, informational, freely handled, but not yet a masterpiece.

The book did very well. Begun in Buffalo in 1870, finished at Quarry Farm in 1871, it was published in 1872. In the same year, at Saybrook on Long Island Sound, he began to plan a much greater book, *Tom Sawyer*.

Roughing It belongs to a purer genre than *The Innocents*. Put it in your library with the series of nineteenth-century travel books of which the American group is in no way least. Irving began with England and went as far as Spain. Dana and Melville took to the high seas, Emerson back to "the old home," Thoreau "traveled in Concord" and then to Cape Cod and the Maine woods. Whitman in his poems wrote "shorts" of American scenes as far as the redwoods. Longfellow, Howells, James, began as travel writers, Parkman preceded Twain across the continent. The Americans, so much written about by foreigners, had now begun to write about others. Finally in *The Innocents* they began to make fun of themselves.

Roughing It was a timely book, though no one would have guessed that it was to become a monument to an era from which innumerable "Westerns," unaware of one of their main sources, would spawn around the world — unhappily with the humor left out. In it, Mark, if he had not discovered his creative genius, had at least developed a technique which was to serve him in most of his best, and some of his worst, work. Perhaps it is the best technique for a travel book — a thread of zestful narrative on which anecdotes are strung. Without the thread there is no information — without the anecdotes there

is no life. The thread here is Mark's own firsthand experience
in a fresh world. In anecdote he reached his peak as master of
the yarn, where he belongs among the great fabulists of history.
I do not say that this is the highest art, but it is about the most
lasting.

I have already spoken of the second piece of unfinished business of Mark's, which was waiting for one success to call forth
another. This was the justly famous book *Life on the Mississippi,* which is really two books, of which one, *Old Times on
the Mississippi,* belongs in this experimental period when Mark
was trying to capitalize on his first success. According to the
story, Howells, his new friend, editor of the almost frightening
(though not very profitable) and very respectable *Atlantic,*
proposed an account of Mark's great days on the great river.
It sounds like the fertile and sympathetic-minded Howells, but
I cannot believe the subject had not been lying for years in
Mark's mind waiting an opportunity. These *Atlantic* articles
made the real book. When in 1882 he added a supplement
after a trip back to the Mississippi, and published it all as *Life
on the Mississippi,* the addition, except for occasional anecdotes,
is mostly a fiddle and faddle of notes in order to make the
manuscript long enough to publish profitably in book form.
The original priceless narrative begins with Chapter IV of the
final volume and extends through Chapter XX. And here again
is the perfect form of the genre travel book, which Mark was
never to equal again — because never again to write, poor fellow, from his enriching memory. *Old Times on the Mississippi* is
concentrated on a skill, like a battle in Homer, or the hunt of
the whale in Melville — and it has the intensity of youth and
the virtuosity of a genius who has learned to write while he can
still remember the entire youthful concentration upon his subject, every shoal and crossing of the river still visible in his
sight. This book is a masterpiece of its miniature kind, a blue-
print of the pilot's trade, made into literature. Nevertheless,

in 1874, at age thirty-nine when he printed it, Mark was still unaware of his greatest talent, which he must still have thought to be description or humorous anecdote. He had not yet come to the great art of creative fiction.

4. MARK BECOMES NOVELIST

I know of no more curious phenomenon in the nature and history of fiction than *The Gilded Age* which Mark and Charles Dudley Warner in Hartford collaborated to publish in 1873. It immediately preceded *Old Times on the Mississippi*. The book has everything! It has a title which has given a name to a whole era of American history. It has an opening section by Mark in which, with consummate skill so simple as to seem artless, he has created Colonel Sellers, one of the ten or twelve great characters in American literature, and now remembered as a living symbol of a continent which opened like a crazy man's dream and became a prodigy. Rip Van Winkle, Hester Prynne of *The Scarlet Letter,* Leatherstocking, Captain Ahab, Tom Sawyer and Huck Finn, Daisy Miller just perhaps, Babbitt — add more such as Dickens and Shakespeare regarded as characters, if you can. The book also contains one of the most savage though ill-written pictures of American politics at its worst period. It contains one of the most deplorably melodramatic heroines ever contrived; and some of the sloppiest and most sentimental passages. As a book it is terrible, and Twain at his worst is quite as bad as Warner; as a contribution to American literature it is a certain proof of Twain's genius, for only genius could make anyone now read it all.

Warner was an essayist and editor of considerable talent. Both were amateurs in the writing of novels; both, like most amateurs, thought they could do better stories than the current best sellers. The book was a "stunt," a challenge by their young wives, now close neighbors, to write a sentimental, melodramatic novel of the kind they were both reading, and make money by it. There was a pretense that the husbands were to parody a bad kind of novel, but it must have broken down after the superb realism of Twain's opening chapters in the backwoods — parody could not follow this. Furthermore, when Twain began to help with Warner's romantic fiction he wrote worse than the novels he was intending to imitate. Twain was supposed to supply the facts, by which he meant his humorous backgrounds and a mass of material from what he had learned of lobbying and rigging juries as a reporter. Warner was to work up the fiction, which was certainly a credit to neither. It is too bad Twain did not turn the attack upon Fenimore Cooper's Indian novels, which every schoolboy reads, upon himself and his collaborator.

We can forget, however, the tripe and the too heavy-handed satire. For Mark had begun with a theme, and created a character to make it alive. Expansion was the theme — the future dramatic expansion of a society and a nation in which only dreamers insane with speculation would believe. In the dull and brutish log villages of Sam Clemens' earliest youth there was one member of the family, James Lampton, who sat for Colonel Sellers, precisely as someone, we do not know his real name, sat for Falstaff. But it is not where a great character begins, it is where he is left that counts. There is no such thing as a photograph, no matter how much that is literal, in a portrait by a great novelist. Grant, however, that it was James Lampton who first unleashed Mark's creative faculty, yet as Colonel Sellers he rises through absurdity into ecstatic prophecy to become a name in history in his own right. For Colonel Sellers is both the triumph and the victim of what historians have come to call the American dream, as it was brought down to earth in Missouri. Colonel Sellers is the optimist who can see a ship canal in a half-dry creek; Nineveh, Babylon, or New York rising in the prairies; a million dollars in every crossroads village (he never mentions a less sum); a rare "imported" turnip for his impoverished family to eat when there is nothing else; and a candle to shine through the stove door when there is no fuel. His spirit was broken only once, when someone said he ought to be in Congress. Nothing, he said, in his conduct justified the saying of a thing like that.

The Colonel's intentions were always good. If he ruined his friends in his speculations, he was trying to help them. If he misled them it was his persuasive tongue which first misled himself. There were hundreds of thousands of him between the Alleghenies and the Plains. Dickens knew one but he was too much for his imagination. He presents him as a crook, whereas he was only a speculator whose hopes were crazy but came true in the next decade. If the Colonel's business ethics seem queer today, these are no queerer than most business ethics in the boom-of-the-West period, and the Reconstruction that followed, to which Mark in 1873 definitely belonged. A sample was the Colonel's idea of buying Negroes cheap in the Border States, sending them into the cotton fields and then passing laws to prevent them from coming back. That was the way that millions were to be made, at least while Negroes were still a commodity.

The Colonel was as native an American product as the Declaration of Independence or the State Universities. If the era of gilded speculation in the vastest unimproved area of good land known in the world was the golden chariot of the Dream, so such characters as the Colonel were the fantastic charioteers. They were by-products of the American passion for education. They were the end-products of the great days of Virginia oratory when a nation was made by persuasion. The Colonel's eloquence could talk the ears off a stalk of corn, and his illu-

sions of grandeur astonish the poor-whites in their clearings.
The powerful use of words he inherited from his ancestors had
become a faculty of self-deception in terms of wealth. He was
vocal in rhetoric as Mark in his Southwestern way was vocal in
"cussing." The possibilities of rivers, soils, mules, wildcat
banks, or patent-medicine flowed as easily, if less accurately,
than the tobacco-spit of his fence-sitting neighbors. It was the
contrast between his dreams and the sodden reality about him
which set him spouting. And the dreams of wealth came true,
though not for him. He was a fool of genius.

What was evident of this gilded age of which the Colonel
was only a backwoods forerunner, was that much of it was
shoddy. And yet the ends at least were not shoddy. Compare
the characters of Balzac who accumulate and hoard franc by
franc with Sellers' millions that were not meant to stick, but
to create, to build, to satisfy noble, or at least grandiose, desires.
As recent historians have pointed out, this has been true of
the vanguard of American capitalists ever since. And if the
Colonel's respect for legal ethics, or any kind of ethics except
kindness and loyalty, is not notable, at least he is on the side of
the honorable man if not of the angels. He and his friends
cheat to rescue Laura from a murder charge, because it is the
seducer they blame; they lobby for "pork" disguised as a
"philanthropic enterprise," but Senator Blodgett who dis-
honestly sells his vote disgusts them all. "Gilded," but very
American. It is best described as a humanitarian morality, an
outcome of a generous people believing in the future and
willing to be rooked if progress goes on. A philosophy, one
fears, which works best in home territories.

A book does not have to be good as a whole in order to be
famous, if in parts or even in single characters it is excellent.
Colonel Sellers has his elements of immortality, like Falstaff,
who also flourished in a good deal of melodrama much liked
by his creator. Mark did not lack guidance in the kind of

literary criticism which could have saved him from a share in making a masterpiece *manqué*. What he lacked was an artistic conscience (except in literary style). Or I wonder if the term should not be artistic integrity. *The Gilded Age* was apparently a continuation of a story begun, or at least planned, by Mark. The original idea may have been satiric fun, but it was equally designed to make money. Others had done so with fiction. Why not take a cut for themselves? So they gave satire a shot in the arm of melodrama and sentiment. "I consider it one of the most astonishing novels that ever was written," he wrote the editor of the New York *Daily Graphic* in a farewell letter to the American people (he was off for England). "Night after night I sit up reading it over and over again and crying. . . . Do you consider this an advertisement?" It was naturally so intended. The book sold in eight weeks after publication 40,000 copies, a record for two months. Now he is proud. Another jackpot! Art is pragmatic, as the Innocents thought. If it pays it is good even if it is so sentimental that one laughs at it. What he lacked in common with so much of the great middle-class experiment in getting wealthy was values. He had almost genius enough to do without them — but not quite.

Anyway, Mark (he still signs himself Samuel L. Clemens, "Mark Twain") has hit the true lode at last in the hardest of hard rock, so we forgive him the mess he left behind him. He has broken through with Colonel Sellers to his own particular treasure — personality, significant, in the round, alive and speaking, unforgettable. That very year of publication he began *Tom Sawyer*.

Chapter IV

JAMES MAKES HIS FIRST
(AND LAST) POPULAR SUCCESS

PLUTARCH'S METHOD in his *Parallel Lives* is to set forth the backgrounds of history against which his eminent men played out their parts; yet it is the exploits of his heroes, usually in battles, or in political crises, or sometimes in morals, which give his Lives the excitement of significant action. This personal action has made his book more compelling upon the imagination of readers than philosophical analyses or the study of a complex of causes, though such as these are not neglected. With a creative writer, however, his environment, his personal conflicts, moral or psychological, even his philosophy of living, are not truly significant unless he has absorbed them into his imagination and made them articulate in books where his experience lives again in representative form. It may be said that the biography of great writers is not really biography unless pointed toward a whole-hearted estimate of what the men really lived for, which means, as has been said before, the books by which they live now if they live at all. Henry James, for example, from very early years was acutely aware that his books were to be his career; Mark Twain at first only dimly guessed that he was to be a writer. Thus the absorption of modern scholars in sources, background, conditioning by psychology and economy, and in general the man and how he lived, and the tricks of his trade, may have been dangerous, even though valuable. Busy with technique or psychiatry, or the economic interpretation of a poor fellow writing for a living, they have often shifted the emphasis from the whole to the part. The final test of a man is not why he functions but how — and so with a book.

2. THE OBSERVER

Despite the somewhat ill-natured remarks upon scholars who neglect books for their authors, let me hasten to assert my impartiality by insisting on the importance at a very early stage of discussing predispositions which both classes and individuals seem to manifest as soon as they can write. Some authors are born romantics and some realists, without more than a restrictive reference to the characteristics of the period in which they are to flourish, just as some seem to be born with good taste and some with bad, without much benefit from education.

All novelists, for example (even those absorbed in self-expression) become by necessity observers. Some novelists seem to make observing a profession, and these remain through their career a little detached from the life-in-fiction which they have created. They protect their sensitive and critical minds from too complete an identification with the personalities they create as if to avoid the danger of emotional strain. This was particularly true of Henry James, who kept his powder dry, especially in scenes of love, where expression might become tempestuous. At first, when still in his very specialized family coterie, he seems, in his earliest stories, to have been most concerned with impressions of moral characteristics represented in observable persons, and thus he secreted, like the silent Hawthorne, moral aspects to which he gave a symbolic form. And indeed many of James' early stories are only dilute Hawthorne, and Hawthorne, thanks to the exquisite quality of his art, always remained an influence.

Yet no sooner has the young Henry begun to see or move in more worldly circles than he becomes a different kind of ob-

server. You can watch the process beautifully in the letters
from abroad to his family, when at first he had for weeks at a
time no one to talk to but his waiter or his language teacher;
when wandering on crowded streets or sitting in the parks of
fashionable spas, he gave his time utterly to observing, observing, almost forgetting, it would seem, his own personality, his
own personal life, though intensely aware of his critical
opinions. Thus in the stories which belong to this period, you
can view the Observer (sometimes so called) in the mass of the
narrative like a separable element. Sometimes it is Henry himself only slightly disguised, a man who preferably makes and
sees action rather than takes part in it. His favorite role is a
wandering bachelor, watching for a group typical of their kind,
Americans representing the traveling breed, or a nervous
mother peering for her young, and at last the girl or woman
herself. But sometimes, and more subtly, he is the center of
the narrative, though not its dynamic hero. The story does
not end with him. For the truly detached Observer neither
fails nor succeeds. He neither dies in tragedy, nor lives happily
ever after. Sometimes what he is (except perceptive) is of no
importance, and then he is the most complete observer; or
what he is may be of great importance, but what he does of no
significance except for its relation to the situation into which
he has dramatically drifted. Clearly a writer like this may be
expected to do some queer things with his novels. For he is
never quite all inside of the narrative. He is like a pedestrian
who keeps to the banks while following a river, or a man devoted to women who never falls in love.

Another influence in Henry James' early career is almost as
outstanding as that of Hawthorne, and this happens to be of a
woman notable among observers. He never, I think, outgrew
it, though in some respects he transcended it. I mean Jane
Austen, and I have collected myself a sheaf of instances, and

especially in his early, though not his earliest, works where the resemblance is too close to be a coincidence. As Jane is said to have written away at her novels while her family talked around her, so James by his own admission was usually a silent listener in his loquacious family, recording among his impressions not so much their arguments as their personalities. Someone, said Henry in one of his Prefaces, must be *aware* of what the situation means, or there will be no real novel. Jane and Henry were always intensely aware, nor do either in their best passages ever make the comments themselves, but leave that task to some character, usually, though not always, a subordinate one.

Here James never reached the perfection of his early teacher. With him, the Observer is usually a pallid if sympathetic figure, most usually an aspect of James himself, but intensely objective. This is generally true of all but a handful of his finest novels. Whereas Jane triumphs by creating a spokesman like Mr. Bennet or Mr. Knightley who is both aware of the situation and also a major personality in his own right. She triumphs also by letting herself as author go when the character who has been the Observer and is the center of the story becomes both author and hero or heroine without important reservations. So it is with Elizabeth Bennet in *Pride and Prejudice*, who, it is generally agreed, is close to Jane herself. Elizabeth does let love conquer criticism at the end, and convincingly also, although it is true that she requires a good deal of shoving by the plot. She becomes all woman as well as a creator's mind. Henry never lets himself fall in love (except as a possibility) in fiction, although he unquestionably resembles some of his characters as much as Elizabeth is said to have resembled Jane, who, so far as we *know*, never gave herself over to love.

In one respect, however, the resemblance between these two great observers was quite complete, and in influence direct.

Such a student of technique as Henry was from early years did
not miss the skill with which, from the simplest beginnings
and the most obvious motives, Jane Austen slips quietly and
swiftly down a delicious country lane or a chatty tea party into
a situation whose drama never relaxes its grip until the end. It
is what Henry means by his favorite maxim "dramatize, dramatize," and as quickly as possible. And if he seldom did it quickly
it was because he was intellectually unable to do so, and well
aware of his fault. The reasons were double. His obsession with
places and their atmosphere, a trait natural to a passionate
traveler from the New to the "dense" and rich Old World,
required pages of description where Jane took sentences. And
furthermore he could not be simple, because, as Matthiessen has
wisely said, James began where Jane left off. He cannot be
simple because his material is too complex; he cannot be obvious because he takes a character whose tangle of motives
requires great space to unravel. Jane was a narrow genius if
deep in plumbable depth; Henry a broad one working with a
microscope upon the infinite manifestations of a surface where
emotion had usually already completed its more obvious work.
Neither ever wrote an actual love scene at its climax with
warmth enough to melt a snowflake. Indeed, Jane dodges such
scenes with a greater reverse of passion than Henry himself.
But she makes a more convincing observer of love because complexity detracts from the force of love, and Henry preferred
always the difficult to the simple. Who shall say that for his
genius he was not entirely right! The "difficult," he said, was
his passion — shall we add, his cherished fault. It is the final
differentiation between the most skillful of our native observers and the parochial Englishwoman he so much admired,
whom Mark Twain alone among our novelists can sometimes
equal as a creator of personality that is more alive (not more
"difficult") than life itself.

3. THE INTERNATIONAL SCENE

When by 1869 Henry James went abroad for the first time on his own (though not yet an expatriate), his quality as an observer was already the best established of his functions. He had learned to observe for his own uses, although he is most articulate about his interests in his letters rather than in his stories. By 1873, in one of the best of his few good very early short stories, he has already entered the story himself in unmistakable fashion. He had dramatized himself as an American student of art, susceptible to impressions, sensitive to the moral difference of races, easily aroused by lively intelligent women, but obviously afraid to get his feet wet! I refer to a *nouvelle*, or long short story, published in *The Galaxy*, a New York magazine. It is unusual for him that he cannot remember its source, so that it is legitimate to guess that it was a daydream while James sat at Saint Germain-en-Laye, over the immense and famous view in which Paris spreads in dusky vastness, "domed and fortified, glittering here and there through her light vapours and girdled with her silver Seine."

It is true that Henry James was perfectly conditioned to be an international novelist. The story of "Madame de Mauves" at the early date of 1873 shows it beautifully. He wrote it in a dark little inn-room at Bad-Homburg, so dark that he could just see his way to and from his inkstand, calling the story later, experimental internationalism. The story in outline told of the woman seen among the mists of Saint Germain, and is conventional enough. She is an American woman, beautiful, strange, lonely, and unhappy, morally entangled in a drama with a "shining, sinful, Frenchman" — only he is not "shining" but plump and quite willing to let her take a lover and let him alone. But the story is lifted into an atmosphere of French life whose tones and undertones make it a masterpiece of subtlety and a tragedy of the moral will, which neither the American woman can relax nor the French husband understand. It is true that (as very often with the early James) it ends with a suicide (of the wicked husband not the virtuous wife) which is clearly because of Henry's feeling that in the hundred pages of the main story not enough has happened. It has, and a thoughtful reader can see there a major novelist not yet skilled enough nor conscious of his powers to know when to stop. But a new talent in English is certainly manifest.

Yet it is not true that Henry wanted to become just a specialist in international reactions — which with the exception of a few of his short stories is exactly what happened to him in his finest work. He says not once but a half a dozen times in his letters that he rebels against his theme, yet he always comes back, with the excuse usually that this is what his public, especially his magazine public, wants of him — that this is what he can publish with some expectation of a reasonable return. His last American novels, such as *The Bostonians,* his purely English novels, such as *The Awkward Age,* might well be regarded as having been published at his own expense — at least of energy and time. Twice at least he determined to sink himself, as he said of Howells, up to his waist in a national scene, and fell back discouraged, only at the end discovering for himself the formula which was international without a limitation of his finest talents.

Was the trouble that the sources of his inspiration in these international complications were too shallow? It depends upon the value of such gossamers of steel as separate nation and nation. This is an important question for my study of parallel lives, where one was to be spent so much in difficult and specialized intricacies.

The word "international" is only a stereotype. If Mark Twain had first and best presented the type of New World man in his Western phase, it was James who first took him, whether from West or East, abroad on something more than a satiric voyage. It is the young Henry who realizes that all types of Americans (now enriched by the Civil War or the Industrial Revolution, and grown powerful, curious, and some of them overrefined) have come to visit or to stay with the Europeans, with social reactions of the greatest interest to a psychological novelist. If he began with a satiric view of the cruder, brasher specimens, using them only as comic relief, he soon lifts above satire, and broadens into a study of manners of a moral type never before familiar in Europe, and with its most diverse individuals more like each other fundamentally than any other race or nation. Thus I answer the question raised above, by saying that this international drama is a great theme, capable of infinite nuance and possible development. A confident, strong-willed people, still largely inarticulate, have come to visit an old civilization, or in representative specimens to live with that civilization, and the reacting cultures are already setting up chemical reactions. Mark, less subtle but more prophetic than Henry, foresaw an American influence (if one takes his work as a whole) as strong in its way as that of the Greeks and the Romans, and he has been proved to be right. Nothing up to the rise of Communism has been so potent in European culture as the coming back from the New World of the Americans. Henry was no historian. This potency he regarded as a "menace" to the old culture which he held so dear. But he was far better able than Mark to assess the finer, the more spiritual, the more intellectual aspects of the drama — and as far as culture in its narrow sense was concerned, he was much better informed. He could make art, as Mark could not, out of social history in rapid motion without too much bothering with broader issues. Many a lesser novelist has been diverted by

these "broader issues" into writing narrative tracts. Both men
(and this is the point of this paragraph) had great subjects,
as subsequent history has shown. It is therefore nonsense to
speak of Twain in that considerable part of his work which
could be called international contrast as only a satirical humorist; or of James as merely an esoteric fictionist in the field of
special types.

But to return to James, it is as a novelist first that he must
be considered — the international scene merely gave him his
opportunity. And that scene was narrowed for him to what
Twain had asserted should be the familiar. It was the French,
the English, and the traveling or expatriate American who excited James' interest. He did not like the Italians (except for
a few aristocrats), thought that they were dishonest, immoral,
and decadent. He emphatically did not like the Germans —
even their music. The Americans, even the "unrefined" but
not the vulgar ones, went deepest with him, although their
sometimes baffling simplicities gave him the least to write about.
The French were his first love, among types of women especially. They had for him in their own way a moral glamour
which no other nation — certainly not the English — could
equal. Next to the American heroines of *The Wings of the
Dove* and of *The Golden Bowl,* Madame de Vionnet of *The
Ambassadors* must be adjudged his most sympathetic portrait
of a woman.

4. THE EARLY NOVELS

I have said that Henry James' first love was France. "Madame
de Mauves" is a particularly good example, since it was written
while he was still only a visitor to Europe. Yet a curious epi-

sode in James' biography shows very clearly why in 1875 it was already certain that James, unlike some later expatriates, might yield his heart to France, but would not, the phrase should be could not, yield his underlying Anglo-Saxon traditions and training. We think of him usually as an expatriate to England, where other and quite different reasons kept him American. Actually, when he went abroad to stay in 1875 his first plan was to settle in Paris, where Rome (the city not the people), which always stirred him most emotionally, would be easily accessible. In Paris his definite idea was to find an entrance to the inner circle of the writers whom he regarded as the most skillful, the most truly professional of all moderns, with results most interesting to a general biography, but rather dismaying to himself.

He was now a correspondent for the *Tribune,* and wanting copy with well-known names in it. Thanks to the right introductions he soon found himself a familiar, if not an intimate, of a distinguished company — a group of reputations which outside of England and America certainly led the literary world. He saw them all and frequently, played charades with Turgenev, and was reminded of "historical games" at Concord, Massachusetts, where he had encountered the same inbred exclusiveness of a self-centered circle. He met Zola once climbing a stair with a pale face after his current serialization had been stopped for indecency; knew Maupassant well, who told him a story which years afterward he remembered but refused to repeat in his letters; the Goncourts, Daudet, and Flaubert were part of the circle, the last the "strongest" artist of the group. Turgenev, an expatriate like himself, was his chief admiration, and he kept his influence for life, an influence, I think, which may be responsible for James' addiction to the *nouvelle,* which is the best term for the brief novel or long tale which James most liked to write. But the experience was curiously frustrating. Forty years later James was being described as too American ever to become really English. Now,

and for other reasons, he decided by 1876 that France was no
nursing ground for him. There were, he said, fifty reasons why
he did not wish to become intimate with his famous acquaintances. They were not *accueillant.* It was a closed circle, interested only in one another, and unaware of or indifferent to
the "warcs" of other literatures. He began to feel a "long-en-
croaching weariness with the French mind." I think, also, from
slanting references in his Notebooks and elsewhere, that it was
the moral attitudes of these French masters that offended an
American tolerant but always fastidious in the relations between the sexes, and perhaps a fundamental difference in
literary purpose, also moral. "I have done with 'em all, forever," he wrote William in 1876, "and am turning English all
over." If he had but a single good friend in England he would
"shake off France like a garment and go thither."

Unhappily he came away with one proud achievement. He
had mastered the French theater, so he said, which he attended
assiduously. He knew all that Dumas, Augier, and Sardou
knew, and a great deal more beside. He is soon to turn playwright, and "will astound the world"! Alas, he was better
than his humorous boast. There was nothing he did not know
of French popular playwriting except how to make a play
succeed in the theater. When the time came he astounded himself by the most calamitous failure in his career.

Slowly, and by gradations, James first drifted, then was im-
pelled, into an obsession with England, the old home. The
English were perplexing, difficult, challenging, rigid, often
stupid and irritating, yet there, in all Europe, and there only
could he slip happily into a residence, which proved to be for
life. By 1877, he was writing to Grace Norton, "I feel more
at home in London than anywhere else in the world" — which
means, artistically speaking, that his international contacts, and
their subtler nuances, are more intelligible, and thus more
analyzable, in England than elsewhere. There was a kinship

of spirit running either way, not unilaterally as in France. By 1878 his first real success was published by Leslie Stephens in *The Cornhill Magazine,* in the same year with another enduring masterpiece, Robert Louis Stevenson's "The Sire de Malétroit's Door."

It is in this eddying of various international reactions that Henry's first important novels were published, *Roderick Hudson,* 1875, *The Europeans,* 1876, and most important, *The American,* 1877. *Daisy Miller* (really a *nouvelle*) was his *Cornhill* success of 1878. Two of these novels James rather grudgingly admitted to his *New York Edition,* and revised. *The Europeans* he left unentered and unimproved; so the reader (as with *Washington Square*) can compare, if he desires, both versions. I doubt whether he will add much to the controversy as to whether James' early and simpler-style novels are superior to his blown-up later stories in which clause and sentence, and especially qualification and included note, make a shining fabric of words as complex as a telephone board. Such comparison as has been elaborately made between the old and the new versions of the earlier and simpler novels bears out James' own statement that he left the fabric of his story untouched, and gave it only the refinement and expressiveness which his words evidently suggested. Whether his adventures into the higher mathematics of diction later are a blessing or a curse is another question. Myself, I vote for the later novels, whatever the strain of attention, with the exception of *The Portrait of a Lady,* which in time is early, in subject matter late. But I do not applaud the strain. He could, of course, have been simpler if he had chosen to be the master rather than (too often) the victim of his taste for the difficult.

It is always interesting to ask what Twain would have been like if he had remained a Western journalist as he well might have done; and what James would have written if he had stayed

at home, as he probably would have had to do if his grandfather had not speculated in real estate. One sees a possible
answer in *Roderick Hudson,* whose hero is introduced as a
potential genius bottled up in provincial New England. The
first part of this novel is such an American story as Howells
must have approved. But it is not Howells, it is Hawthorne
who is his literary inspiration. James had a glamour for
Howells which seems to have misted that honest editor's eyes.
Perhaps it was because he was not yet firmly settled in Boston
from the West, and was dazzled by a precocious example of
what he recognized as deeply cultured writing. But any editor
would have been impressed by a young man who still looked
like La Farge's portrait. With Mark the glamour was upon
Howells. The prestige of the *Atlantic* and the Brahmins was
still such as to make him feel honored to be paid sixty dollars
for a contribution, by this time a pittance for the lion (or the
jackass as some called him) out of the West. But Howells was
sufficiently unsettled from his critical bases to publish in 1871
a James novel called *Watch and Ward,* already mentioned,
which later readers, including Henry James himself, have
agreed was a rather absurd failure.

Howells' judgment was much better when Henry, his imagination enriched by the international scene, began *Roderick
Hudson* in Florence, continued it in the Black Forest, and
finished it in New York. He wrote it, so he says, with no impulse but to "ease the inward ache" of leaving his beloved
Italy, and to "prolong the illusion of its golden air." With
much more truth and less sentiment, he added that he was trying to catch "the related state, to each other, of certain figures
and things." The "things" were of Rome and New England.
The "figures" were New Englanders and Romans, and a new
international type, as beautiful as she was strange — a complete
feminine expatriate.

What chance, Henry asks in the beginning of *Roderick*

Hudson, has a genius living in Northampton, Massachusetts, in the eighteen-seventies? A genius who is a "common" fellow, who wears "swagger" clothes, is lazy and worthless in the eyes of the townsfolk, both morally and emotionally unstable, and without conscience for his friends? It is, one sees, a real Hawthorne question as to what is the relation between morality, environment, and genius. Henry's novel sends young Hudson to Rome under the patronage of an Observer of culture, who is not too unlike Henry himself. Hudson has already molded a beautiful child who has rather shocked the town by its nudity — which is a little shocked already to find that they have produced in their midst his patron, the Observer, who has no trade except to be a man of leisure. And so Hudson the prodigy is sent abroad and is evidently worth sending, but the worldly, witty, essentially corrupt expatriate society of Rome is too heady for him. When he makes his first success, he is not equal to the labor required for perfection. Instead, he finds it easier to become infatuated with an incredibly beautiful girl (we shall meet her again years later as James' Princess Casamassima) who has been put upon the marriage mart by her American mother. Like his art, she requires a higher bid than he can make. And so he kills himself, much more credibly than most of James' suicides, in a final gesture somewhat reminiscent of another egotist, Hawthorne's man with the marble heart.

Hawthorne was James' guide to such a New England town as Northampton, which James had merely visited. Hawthorne, before James, filled pages with discussions of art (not always good art). With Hawthorne, morality was something bred into a race, which, when violated, led to disaster. It is difficult not to conclude, that if Henry had stayed at home, away from the international scene where he learned that morality was a basic relationship which made civilization, and was usually concrete, then he might have been marked and limited by the old master for life, a victim of his persuasive style. As it was, some of his

early short stories, but not *Roderick Hudson,* which has its
great moments, are only jejune Hawthorne. He escaped into
his own originality precisely by way of this *mondaine* society
too trivial seemingly for Hawthorne, and so much more brilliant and artistically no less significant than the moralities of
The Marble Faun. Of this James seems to have become well
aware. When he came to revise this story, he realized that he
had missed a dramatic antithesis, which for his talent was far
more promising than a moral apologue. The girl at home,
Mary Garland, lovely but too ethical for Roderick, was the
shining contrast with the charming Christina whose brains and
beauty were her morals. These two, with the "innocent" American genius fumbling between them, were the real story, one of
those subtle pressures of European and American tradition
upon the individual which were to make James' fame.

I have digested *Roderick Hudson* into a simplicity which
belies the richness of its fabric and the gay glitter of the minor
characters who are disillusioned without being hard. I am,
indeed, desirous of escaping a descriptive catalogue of James'
work, even at the risk of omission of parts or wholes. After all,
this book is a study of men and their work against a background, not a handbook for quizzers. Yet the reader must remember that with James, who had so little personal history of
his own beyond his art, a fortunate conception of a book was
a dramatic moment of life. If I omit or hurry over certain
crises of such creative experiences, it is not for lack of importance to him but for relevance. And if I seem to scant many
aspects of his books, as I do in this one, it must be remembered
that without making my study of parallel lives an anthology,
it is impossible more than to suggest by description the wit, the
sharp but urbane criticism, by which this still young man
brings into reality, as early as in *Roderick Hudson,* the expa-

triate society of Rome, playing its own drama of greed, ambition, vanity, and the purchase of Old World distinction among the faded glories of Papal Rome, and in the presence of the still more faded descendants of the great.

But no omission can be made of the second of James' first mature and masterly novels, *The American* of 1877. *The American* is exactly contemporary with Mark's *Tom Sawyer,* and both represent men of the greatest ability reaching into new fields of endeavor. Mark was turning from travel books and semi-journalism to his own past, when

> *A boy's will is the wind's will,*
> *And the thoughts of youth are long, long thoughts.*

James, committed to international reactions, was leaving his half-baked geniuses and "refined" Americans trying to learn how to live a life of cultivated leisure for an American type which he had avoided (or was ignorant of) at home, but which now began to fascinate him. As he learned to know familiarly the European scene he became aware of an American who had already made himself rich and powerful in that development of a continent which hitherto had seemed to Henry a menace to "culture," if not a cause of vulgarity. Here was a dramatic American whose first acts had been played beyond his scope and even his knowledge. They had been played either in that downtown region of business, as he called it when he lived in New York, which was more foreign to him than Rome or Paris; or, as in the case of the character who now engaged his imagination, in the dim West where men grew rich by selling plumbing or speculating in silver and gold, like Twain's acquaintances. These Americans now encountered abroad were not trying to become as European as possible, they were confident of themselves, strong-willed, idealistic, yet still innocent of the "poisons" of Europe in its glamorous old age.

I recall [wrote Henry in his later Preface — and this is a good instance of how stories came to him, when not by someone's anecdote]
that I was seated in an American "horse-car" when I found myself,
of a sudden, considering with enthusiasm, as the theme of a "story,"
the situation in another country and an aristocratic society, of some
robust but insidiously beguiled and betrayed, some cruelly wronged,
compatriot: the point being in especial that he should suffer at the
hands of persons pretending to represent the highest possible civilization and to be of an order in every way superior to his own. What
would he "do" in that predicament, how would he right himself, or
how, failing a remedy, would he conduct himself under his wrong?

And before James left the horsecar he had the answer:

Stricken, smarting, sore, he would arrive at his just vindication and
then would fail of all triumphantly and all vulgarly enjoying it. He
would hold his revenge and cherish it and feel its sweetness, and then
in the very act of forcing it home would sacrifice it in disgust. He
would let them go, in short, his haughty contemners . . . and he would
obey, in so doing, one of the large and easy impulses *generally* characteristic of his type. . . . All he would have at the end would be
therefore just the moral convenience, indeed the moral necessity, of
his practical, but quite unappreciated magnanimity . . . a strong
man indifferent to his strength, and . . . the assertion of his "rights."

And here was an American type which gave to James for the
first time, I should say, a heroic aspect of our material conquest
of the continent. This hero for an international novel had not
only made his millions in the mysterious hinterland of "culture," he had looked beyond them into the "what next?" of his
own personal life. Distinguished in the Civil War as well as
in industry, he had kept a "wary freshness" and a strength that
was moral as well as intellectual. And like the Romans in
Greece he is determined to conquer values that he did not
possess, the values of an old civilization. The attitude and
carriage of this American, as James sees him preparing for a
slow conquest of Paris, have a liberal looseness. His coun-
tenance had that "paucity of detail which is yet not emptiness,

that blankness which is not simplicity [we call it "dead-pan"], that look of being committed to nothing in particular, of standing in a posture of general hospitality to the chances of life, of being very much at one's own disposal, characteristic of American faces of the clear strain." His eye was "frigid and yet friendly, frank yet cautious, shrewd yet credulous, positive yet skeptical, confident yet shy, extremely intelligent and extremely good-humoured, there was something vaguely defiant in its concessions and something profoundly reassuring in its reserve." Prosperity seems to have been "within his call; he is evidently a man of business, but the term appears to confess, for his particular benefit, to undefined and mysterious boundaries which invite the imagination to bestir itself."

You could scarcely ask a better, a shrewder, and a more flattering portrait of the American of the "pure strain," who has been an often maligned and misunderstood leader of our industrial development. Indeed, the history of American capitalism has seldom been without its "practical, but quite unappreciated magnanimity." Young James as observer of an American type has done as well as younger Huckleberry Finn with his equally American, if more local, specimens on the river. And Newman, for that is the name of the man himself, is obviously an admirable choice for a novel of the American invasion of Europe — quite possibly for a great novel.

James set about it with "eagerness," and put all his winnings of European and especially French experience on the result. Newman was not to be content with pictures and palaces, nor with the accessible society of expatriates. He sought the fruit of all this rich beauty in history, and was determined to find it in a woman. He made his goal Madame de Cintré, precisely the most aristocratic, most handsome, most winning, and most inaccessible of the old noblesse, and thus encountered in determined and not unskillful battle her beaked, clawed, and greedy family, joining insult to arrogance in their resistance to the barbarian, except as one who could be stripped for their benefit.

The conflict between American "innocent," innocent only in my special sense, and French aristocracy is excellently conducted, dramatic, brilliant, with a subtlety by no means confined to one side. Newman wins, and then is frustrated. Madame de Cintré accepts him. But in the course of the family intrigue, she discovers a foul murder which blackens the family past. They are put in his power. But she deserts him, not for them, but out of a fanatical sense of family honor. He loses her — has nothing left but his magnanimity in refusing to follow his revenge.

Even James felt that this was a weak ending for a magnificent story. She loves him. Why did she not desert them, marry him, and go to America to live? Years later, in a private letter, Henry explained that Madame de Cintré could not be allowed to marry this admirable American, since life for such a woman was impossible anywhere but in France, and certainly not in America. Perhaps — and James tried to prove it later in the much inferior story of Lady Barberina who could not take it in New York. But actually, the difficulty was, that while James was by this time familiar with his Paris and enough of the habits of its noblesse, he was not at all familiar with either the environment or the men of that America outside the Jamesian and Newport circles where Newman was a power. Good realist that he was, he sheered away from the problems of settling a Cintré in a possible environment which might have saved Newman from frustration and Madame de Cintré from a living death in a convent. Newman, a whole man and presumably as powerful as likable, and as skillful in love and friendship at home as in Paris, was beyond James' sure comprehension. And the proof, I should say, is that never again with any emphasis did he use an American man of this type to command a story. His rich and successful Americans from now on were to be old men, long since retired from unknown regions and "mysterious activities." For Americans of the heroic mold, capable of encountering Europe and triumphantly succeeding, or tragically failing, he substituted young American women, with no "downtown" blank spots in their past. And chose well. The drama of the American woman's cultural needs of an old civilization was quite as good a subject, and for James, always intuitive of woman, more intelligible to his genius.

The young Henry in 1869 was taken to call on the redoubtable George Eliot, whose works had won his imagination, possibly as combining strong moral background with a skillful and purposely analytical art. "I have fallen in love," he wrote his father, with this "great horse-faced blue-stocking." Nine years later his current social patroness, the amiable but rather foolish Mrs. Greville, "a cousin by marriage of the Greville papers," took him again into the equine presence, made more portentous this time by her protective mate, G. H. Lewes. James felt that the two might come to like him but only after Mrs. Greville, who was a "rattle," had said good-bye. Unfortunately that "ridiculous" lady, without consulting him, left behind her as a gift two slim volumes of Henry's latest novel. They were entering the carriage when Lewes hurried after them shaking high the uninvited present: "Ah those books — take them away, please away, away!" The bruise to the author's vanity, even though his identity was unrecognized, was "sharp."

The little volumes were certainly his *The Europeans* published that year. Already his brother William, with his usual obtuse criticism of Henry's fiction, had deplored the book as light, and it is not impossible that these unhappy auguries from great moralist and great-to-be philosopher were one reason why James never included the novel in his *New York Edition*. It was an error, for this is a delightful story and very relevant to the present discussion.

For here is a different attempt in a lighter mood and with more familiar characters to reverse the theme of *The American,* and bring Europe, or rather two Europeanized Americans, home to encounter a contrast in manners in their almost forgotten New England where they hope to place themselves with their rich relative. If it lacks the somber undertones of *The American,* its plot is much more plausible. The Baroness Münster is precisely such an impecunious but highly connected aristocrat as James found always fascinating in expatriate society. She and her dilettante artist brother are quite de-Americanized, and he with his kindness and good sense is well fitted to be the Observer of the story. The Baroness presents a theme often repeated by James, admirable social manners which lack in *mondaine* society the moral integrity, or, as with Madame de Cintré, the moral firmness, of the "clear-strain" American. Her cynical wit and polished skill are contrasted in this novel of the Boston area with the rigidity of New England, where her uncle, Mr. Wentworth, the head of the family, regards "pleasure" as dangerously including art as well as drunkenness. "They are sober," says Felix to his sister, "they are even severe. . . . They take things hard. I think there is something the matter with them; they have some melancholy memory or some depressing expectation. . . . My uncle, Mr. Wentworth . . . looks as if he were undergoing martyrdom, not by fire, but by freezing. But they are wonderfully kind and gentle." Two sisters are in the family, one a conformist, another a rebel ignorant of what she rebels against in this atmosphere. "We shall cheer them up," says Felix, and does so, while describing their venerable New England homestead as a three-story bungalow in a region of dirty woods! No wonder William found the novel deplorably light. Actually it is James at his best in his Jane Austen vein. The novel could have been called *Morals and Mores,* if anyone had known then what mores meant. One regrets that in his later search for difficult subtlety, James did not more often indulge in the Jane Austen touch. But it appears more commonly than is generally supposed. *The Europeans* is not one of his most important, but quite one of his most readable books. It should be reintroduced to the American public, the more so that Felix's whimsical comments on the difficulty of describing so primitive a place as the "tremendously natural country," under its "strange white light," and its "faraway blue sky" are clearly James' own. Unlike Jane Austen or Howells, he never knew any one country to its grass roots, and was constantly being surprised by his own birthplace.

So far Henry has been consciously experimenting in international reactions, which is not to say that *Roderick Hudson* and *The American,* at least, were not major efforts, and that *The American* does not include some as fine fictional writing as he was ever to do. He has not attained a success commensurate with his labors; although much critical esteem — one can scarcely use a stronger word. Ironical, that this success did come not only with another avowed experiment, upon which, so he wrote his brother, he did not wish to waste a bigger subject. In *Daisy Miller* (first published in 1878) which is still one of the few Jamesian titles known generally to the public, he wrote a *nouvelle* of contrasting morals and manners, but this time his mood began in cruel satire, lifting at the end into intense pathos. It was a success, he wrote Howells, spreading his fame in two hemispheres, but as so often with young writers, when they write a masterpiece, it brought him in little, only two hundred dollars from his native land, although Macmillan's London publications must have yielded more. Even the success was somewhat grudging, since an unnamed Philadelphia editor in rejecting the story called it an "outrage on American girlhood." Yet the reputation was great enough to persuade Henry that if he wanted to be read he would have to stick to the international. It would have been more true, if he had said that if he wanted to be read widely, he would have to make his novels as emotionally moving as is *Daisy Miller*.

The story of Daisy, an unusually crude and naïve American girl abroad, tricked by her own moral innocence, came to Henry by way of gossip (his favorite source for stories). He was well prepared to dramatize it for, like Winterbourne, the cultivated drifter of the narrative, he was a stroller on terraces and through sightseers' haunts, and, like Winterbourne also, had seen many a crude compatriot snubbed by sophisticated expatriates. He had met the "dyspeptic" American mother of the story, who, with increasing wealth, had lost her position in the household when freed from domestic responsibilities. He had observed the incongruous diamonds in her ears, and heard her querulous voice. He knew her precocious children over whom she had no control — the shrewd, hard little boy, a hotel pest, and Daisy, the surprising flower grown out of democratic commonplace, her atrocious English, her exquisite dressing, a good girl, ready for love and shockingly candid in her attempt to find it. Winterbourne, like James, was also an Observer, nor did his snobbish aunt prevent him from estimating at its true quality the loveliness of Daisy. But as James said of him, and might have said of himself, he had "lived too long in foreign parts" to be convinced easily that this uninhibited American girl, so beautiful and so frank, was really innocent, or that in her chatter she was offering him a love of rarest quality. He had become an expatriate accustomed to consider American simplicity as a comic strip. And so it was not Winterbourne but a nondescript Roman, seeking to marry Daisy, who played upon her innocence to the cost of her reputation with the old hens of the expatriates. Winterbourne was too cautious to save her. By a girlish gesture of challenge she lost her life, not too accidentally, as a result of the feverish and forbidden night air of the Coliseum, alone with the Roman who loved her but knew that she would never marry him.

And something very curious happened in the last pages to this story. It had begun as a cool study, realistic, satiric, of contrasts in codes of behavior, but ends as poetry. James says so himself, answering in his Preface one of those rhetorical questions he was all too fond of in his later manner — a question which no one living except himself could have got through with orally without a syntactical breakdown. He had lifted naïve little Daisy with her small-town voice, and small-town manners, and small-town sincerity, into poetry, the poetry of pathos. He had done so without making her less true, and so achieved a warmth which is felt even through the Observer's reticence and caution in the presence of unanalyzed emotion. Winterbourne gives his own answer with tight-lipped intensity in a single remark after her death — to which William James, so curiously insensitive in the presence of art, strongly objected — "She would have appreciated one's esteem," by which he meant that he should have given her his love.

This decade, roughly of the eighteen-seventies, which has been the subject of the last chapters, conveniently ends at 1876 for Mark and 1878 for James. Intellectually as well as biographically it was essentially a European experience for Henry. The letters Lubbock chose for reprinting in these years are written from London, Florence, Rome, Great Malvern (the sanitarium), Cambridge, Massachusetts, Heidelberg, Berne, Paris, Etretat, and from 1877 to 1878, England and Scotland, which indicates only partially the extent of his wandering, and emphatically his gradual settlement upon England. Like Mark he was writing carefully about scenes and people with which he was in most cases at least reasonably familiar.

We are approaching the peaks of achievement for both James and Twain, and they are in sight by the latter seventies. It may seem curious, yet it is natural for nineteenth-century Americans, whether turning West or East, that the sources for the books of both are usually travel — an inevitable subject for a mobile people. Mark as late as 1878 is busy with *A Tramp Abroad,* where he tried to repeat the same compound of satire and information, stuffed like a cake with wisecracks and anecdotes, which made the success of *The Innocents Abroad.* James' first four considerable works of fiction are not by-products but main-products of travel, by a man whose extra income came from writing foreign correspondence. He was not yet the sure master of the art of the novel; Mark never was, but then he was the kind of genius that can absorb errors, pervert technique, and still (at his best) get away with it. James, as we can see in these years, was determined to be a master, at least of craftsmanship.

Chapter V

TWAIN FINDS A TREASURE IN HANNIBAL

I HAVE WRITTEN before of Mark's drift toward respectability. In the next stage of his biography he became, in its best not its worst sense, the thing itself. After preliminary visits with friends, he and his family came in 1871 to settle down, intending it to be for life, in one of the most respectable (again in its best sense) cities of New England, or for that matter of all American cities — Hartford, Connecticut. The surprising thing is that modern enemies of all things called respectable in American life should have failed to understand why he did so, and with such great satisfaction, and have supposed that it was Hartford and its unquestioned respectability that dropped a soft blanket of comfortable worthiness upon his career in the adventurous and supposedly radical West. I hope to show that of all probable choices of a residence for Mark as a creative writer, Hartford was one of the best.

I shall not endeavor to describe the intellectual circle of Nook Farm, a community that grew up slowly from the eighteen-fifties on a hundred-acre tract of the lovely West Hartford territory, just suburban to the city itself. Kenneth R. Andrews has just done so with charm, erudition, and insight in *Nook Farm: Mark Twain's Hartford Circle* (1950). There Mark lived for twenty years from 1871 to 1891, in more or less close communication with a group of intellectuals, all sympathetic neighbors; all vigorous, and some exceedingly vigorous, minds, none of them "stuffy," all of them vitally interested in vital movements of contemporary life. If in association with Charles

Dudley Warner, Harriet Beecher Stowe, Joseph Hopkins
Twichell, and in the auras of Horace Bushnell, Henry Ward
Beecher, Isabella Beecher Hooker, the air often breathed of
reform, and if a good life which was usually a moral life was a
visible ideal, there was nothing deleterious to a writer whose
deepest concern was to be with the American past, and whose
interest was essentially in persons, whatever their social and
religious doctrines. And it is a factor of great value in this
friendly society for an intensely individual creative imagination such as Mark's, that none of the numerous professional
writers of the Nook Farm group in any sense rose toward greatness, or even high originality, except Harriet Beecher Stowe.
And she, I should say, did no more than make abolitionism respectable, if not loved, by Mark, whose humanitarianism would
have made him anti-slavery anyway as soon as he got out of
Missouri.

This, however, is negative, but the positive advantages of
Nook Farm are also evident. There, after his Hannibal childhood, Mark at last settled down (relatively at least) in a "dream
house" of his own building, a refuge from boardinghouses,
hotels, or lecture circuits, and a relief from the wanderings of a
man whose profession had been travel for twenty years.

And I should add some items. It was still Reconstruction
days when Mark went to Hartford, when the momentum of
industrial development and agrarian expansion was being
turned toward private profits, in a boom which soon ended in
a great bust, and began again in an intenser materialism lasting
at least until President Coolidge could announce that the business of America was business. Nook Farm, in the heart of the
American Industrial Revolution, was an idealistic community
but busy with finance and investment also, as Mr. Andrews
emphasizes. There was plenty of business talk and very little
of even the mild socialism that Howells was trying to bring
from Boston. Hartford was industrially a progressive city, like

all urban Connecticut, but not speculative, and with few exceptions not a region acquiring vast profits then and afterward. It was a good place for Mark, who in one of his aspects was a sound entrepreneur of his own works, an even more eager promoter of business relating to them, where he was not always sound, but a reckless speculator in other people's attempts to make money. He wanted desperately to make and keep and be sure of a fortune. It was a dream of security, with the price going higher year by year. His letters are full of this. It differed only from the dream of the great "empire builders" and smaller magnates of the period, in that he did not seek power, he wanted money, security with an S. "The years between December, 1884, and December, 1889 — the longest period between 1867 and 1910 in which Mark published no books — " says Mr. Andrews cogently, "are those of his greatest involvement in business enterprises." He was thinking of himself as "a captain of industry." Hartford, for all its high level of education, was quite as keen as Athens on making profits, while in its Nook the good talk of ideas went on. Yet it was a better and safer place for Mark than Washoe or San Francisco or New York, while his fortune was in the making. He must have felt that a conservative community, interested in both thinking and business, was good for him. Of course, he did not always or often take its advice.

Mark, in fact, was reverting to family tradition. The "Judge," his father, did not want to go back to Virginia, but he did emphatically want to go back to the secure life of dignity, the kind of respectable living, the "barouche," and the memories of servants with which he had started West. All the family did — Orion most of all, who, in his desperate efforts to get rich securely and quick, went (among one hundred other enterprises) into the chicken business on a large scale, without estimating the cost of the feeding, and lost all of one of the numerous donations Mark sent him. A secure and respectable prosperity was the ideal (not literary eminence) which his mother, with her difficult past, never failed to hold up before her puzzling son, in many letters. My final argument that Hartford has reason to be proud of Mark is that he wrote his best books when his life centered there.

This last, of course, requires some explanation. For no part of Mark's best literary material, with one partial exception in *A Connecticut Yankee in King Arthur's Court,* comes from Connecticut or the East. It is all from the West — every living character (except the Boss) is entirely from the West. And it is all the substance of his youth. This was not Hartford's fault, which did in his Nook Farm circle give him some literary ideas — not many. It was the curious nature of Mark's own genius. Like Shakespeare (though for very different reasons) he would not, and in Mark's case certainly, he could not write his best about his own immediate times and environment. To begin with, he did not want to. He read history with passion — the scandalous Suetonius was his bedside companion, but Paine quotes him, "I detest novels, poetry, and theology." If he made exceptions for fiction it was for *Don Quixote* and *Gil Blas* which are stories of the past. He did not want to do, he could not do, and said so, the society in which at the moment he was living — and proved his point in *The Gilded Age,* which in the worse half is substantially contemporary. The reasons for this I have touched upon before. First was Mark's palpable failure to grow up, to become a "mature mind" in Mr. Overstreet's definition of the term, except in the management of his own literary properties, and not always then, and in his successful married life, where, however, he did not mature personally so as to escape the almost self-destroying effect of any family loss. He was a boy endowed with the super qualities of a first-rate creative mind, not a critical, not a judicious one. His zest for experience, even in talk, his obsession like a boy's with new personalities, his ill-directed but prodigious energy, his explosions of wit and spurts of humor came from a mind as fresh in the years of his decline as in youth. Read ten pages of Mark Twain, whether of boys or adults or ideas or things, and all this will need no more argument, especially in his later attempts at philosophy, where he is often youth incarnate. Only in his superb and perfectly developed diction does Mark seem utterly mature.

The conclusion, it seems, is very simple and needs no elaborate psychiatry. Mark, as he grew more creative, was driven back upon his early youth both by predilection and inability to nourish his imagination from the contemporary scene. He could satirize it; he could not make it live. His new friends, his new interests, his new environment satisfied him deeply, but did not stimulate his extraordinary faculty for recreating life. This life had to be young in order to be felt, for he was young regardless of age — and to be young it had to be retrospective, rising from the memory. In the rich material of his reporter's books on the West and the River, there were brilliant glimpses of his power to make personality and invent fictitious incident. But back of and deeper, more mellowed, more taken into the depths of the consciousness, lay the most intense life of all — the sensitive years of his first adventures into the glamour and excitement of a free life on his own, in what seemed an illimitable world of promise. Then this fortunate American boy was growing up in the morning time of the West, in a boy's realistic Heaven, even though aspects of Hell and Purgatory lay beneath his innocent bare feet.

I submit that Hartford (and Quarry Farm), not the West itself, Hartford where he lived in a society which engaged his other necessities and interests, but let him alone to write out his "long thoughts" of a lost, but not irrecoverable youth, was precisely the place to pass the veil of time and space, and create Tom Sawyer and Huckleberry Finn.

2. ITEMS OF BIOGRAPHY

It should be clear from the previous paragraphs that the important biography of Mark in these years is of his life as a writer in, say, 1875 to 1885 at Quarry Farm near Elmira or elsewhere on leave, so to speak, from Hartford. But for convenience I shall list, not all he wrote — he sometimes wrote four thousand words a day at Quarry Farm — but the well-known achievements of this period. In 1871, when he moved to Hartford, he finished *Roughing It,* published 1872. In 1872, he began *The Adventures of Tom Sawyer.* In 1873, he published *The Gilded Age.* In 1874, he published in *The Atlantic Monthly, Old Times on the Mississippi.* In 1874 and 1875, he worked on *Tom Sawyer* and published it in 1876. In 1876, he began the *Adventures of Huckleberry Finn.* In 1877, he began *The Prince and the Pauper,* published in 1881. In 1878, he began *A Tramp Abroad* and published it in 1880. In 1880, he took up *Huckleberry Finn* again ("*I* shall *like it,* whether anybody else does or not"). In 1883, he published *Life on the Mississippi.* In 1884, he published *Huckleberry Finn,* not distributed until February, 1885. And in 1885, reached his fiftieth year.

What did he look like then to his most devoted, and sometimes his most perceptive biographer, his daughter Susy. She used to keep her biography under her pillow at night.

We are a very happy family! We consist of papa, mama, Jean, Clara and me. It is papa I am writing about, and I shall have no trouble in not knowing what to say about him, as he is a very striking character. Papa's appearance has been described many times, but very incorrectly; he has beautiful curly grey hair, not any too thick, or any too long, just right; a Roman nose, which greatly improves the beauty of his features, kind blue eyes, and a small mustache, he has a wonderfully shaped head, and profile, he has a very good figure in short he is an extraordinarily fine looking man. All his features are perfect, except that he hasn't extraordinary teeth. His complexion is very fair, and he doesn't ware [Susy's spelling] a beard.

He is a very good man, and a very funny one; he has got a temper but we all of us have in this family. He is the loveliest man I ever saw, or ever hope to see, and oh so absent-minded!

Susan's portrait omits only the piercing flash of Mark's eyes when in a temper, the self-dramatizations of his movements, especially his entrances and his exits, his drawl, and the quick reversals of his temperament.

It was at this period of the latter eighteen-seventies and early eighteen-eighties that Mark became a national figure. This resulted not so much from his books — not even *Tom Sawyer* and *Huckleberry. Finn* — as from his lecturing and his *obiter dicta* lifted from his speeches or passed on from his stream of talk, that went across the country. For his wit was as native to him as breathing. It was a lighthearted wit that broke easily into anger and scorn. The letters he wrote to Mrs. Fairbanks (the Mother Fairbanks of *The Quaker City*), recently published by Dixon Wecter, show far better than his family letters what a reckless, caustic talker he could be, and how much even of what he wrote for publication then had to be thrown overboard. It is not surprising that as he gained in power, his "wit and wisdom" as they called it in the old anthologies was bound to make him a celebrity. Indeed, it was orally that his books — especially their humorous portions — made their deepest impression — sometimes, as with *Huckleberry Finn*, in extracts before they were published. Like Dickens, he could deliver with such dramatic effect that his audiences were prepared in advance to laugh as Dickens' audience was ready to cry. And inevitably his fertility in epigrams spread his ideas because they were so quotable. Already he had become a public voice for America, and usually in good causes, political, or humanitarian, or in reform (the laws of copyright, for example), as also with his neighbors at Nook Farm.

In politics he had been a satirist of corruption and misman-agement, but until the campaign to elect Blaine for President, he had been like most of his friends an unreflecting Repub-lican, the party that had saved the Union. He could stomach Grant even in his second term, but inevitably when Cleveland challenged the Republicans this Missourian found it easier to break away from the Grand Old Party than did his friends in Hartford. He became a Mugwump (a horrid word used to describe an independent) and his closest friend Twichell joined him, to the scandal of his associates, although not to the extent to which both Twain and his biographer Paine described their disapproval. Susy as usual has the right quotation, "Papa said the other day, 'I am a mugwump and a mugwump is pure from the marrow out.' " But I think Mark was referring not to the relative chastity of the candidates then in dispute, but rather to the hypocrisy of his respectable associates who preferred an obviously corrupted party to a democrat such as Cleveland.

For the rest — and away from creative writing — he was a Yankee on the make, determined like his neighbor Colt, the revolver man, to make it big. But his ambition was for se-curity (the necessary amount constantly expanding), not that vulgar vanity of the new millionaires which made America of those days a show place of bad taste for the world. Note, for example, his own pleasant though commodious house in com-parison with the drunken fantasias of his old acquaintances, on Telegraph Hill in San Francisco. Yet it was in these years that this Mark, become expansionist like Colonel Sellers and Tom Sawyer, those gilders of life — planned (and for a while succeeded) in making the biggest publishing house, the big-gest royalties for others as well as for himself; entered the biggest speculation to make the biggest success of a typesetting machine, and crashed finally in the biggest literary bankruptcy, followed by the biggest journey all around the world in order to pay his debts. And all the time security, if he really wanted it, was running from the nibs of his pen. Of course, he did not really want security — any more than power or ostentation. He wanted to be able to gamble through life, with a large enough sack of nuggets in reserve.

3. TOM SAWYER AND HUCKLEBERRY FINN

The limitations of this book make it necessary to turn from Mark the wit who said that the report of his death had been greatly exaggerated, and other classic wisecracks. Probably many of Mark's epigrams will survive, perhaps attributed to someone else, after his books have all been lost; but the concern in these parallel lives is with a creative representation of personality, and especially American character. If he succeeds there he becomes a maker of history where history comes nearest to important truth by rising to an art. I have tried in an earlier chapter to identify one aspect at least of Sam Clemens' personality, temperament, and character with Tom Sawyer or Huck Finn. Now I shall try to separate them, as one must in discussing not a person but a book which projects, like all art, the author's imagination into the representative, the symbolical, and, if it is strong enough, into the universal. It is not a platitude to say that Tom is the eternal boy, but merely a too broad assertion that the success of *Tom Sawyer* is not to be explained only by the material Mark brought to the making of it.

There was nothing new in the nineteenth century at least in the subject — a small boy's biography. Before that century with its flood of humanitarianism, the child in neither Christian, nor Arabic, nor classic literature had seemed worthy of a book about him. Glimpses of children — pathetic, charming, ethical, or, as in the picaresque, immoral — are abundant. Shakespeare's Mamillius lives through a few speeches, Chaucer's Hugh of Lincoln in a few lines. But small boys and small girls in literature are usually seen but not heard, or are characters minor to the action. Their life, except that they should be kept alive, was neither interesting nor important to novelists of manners or pre-Wordsworthian poets, or philosophers before Rousseau. Yet after Thackeray and Dickens it would be absurd to call Twain the inventor of the boy's story. His originality must be sought elsewhere.

Mark wrote *Tom Sawyer* with passion, but he was curiously dubious of its merits and indifferent to its success except as a money-maker. In advance of reading, he offered Howells half the rights if he would dramatize it; and (incredible) when he did leave the manuscript with him to be read, said that if it got lost in the express on the way home, "it will be no great matter." Was there some reluctance at publishing so personal a story? We know that Livy was a good deal bothered in her respectable soul by some of the incidents, and more by items of language. Howells and she left one "hell" in by accident which came out in a hurry when Mark told Howells about it. Perhaps he had *Tom Sawyer* in mind when he told Orion that some day he would give up "bosh" written for others and please himself. Which, if you remember the real intimacy of the story, and its wide difference from his idea of a successful novel as illustrated by *The Gilded Age*, may account for some of his doubts. What is surprising, and very interesting, is that he wrote it for adults, meaning undoubtedly the innumerable perennial adolescents like himself, and it took Howells to persuade him that it should be edited and published as a boy's story for boys. For once Howells was wrong as an editor. The ideal audience for *Tom Sawyer* is the man recalling his youth. Boys read it for its excellent adventure, not always humorous; men, for a quality in Tom's imagination which they do not always understand.

The peculiar quality of *Tom Sawyer* is not easy to define. The graveyard murder, the trial, the Sunday School episode in which the tenderness of Mark's memory saved him for once from burlesque, the fabulous pirates' island, and more and more are easy to value — although I for one think that the cave and Becky and Injun Joe there and the hidden gold are on a very thin ice of contemporary sentimentalism. But none of these make it the so definitely *American* masterpiece that it unquestionably is. Part is in the realism of background, so vividly created that it may be said to have turned Mark Twain's small town on the river into a homing place for the American imagination. Compare in this respect another famous boy's book, Stevenson's *Treasure Island,* where pure adventure, if less humorous, is as memorable as in Mark's story. The literary merits of writing are said to be equal, though I do not agree. But Mark's hero is a projection of a personality infinitely deeper and more interesting than Stevenson's rather unoriginal youngster of pluck and invention lifted into adventure. Indeed, except for Long John Silver, *Treasure Island* would not be notable for personality. And the background of *Treasure Island* does not leave pictures that become part of the furnishing of memory, not even for tropical islands. For Stevenson at the time of writing had never seen a tropical island, and his scene is drawn from the coast range of Southern California, with even a redwood, California azalea, and improbable nutmeg trees from the East tossed in to make the island seem tropical.

Tom himself, I mean the Tom as Mark created him, not the Tom whose tricks and adventures were undoubtedly much like those of young Sam Clemens, was actually the Colonel Sellers of St. Petersburg. The analogy, like most analogies, is incomplete, but in essence it is true and convincing. The Obedstown where Colonel Sellers dreamed and ate raw turnips was by Mark's own merciless description a run-down backwoods settlement of the decadent survivors of the pioneers. The rail-sitting inhabitants were kindly and picturesque, yet that is all that could be said for them. They were, as the Colonel said, less industrious than their own pigs, no more forward-looking than their slaves — nomads camping in a land whose promise had only been scratched. It was the Colonel, his mind, like Don Quixote's, unsettled by too much reading, who gilded the doomed village until he believed all he said.

And what was St. Petersburg itself without the expansive imagination of Tom? A sluggish, lovable small town of the kind familiar to all Americans of the old stock, with only one half-breed Indian and stories of sordid river pirates to recall its less respectable past. Such it was in its own eyes, and it was only Tom's imagination that made it a memorable experience to have grown up there. For Tom was not only the eternal small boy who feared God and hated the Sunday School, but also the only begetter of romantic and heroic dreams drawn from what he could remember of his reading. The river was just a river to the tobacco-spitting loafers, but to Tom it became seas and deserts, and also to the boys he led, even to that eminent realist Huck Finn, until they got tired and went home. You can say of old Sellers and young Sellers, each in his way, what Chaucer said of Petrarch:

> *Petrak, who with rhetorike sweete,*
> *Enlumined all Ytaille with poesy.*

Only it was a very expansive, American type of rhetoric, with Southwestern trimmings.

Most of all, *The Adventures of Tom Sawyer* is a story of a

New World boy. Whatever its humor and its romance, the intoxicating element is freedom, freedom in this half-tamed river region of space, and freedom from effective control. Pap Finn complained bitterly of his loss of complete freedom which had led him like the Indians to take to drink. The boys, however, though still in the margin of regimented life, could be and were free to carry out anything Tom's inventive mind would propose. It was not only in their power, it was very definitely part of their share of the West-moving American tradition.

Finally, Mark had succeeded where usually he failed. By limiting himself (with Howells' and his wife's assistance presumably) to the expansive imagination of a gifted boy, he had run a measured mile without a break. This for a lecturer who followed the laugh into every good and bad was an achievement.

I do not wish to add unduly to the extensive literature that has already gathered about ragged, dirty, shrewd, freedom-loving Huck, the little river rat. A controversy must have begun in Mark's own mind, since he put the story aside after writing several hundreds of pages, ostensibly because he felt doubtful of his American readers, although he may of course been merely "stuck." Were they likely to welcome a tough story of a ragamuffin? He gave them in 1881 a pauper boy without too resounding a success, and a prince thrown in with him, and a realistic background far enough in the past not to offend. Twain, speculator that he was in "projects," liked at least calculable risks in publishing books. His visit to the Mississippi in 1880 probably warmed his enthusiasm again, yet he had reason for his foreboding. Two years after Huckleberry Finn was born in print, Mark's American readers made a cult of moral, sentimental Little Lord Fauntleroy, and dressed their small boys in velvet and curls in imitation, while the Concord, Massachusetts library added to Concord's other fames by banning Twain's book. It was not, I should say, regarded as a masterpiece, even by its author, and certainly not by the public — for a long while. Mr. Andrews quotes a contemporary reviewer, Henry Vedder, who deplores the relative failure of the more elegant *The Prince and the Pauper* because "it is only when as 'Mark Twain' he writes some such trash as the *Adventures of Huckleberry Finn* that this really capable writer can make sure of an appreciative reading." It was Mark himself who had described "The Celebrated Jumping Frog of Calaveras County" to his mother as a villainous backwoods sketch, which, though it did not represent his own opinion, certainly did hers. Mark, like his mother and Mr. Vedder and Livy, was not genteel, and knew it. This sometimes made a coward of him.

Huckleberry Finn, the character in a book, was even more different from the real Huck, who is presumably drawn from young Tom Blankenship of Hannibal, than was Sam the actual boy from Tom Sawyer. Tom Sawyer, the go-getting dreamer, is a small boy's version of the American dream of expansion. He lived, of course, in the real Sam Clemens' imagination, and was well represented in the real Mark of the future, whose financial speculations were unsuccessful sequels of Tom's hunt for the treasure. Huck also was part of Mark Twain's character and of his imagination, but he lived squarely in the present, with an unfailing eye for its possibilities — old clothes, pleasant companions, an empty hogshead to sleep in, and freedom to be himself. When the Widow Douglas told him about Moses, he lost interest as soon as he learned that he was dead. If Tom Sawyer still represents ten out of a hundred Americans, Huck stands for a good share of the proclivities of the other ninety. The environment, of course, is very different, yet Huck was as easy in this environment as Babbitt until he began to try to keep up with the Joneses, or as one of Melville's Marquesans, who also objected to being "sivilized," or as the "mountain men" of the Rockies. He knew the face of everyone in St.

Petersburg, and the private lives of all that interested him —
as Mark did when he was in the Far West. He knew woods and
waters, and "signs" that threatened misfortune, and Nigger
Jim's portents of wealth, which did not worry him because that
didn't have to happen right away. Hence as a reliable reporter
of the nature and quality of mankind he was worth ten Tom
Sawyers. He was a realist, not cursed as so many realists are by
the belief that there is nothing in the world mysterious or
inscrutable. He could size up a man or a woman as accurately
as Mark the pilot had learned to distinguish with an indelible
memory the shoals, towheads, and snags of the Mississippi. He
had what James required if he were to write of Americans at
home, and thought he ought to acquire, and did not want to,
and never really tried, and so stepped out on the far thinner
and more perfect ice of international experience.

With this as a preliminary, let it be said that the American-
ism of *Huckleberry Finn* is not, of course, its first importance,
except for social historians who must always regard it as one
of their outstanding documents. It is a work of art, not a tract
or a travel book, though good as both. Mark's prefatory
"Notice" should be accepted verbatim:

"Persons attempting to find a motive in this narrative will
be prosecuted; persons attempting to find a moral in it will be
banished; persons attempting to find a plot in it will be shot."

He ought to have been shot himself for attempting to insert
a plot, and a bad one, in order to end melodramatically Huck's
voyage by importing Tom and one of his egotist fantasies, by
which runaway Jim turns out not only to be free already, but
is forced to dig himself to freedom all over again. However, his
assertion is correct. He did not write the book to moralize, although those pages in which Huck knows that Huck as a
"nigger-stealer" is in a low-down business, yet loves Jim anyway, and steals him even if he will go to hell for it, are more
cogent as real satire than *Uncle Tom's Cabin*. Twain did not

write Huck's book to describe a river, even to crack jokes (its humor is far deeper than jokes), or to reminisce. Yet he had a purpose as definite as Shakespeare in his best comedies, and I do not mean making money, at which both were extraordinarily keen and successful. No, Huck's book is primarily a portrait book, which can be either a rather low or a very distinguished form of literature. That, as Buffon would have said, is its "style." Even *Hamlet,* in spite of its complex motivation, belongs in this "style" also. Shakespeare certainly did not set out to write a tragedy of indecision. He wished to write about Hamlet and his friends and enemies, and Mark wanted to write about Huck and his associates, in portraits too dramatic to be forgotten. Obvious perhaps, but not to most commentators on play or story, who wish to discuss the philosophy and background and historical climate before they note that the writer thinks first of all of the man (or boy) who, unless he is intensely alive, will never stir enough imagination to make his works and deeds worth arguing.

Henry James was a great artist in dramatic fiction, but his achievement was not the greatest kind of achievement in that art. He is almost unexampled in subtlety, in depth of analysis, in one kind of originality, but he does not seem to have been able to create personalities who, as persons, not chiefly as psychological types, were able to extend their life far beyond their books. In English, Shakespeare obviously was such a portrait writer, so was Dickens, Scott, in lesser measure Fielding, Jane Austen, also Twain, with a more limited talent, and not too many others. James makes up in part in analytic for his failure to attain the highest synthetic powers. Such portrait writers simply *have* the imaginative transformation of experience; they do not as a rule go out to get it. What excites them seems to be a recreation of a person, who can often be identified with reality, but new, more vivid, more realized, and equally integrated in life. Then they seek or see the implications of a stream of action — with Huckleberry Finn it was the flow of the river — which bears such characters onward and lets them speak and act their recreated selves. This is a greatest art — apparently an instinctive art in its origin — the greatest in fiction or drama, though not in poetry, or elsewhere in the practice of writing.

It was no failure in narrative skill which kept James from this supreme achievement, for his skill was far more perfect technically than Twain's. Yet when, in "The Turn of the Screw," he came to analyze the story of a boy experienced (like Huck) in evil, he invented an exquisite creature who spoke, not one of the seven Missouri dialects, but James' own inimitable elaboration of English into a tongue of the more intellectual angels. For re-creation of universal experience, his imagination was too specialized. There was no "density," he felt, in backwoods adventure. Yet the vigorous uncultured level of American life was as "dense" in its way as Elizabethan England. James not only lacked the knowledge of this society, he lacked also the portrait-making faculty which in such people is more effective than analyses. Twain had it, though it must be admitted that he could not have applied it to such a superb creature, ungraspable without analysis, as Strether in *The Ambassadors*. Even Jane Austen's portraits of gentlemen and gentlewomen were out of his range. As he said, they "maddened" him.

And now to Huck. It was an accident, of course, that a man with Sam Clemens' imagination should have been born in the welter of a pioneer civilization in rapid transition, and on a great river where a novel could be floated like a showboat. Yet it was not accident, but a miracle, that brought a genius and such a scene together at the right time. For Huck's book is not naïve, it is not reporting or just great storytelling, it is a careful work of conscious art by a man who this time settled down to make his story true to his own unusually sensitive, deeply

recording, and highly intelligent memory. Huck was thirteen
or fourteen, so he says, when he floated down the river. He was
an adolescent (not a romantic small boy like Tom in his own
book), and, as with David Copperfield, had a deep experience
of brutality, which had made him as wary as a cat in a strange
street, without inhibiting either his loving or hating of experience. He was an adolescent in what was, broadly speaking, an
adolescent civilization, much of which he understood as well
as Dickens the London slums, some of which, since he had been
a river rat, so absorbed him as to make him as observant as Sam,
the river pilot's apprentice. He had a great gift, inventive lying,
which was like Deerslayer's skill with the rifle, a necessity for
survival. Yet what he saw he saw honestly, which was impossible for Tom Sawyer. He was given (by Twain, of course) also
the extremely difficult power of convincing and consummate
self-expression so that he could recreate orally the flow of life.
Shakespeare gave it to Falstaff who was a (fat) waif of fortune
whose career, like Huck's, depended upon successful lying and
persuasive self-portraiture. And so Huck described the Royal
Nonesuch and Colonel Grangerford, and his drunken father,
Pap Finn, upon whose humors (as Falstaff upon the Prince) his
life literally depended, as we readers have seen them ever since.
Let him tell about Pap Finn, just back after an attempt to get
the $6000 share of the gold that Huck and Tom had found in
the cave. "Govment" and the law have entangled this free
American citizen and driven him to drink and the indignity of
a night in the gutter:

> Call this a govment! why, just look at it and see what it's like.
> Here's the law a-standing ready to take a man's son away from him
> . . . a man with six thousand dollars and up'ards, and jams him into
> an old trap of a cabin like this, and lets him go round in clothes that
> ain't fitten for a hog. They call that govment! A man can't get his
> rights in a govment like this. Sometimes I've a mighty notion to just
> leave the country for good and all. Yes, and I *told* 'em so —

Always, as in *Tom Sawyer*, Twain, with a few minor exceptions, limits his art to an adolescent river boy's experience and imagination. And it is not any boy. If Tom has been not improperly described as universal small boy, he is only one kind of universal boy, and Huck, when you get him out of his hogsheads, has a wisdom and a kindness and a realism which are at least as common in boys worth writing about as Tom's more dramatic gifts. And Huck is more completely individual than Tom. You cannot use his name as an adjective, as I have used Tom's.

The romance of *Huckleberry Finn* is a romance of space, the unending river, the ever-bordering forests, the Plains and Indians beyond, the strange built-up East behind. This is why it is commonly said that the book is so American. I think this statement is oversimplified. There are other books in other literatures where space is the romance. Turgenev and Tolstoy can both suggest it of Russia. One gets it in *The Odyssey*. The distinction of *Huckleberry Finn* is that space is absolute, it is a story of a permanent possibility of as much freedom as a boy can wish. This is at the heart of the American experience. To Huck, the home-lover, who liked everything about St. Petersburg except school and clean clothes, an extension of his freedom seemed a matter of will. The great lumber rafts came from the North — he would always be able to go there. The steamboats came from a vague South which someday he can see. Injun Joe was headed for faraway Texas. He could go there anytime if there was a cause. He lived in a mobile civilization which in his experience had always (except for the slaves) been free to move. His father felt the cramping of departing space, but not Huck. His romance was a free world limited only by a boy's handicaps and wishes.

There is another space book more comparable to *Huckleberry Finn* than any I have mentioned. This is Tom Collins' *Such Is Life,* a free-and-easy saga of nineteenth-century Australia, where

men and their bullocks voyage across those vast grazing spaces
as uninterested in the outside world, as ignorant of the transi-
tory nature of their freedom, as Huck himself. But Collins
himself tells the story, and he was an educated, a rather over-
educated Britisher, who sees the drama through sophisticated
eyes, turning it into philosophical history. He is often as vivid
as Twain, and immensely worth reading, but he is not a creature of freedom of space, he is its elegist. So was Mark himself,
but not in this book, not as Huckleberry Finn.

The drama of *Huckleberry Finn* is, of course, its characters
in action and conflict. Here Mark had a great advantage over
Henry James who cried to himself constantly "dramatize,
dramatize" and did so in eloquent words so often impossible of
utterance by anyone but Henry. James deals with a drama
revealed by analysis, which is perhaps his greatest fascination
for the attentive reader. Mark's drama is self-evident once the
scene and the characters are set. His art is to sharpen it, to make
it, as a playwright would say, act. Consider that chapter from
Huckleberry Finn which has been called, and justly, one of the
finest short stories in the language, the Grangerford-Shepherd-
son feud, which is all action and description, as told by Huck.
Here is the aristocratic parallel to Pap Finn and Injun Joe —
a culture breaking down into survivals heroic to the point of
absurdity. The Colonel's arrogant nationality was one of the
causes that brought on the Civil War. Yet even in his backwoods simplicity he is an aristocratic type deplorably lacking in
the present, who belongs with Harold's bodyguard that kept
the shield-wall until all were slaughtered. And yet he is so
clearly an American type where violence seems always to have
a core of sentimentality. How superbly Mark brings out this
familiar trait, stopping just short of burlesque, in Huck's
fascinated description of Emmeline Grangerford's art and
poetry. With the least knowledge of American social history,
one has to say that both the Colonel and Emmeline are true, a
little of each in each.

And finally, you have really to like Huckleberry Finn (as the librarian did not) as you have to like Falstaff in order to appreciate the subtlety of that combination of rascal, sensualist, and poet. And you have to like Pap Finn, and even the King and the Duke (Nigger Jim is easy), if you are to feel how much more than a boy's tall story Huck's book really is. And you have to like Mark Twain if you are to forgive him for letting the Tom Sawyer in him, and Tom himself, escape in the last chapters where the action is not seen as Huck would have contrived it, and the only compensation is Huck's realism, and his reflections upon conscience which deserve a place beside Falstaff's discourse on honor. For Mark, even in his masterpiece, was, here as always, both the creator of the script, and also the moving-picture director, who can be counted upon, sooner or later, to insert a blonde, a wisecrack, a great lover, or a burlesque, at the high point of a saga.

Chapter VI

JAMES WRITES HIS FIRST GREAT NOVEL

By 1880, Henry James, permanently settled in London, had made up his mind about the English. They were "dense," by which here he meant deep and rich in character, they lacked all sense of irony, were often rude — and probably the greatest people in Europe. They could also, to use an American figure, be as slow as molasses in January. He had an opportunity now to know them well in the upper registers, including the intellectuals. In the winter of 1879 he had dined out 107 times. In 1880 he was spending a week-end at Lord Rosebery's great country house with John Bright, Millais the painter, and Lord Northbrook, the last Liberal Viceroy of India. He was watching at one time the Derby winners being trotted out from the stables. At another he was waiting for the footman to ventilate his shirt, and turn his [red!] stockings inside out in preparation for dressing for dinner. Fanny Kemble, the great actress, in what James called her indifferent look, appears as a glamorous person in spite of her age. She was for him like an uncovered cistern into whose secrets one plunged with a splash. In the spring of that year he was leisurely picking up Europe again, city by city, from Paris to Rome and the Riviera. It was a good life, especially for a bachelor who liked attractive, intelligent women. The contrast in outer circumstance between his life in Cambridge and this was emphatic. Yet it was not so great as that between Mark Twain's in Hartford and in Virginia City.

Both men at the moment were determinedly writing about

Americans. All three of James' next novels, in 1880 and 1881, were primarily about his compatriots, and one of them was laid entirely in New York. For James' desire to write about his country as well as his countrymen abroad died hard — perhaps its first severe blow was *Washington Square,* which he himself called a "poorish story," and complained that he had not enough "paraphernalia," by which he meant such riches of remembered background as Twain put into *Huckleberry Finn.* For that, he would have to go to the expatriate, the American turning East, as Mark to reach the height of his achievement had to return to the childhood of the Americans whose ancestors had turned West.

2. ON WRITING A NOVEL

The steps upward or downward which lead to the climactic success or failure of an eminent man are sharply indicated in Plutarch, which is probably the reason that his influence has been as great upon literary as upon historical writing. With him, these successive impacts of circumstance and revelations of character are selected from the results of opportunity, of native ability or its lack, and of the moral qualities of man. Plutarch oversimplifies, sometimes from a lack of knowledge, more often from design. In literature, in a historical novel for instance, oversimplification is usually purposeful: it is the only way to draw the story from the known facts, which usually the novelist finds too abundant. He is after symbolical truth, rather than statistical and analytical accuracy. Yet, of course, all history is selective. The historian has the choice whether to contribute facts for a stockpile of evidence, or to use his time in interpreting a stockpile, already available, of what he thinks relevant. Of course, he is sure to go wrong in one direction or another. Even the tireless Gibbon failed to interpret the visible facts of the art to qualify his generalizations as to the decadence of Byzantium. In literature, the problem is both easier and harder. It is easier to select the evidence that supports the known behavior of human nature, harder to draw out an imaginative truth which fits a given situation. Compare a "scientific" account of Mark Antony with Plutarch's, and with Shakespeare's based upon Plutarch.

In the case of a powerful novelist's first masterpiece, the sources of his narrative and his character studies are as of above, with an addition that there is another important selection not often given enough emphasis. Usually the artist's imagination turns instinctively to that part of his consciousness which holds his warmest, his deepest memories. This was emphatically true with Twain, less so, except in his greatest novels, with James. The book which he then writes may owe its success to many other qualities, such as a matured technique, or good fortune in its choice of a subject appealing to his readers. But it will have a communicable emotion, an authentic firsthand testimony, which makes it a more human document than its predecessors. These begin to seem experiments or by-products of a searching genius, which is settled at last in its proper nest. To change the sex in order to get the figure right, she flies off from time to time to try other nests, yet for great achievements comes back.

I am sure that Henry James would have approved of this analogy, refined it, and put it into much longer sentences. Even crudely stated, it is true for him, and emphatically in this period of his first triumphant book, and the two experiments that preceded it.

3. HENRY'S IMAGINATION TURNS HOME

I could omit the first of these experiments, a brief one, if it were not interesting at this stage to watch Henry at work. He was far less the perfectionist than his more slavish admirers suppose. No one seems to have liked *Confidence* very much, including its author. James apologized for it to his brother, saying that *Scribner's* magazine had paid him well for it, which was an unusual experience. When the book came out in 1880, it should have been recognized that there were a score of scenes and dialogues in it as brilliant as Henry ever wrote. But although he was familiar with expatriate ladies in search of a rich husband and young gentlemen from Harvard trying to live beautifully, still the novel did not jell, and why? The proposed end he had written down in his notebook was a murder and a moral collapse. It was a Hawthorne plot. Everyone concerned lacks confidence in everyone else, but no one as the story worked out would by any possibility become a party to a murder. So he shifted the story to a novel of moral manners, more or less in the Jane Austen tradition, ending it happily and in part because he had decided by this time that American magazines liked happy endings. Also the Observer, who should have spoken for James himself, fell in love and married, and James could no more carry himself there than into Wall Street. He had begun with a plot and found too late that the psychological effect of a lack of confidence which it required did not interest him as much as a study of manners. Of course, Jane Austen also began with plots but their simplicity was such as never to bother her. But Henry is often a victim of his own intricacies. In this case he floundered, but saved the book's readability.

Washington Square, published in book form in 1881, has the most ironical history of James' novels. It pleased him less even than *Confidence,* so that he omitted it from his *New York Edition.* If it seems vivid to us, it is perhaps because *Washington Square,* in part at least, still exists, and has acquired the "density" of another age. Yet it was this book, which he had discarded, that, when picked up by competent playwrighting in *The Heiress,* has begun the new reputation of James as a writer for the theater, which he never could achieve for himself.

Washington Square is a twentieth-century story written, in part at least, in an eighteenth-century manner. The brilliant, arrogant doctor, whose neurosis it was to revenge upon his dull and plain daughter the loss of his beautiful wife, provides drama and psychological opportunity enough to satisfy everything that James craved. Why then call the novel an experiment? Why did he think he had failed? Mrs. Penniman, the doctor's silly, matchmaking sister, is a figure out of *Sense and Sensibility,* and worthy of a place there. The book, indeed, might have been called *Sense, Arrogance, Selfishness, and Sensibility.* But Henry lacked both the ability and the will to stay upon the surface of a situation. What touched his imagination was a fine girl wrecked by an unconsciously vindictive father. He was skillful on Jane Austen's plane of ironic personalities, but his real interest, like Hamlet's old mole, kept working beneath the full consciousness of anyone in the story.

For such a story he needed "paraphernalia" to support its reality. He took this story from an English anecdote told him of her fortune-seeking brother by Fanny Kemble, but added the real plot himself, and placed it, unnecessarily, in an American setting. The setting became vague the moment he left the Square and the great house doors that shut in more than they shut out. It was a tale, so he thought, in a vacuum, and James, even more than nature, hated a vacuum. Balzac had taught him that readers feel the want of "manners, customs, usages, habits, forms . . . matured and established," upon which a novelist lives. James' provision from America was only sufficient, he felt, for an occasional *nouvelle*.

It was an American experiment he never tried again in a novel but once. Like the would-be lover in *Daisy Miller,* he felt he had stayed in foreign parts too long. I think his artistic prejudices, which sometimes became dogmas, misled him. *Washington Square* is a far finer book than his American contemporaries, with whom it was not successful, thought, or than he thought. Catherine is probably the best of his frustrated women. But psychoanalysis was not yet familiar, or acceptable, in Washington Square.

The book of Henry James toward which all this chapter leads is *The Portrait of a Lady,* begun in 1880, and serialized (before it was finished) in 1880–81. No book of his, as his notebooks show, was more carefully developed and written, none written in the course of a more "charming life," especially in Venice above "the far-shining lagoon, the pink walls of San Giorgio, the downward curve of the Riva." This novel, to revert to my Plutarchian analogy, is to be compared to the crisis which brought to the Greek or Roman hero, not final triumph, but a revelation of such masteries of his problem as can indicate to the intelligent observer the nature of his genius. Such a discovery is the final fruit of good reading. It is like the after reflection upon a good dinner, a matured marriage, or, to a military expert, a battle fought and its results achieved. "With strong handling," James wrote of *The Portrait* in his notebooks, "it seems to me that it may all be very true, very powerful, very touching." It was, and most of all (an effect which James did not often aim at), very touching. The most moving, to my thinking, of all James' scenes, is to be found toward the end of this novel.

Probably the worst way to read Henry James is to begin the
novel or short story with the Preface which, often many years
later, he prepared for it. With very few exceptions these Prefaces are much more difficult to follow than the stories they are
supposed to introduce. They should be read afterward, not
before. And furthermore, while this master of involution succeeds brilliantly in explaining how he devised the technique for
elaborating his situation, he usually fails more than to hint at
why some of his novels lift and carry the imagination where
others of equal technical excellence leave the reader cold and
a little bilious from trying to digest a dictionary of words.
Certainly, when he does include the "key" to one of his books
that has become a successful masterpiece, you have to search for
it as for the key to a car in a lady's handbag. There is such a
key in the Preface to *The Portrait of a Lady,* and it is the right
key.

Henry professed to despise plots, yet he did make magnificent
ones — as later dramatizers of his novels are beginning to discover — magnificent because they were the inevitable results
of dramatic situations. He could overstuff a plot with words as a
too affectionate mother may overfeed her baby, but he never fell
off and out of it into vaudeville as Twain was too likely to do.
Look at the drama, the potential melodrama, of *The Portrait
of a Lady.*

Isabel Archer is a good girl, so American that only a new
continent could have produced her, and yet as "dense," as self-
scrutinizing, as a member of the James family. She is determined, a little hard, innocent of the sophistications of evil,
contemptuous of what is said to be the impossible. She is a
rebel against the American pioneer doctrine that suffering is a
maker of character, and convinced that the fine spirit can
ignore any defect in others but disloyalty. She has not a grain
of pettiness, and is not even aware that she is poor, for she has
never encountered poverty. What she wants is life for life's

sake, and, like Henry Thoreau, she will accept nothing less than all of it for fear of missing something essential. She is sure of success, and three words are always on her lips, freedom, liberty, and independence.

This brilliant creature, for she is brilliant if not beautiful, sets out for Europe with Excelsior on her banner. And as with so many Americans, the breaks at first all come her way. Her uncle, a rich and wise expatriate American, loves her for her candor and her courage. His son, Ralph Touchett, a tubercular forced to hold back from "the riot of expression in living," is a man of infinite subtlety, even more generous than he is subtle. He loves her because she lives what he can only imagine. A neighboring nobleman wants to marry her, but she still carries her banner, and Ralph persuades his father, now dying, to halve his own inheritance with Isabel, and so give her the chance for personal independence. He knows that it is an equal chance for ruin in the actual predatory world of Europe, but bets on her integrity, still more on her loyalty to an ideal. .

Madame Merle, an enigmatic American, is the villain of the plot. She is, to appearances, the finished product of adaptation to the rich life which Isabel covets. Actually, she is the discarded mistress of Gilbert Osmond, an expatriate American esthete, whom Ralph justly calls a sterile dilettante. He is also a man of impeccable taste, an egotist who has made himself an aristocrat of culture by despising his inferiors. His lovely and pathetic daughter is also Madame Merle's, who is willing to be a villain in order to capture Isabel for Osmond and assure her daughter's future. One thing only is needed to perfect Osmond's egotism by making possible the conventions by which he lives — money.

It works. Isabel tires of independence. Like many Eastward-turning Americans she longs to blend her young strength with an old culture. And Osmond's charm arouses the first passion she has ever felt. It works, but not for long. "You seemed" said

Ralph to her, "to be sailing in the bright light over the heads
of men. Suddenly someone tossed up a faded rosebud — a
missile that should never have reached you — and straight you
drop to the ground. It hurts me." It was worse than that. Her
clear and powerful innocence is vulnerable only to what for her
had been unimaginable — a life without character, Thoreau
would have called it. She is in a trap, food for an unprincipled
hunter of his own advantage; trapped, too, by her own loyalty
to the obligations of a vow.

In two great scenes James resolves the story. In the first, this
devotee of dialogue describes Isabel's bitter analysis before a
dead fire in a night up to dawn. He says it is his best chapter,
and it is certainly his most dramatic. The second is Ralph
Touchett's deathbed in England, whence she has gone against
her husband's peremptory and contemptuous refusal. It is one
of the noble death scenes in fiction. For Ralph has not again
risked a bet on the power of innocence. Thanks to him she can
still buy off her evil egotist by the gift of a fortune, but he has
left her nothing now, so that she will never be exposed to the
hunters again. He guesses that only one thing can save her, a
man who loves her with such aggressive passion that he can give
her the freedom she has never possessed, to be loved for herself alone. The story has had him in waiting since the first
chapter. Does she marry him? James seldom writes the last
chapter of his best books. "The *whole* of anything is never
told," he wrote in his notebook, "you can only take what
groups together. What I have done has that unity — it groups
together. It is complete in itself — and the rest may be taken
up or not, later." He never did take it up — which would have
made a moving-picture director commit suicide. I wish he had
married her off, for there were clear indications. But for James
that was in "another part of the forest," as they say in Shakespeare's play.

It is a good plot, but there are plenty of others as good. As a plot it would never guarantee a Jamesian masterpiece. For once, his account in the Preface goes beyond the descriptions of how he built a story on firm arches and how he erected a perfect building on them, and proceeds to the subject matter itself. Turgenev gave him with his own lips the formula for such a story as this one. Find the vision of your character, he said, and then let the chances and the complications of existence to which she and she only is subject provide the right relations to her, those that would most bring them out — the complications she would be most likely to produce and feel. But, says James on his own, the "moral" sense of a work, which makes it more than plot, more than situation, depends upon the "felt life concerned in producing it." The question comes back to the artist's sensibility and its quality and capacity, its ability to "grow." Any vision of life depends again upon "some mark made on the intelligence, with some sincere experience."

Evidently in this succinct and cogent analysis James seems to be pointing at some personal experience back of and behind the persuasive emotion of this novel, which makes it more dynamic than a story heard at an English dinner table. Is there "felt life" in *The Portrait?* There surely is, and it is not difficult to trace the source. The felt life was his own. The sincere experience was his deepest (as far as we know) with a woman. It was his long association with his cousin, Minnie Temple. Her death of tuberculosis in 1870 marked for him, he said, the end of his youth.

The great characters of a major novelist are always taken from a felt life, that is, from a personal experience, but are never copied, except in useful detail. Minnie Temple was one of Henry's Albany relatives, where Isabel was from. She was not Isabel in any detail of worldly relations, but rather a prototype of Isabel's character and imagination, and, being real and Henry's dear friend, she was warm and alive in his memory. After her death, he wrote a very remarkable letter to his

brother, William, who was, if anything, even closer to Minnie.
"She was at any rate the helpless victim and toy of her own
intelligence. . . . She was a case of pure generosity — she had
more even than she ever had use for. . . . She *represented,* in a
manner, in my life several of the elements or phases of life at
large — her own sex, to begin with, but even more *Youth;* with
which owing to my invalidism, I always felt in rather indirect
relation." She served her purpose so far as James was concerned by "standing well within the world, inviting and inviting me onward by all the bright intensity of her example. She
never knew how sick and disordered a creature I was. . . . She
was a breathing protest against English grossness, English compromises and conventions, — a plant of pure American growth.
. . . I can't put away the thought that just as I am beginning life,
she has ended it. . . . Twenty years hence we shall be living with
your love and longing with your eagerness and suffering with
your patience."

Isabel is less close to Minnie than the heroine of *The Wings
of the Dove* whom we shall encounter later, but in vital respects
she is a Minnie not doomed to early loss of strength and death.
As James said in his Preface, character changes under the stress
of invented circumstance. But Minnie was surely the single
small cornerstone, the conception of a certain young woman
affronting her destiny, which had begun, so he said, by being
"all my outfit" for the large building of *The Portrait of a Lady.*
And, of course, Ralph Touchett is in his essential situation
Henry himself, in his fortunately brief experience of sinking
out of youth and brightness into decline, with Minnie beside
him inviting him onward by the brightness of her example. It
was an inversion of the story of Isabel and Ralph and neither
is a portrait nor a self-portrait, but as Isabel's warmth comes
from a cherished memory, so does Ralph's from a deep layer of
Henry's consciousness of a "sincere" experience, and especially
from the too little noted resignations of his invalid youth.

4. CONCLUSIONS

The Portrait of a Lady might itself be called another portrait book, but this would be to give a false impression of a story where the "moral" sense acts deeply upon felt life. Osmond is not only a portrait of the real dilettante as the Italians understood the word; also he is nearer a creature of pure egotistic evil than any character in Hawthorne's Rome. Even Henrietta Stackpole, the roving American reporter, is not chosen for comic relief so much as to oppose whenever necessary the "innocent" ideas of America to the deadly conventions of an arrogant tradition, which brought down Isabel fronting her destiny in the upper air, with a poisoned, wilted rosebud.

No two books could seem more dissimilar at first thought than *The Portrait of a Lady* and *Huckleberry Finn,* upon which Mark was working or meditating through much the same years when James was writing. Yet Mark, like Henry, might have got his formula from the great Russian Turgenev, who was contemporary with both. All three selected the situations most likely to express the central figure of a story — which is more valuable in the kind of stories all three wrote than a plot. And as backgrounds, both Henry and Mark used the richest: Henry, the soft lawns of an English country house and its pictured corridors, and Rome; Mark, the incalculable Mississippi. More cogently, both for Isabel, the would-be intellectual from the Hudson Valley, and Huck from the new West, the theme words were always, freedom, liberty, and independence. Huck was wiser for himself. The Widow and convention were always on his trail, but he knew how to escape, while, as Ralph said, Isabel was ground in the very walls of the conventional. Most

important in the comparison, however, is this: Isabel and
Ralph have a warmth of life that makes you care deeply what
happens to them in the course of the story, and what happens to
Isabel afterward. They, like Huck, are the products of "felt
emotion" and they produce it — which is by no means true of
most of James' great gallery of characters, who stir the mind
more than the heart and are remembered by their brilliant
characterizations more often than by their personalities, or even
by their names.

Chapter VII

MACHINE-AGE YANKEE

In 1886 Henry James published a novel on women's rights and the social conscience. In the same year he published another which had, for subject matter, international socialism and Communism, and for characters, terrorists, fellow travelers, "pinks," and a member of the pre-British Labor Party. In 1886 Mark Twain was writing a book on democracy *vs.* feudalism, meaning by democracy an equality of opportunity for man, to be won by technology. He outlined the philosophy of productivity and prophesied the triumph of the gadget. No one would be more surprised than Henry James to learn that in his book he forecast familiar types of the Industrial Revolution in the twentieth century, a generation ahead of time. The definition I have given above of a *Connecticut Yankee in King Arthur's Court* might have surprised Mark Twain, but he would certainly have agreed as to its truth.

There is, of course, nothing in the coincident interest of two such diverse men (Henry's a passing interest) in social conscience, the labor question, economic theories, and the proletariat. Neither man, I suppose, had ever heard of the Industrial Revolution or knew anything about Karl Marx, and if James had heard talk of Communism it would have been among his French literary friends, Zola perhaps, and the reference would have been to the fierce Commune of Paris after the Franco-German war of 1870–71. Social revolution was in the air, and, important for novelists, its protagonists were becoming familiar and possible characters for fiction. In Europe anarchy and terrorism were being suppressed in Russia. The blow torch which was to ignite the world, Marx and Engels' *Communist Manifesto,* had been published in 1848. The second volume of *Das Kapital* was issued after Marx's death, in 1885, but Marx and Engels would have been only names for our writers. Both may have seen Edward Bellamy's novel of a Utopia, *Looking Backward,* 1888, since it was fashionable reading. Henry George's *Progress and Poverty,* 1879, protesting against mere morals and idealism in reform made no impact on either. Yet Mark was aware that the air was vibrant with social betterment, and did not too much like it when it came under the banner of reform. And in the brilliant circle of talkers where James was living in London, economic ideas were beginning to elbow politics. He had known the intellectuals of his father's generation who soothed their consciences by proclaiming with Emerson the infinite possibilities of the individual human being, man or woman. Now he met aristocrats of privilege, mostly women, whose consciences were also tender from a contrast between the classes, where they lived at the top. Twain's own radicalism was still Jeffersonian, and philosophically as old-fashioned at least as Jackson. But he had moved to Connecticut where they were making mass production possible by the precision tool and interchangeable parts, which was to hasten a revolution compared with which the dictatorship of the proletariat is probably already as old-fashioned as Jeffersonian political democracy. The second American revolution, this time without bloodshed or political theory, was to be based upon technology.

2. MARK LEARNS FROM THE EAST

The biography of Mark Twain, as Bernard DeVoto has noted, is from beginning to end the story of a restless man. Even when he was well settled down in Hartford in 1874 and adjusted himself to respectable living, he was never quiet for long. "He never spent a full year in Hartford, he made at least twelve trips abroad, and he once expatriated himself for nine years." If he ever concentrated exclusively on his writing, it was at Quarry Farm on vacation from Hartford, or in some resort in Europe. Even then he worked surrounded by unfinished manuscripts, tearing off hundreds of pages a day, overwriting everything, until he stopped from sheer fatigue or disgust. He was too like the Paige typesetting machine on which he spent a fortune — too delicate, too intricate, too energetic, to submit to control.

It is easy to say that this was a pioneer trait acquired from a mobile family ever moving, or planning to move, in search of something better. But Mark's restlessness went deeper. It was very different from the frequent wanderings of Henry James abroad; rather it seemed to come from an inner necessity strengthened by a need to escape from his own financial uncertainties, later from his own success as the world's funnyman and wisecracker. Henry ripened in Europe. Mark took the West and his own neuroticism with him. His satire, his irony, his inner revolt, which he said was against the species man, but which was really against himself, increased. DeVoto quotes a sentence which is omitted from the autobiographical letter with which this book begins because Mark had crossed it out in his copy, probably because it was not very articulate. "And yet I

163

can't go away from the boyhood period," he wrote in his account of his material for writing, "& write novels because *capital* [he means personal experience] is not sufficient by itself & I lack the other essential: interest in handling the men & experience of later times." "Essential interest" — he could not find it in "later times," either in Nook Farm, or in Europe. Yet his correspondent who, to judge from the references of Mark's letter, had been complaining that his admired author had chosen King Arthur's Court rather than men and experiences of later times, had not noted, nor had Mark in his reply, that in *A Connecticut Yankee in King Arthur's Court* Twain had found in Connecticut one essential interest, one character who, like Tom Sawyer, was an aspect of Mark himself, that was very definitely of his own time. This, of course, was the Boss — a boy in spirit, though a giant in achievement, a cock-sure adolescent, let loose in what he regarded as a cockeyed world.

3. A CONNECTICUT YANKEE IN KING ARTHUR'S COURT

A Connecticut Yankee in King Arthur's Court, which Mark finished and published in 1889, has gone down in critical estimation as fast as the *Adventures of Huckleberry Finn* has come up. DeVoto, in his recent volume in *The Portable Library* series, omits most of it, although in his Preface he says that it contains some of the best as well as some of the worst in Mark Twain, and elsewhere describes it as the last of Mark's books of the first rank. Its taste, indeed, is often worse than a barker's in a circus side show. What lover of Twain has not tried to forget those shameful knights, cured of chivalry, who ride about the kingdom like Fuller brush men, advertising toothpaste. It is not a parody of Malory's *Morte d' Arthur,* which was one of Mark's favorite books. It is not a satire based on Tennyson's too noble Arthur. It is a burlesque which dirties the idea of chivalry.

Twain attacked the processes of representative government in *The Gilded Age* with a fierce humor, fierce because in Congress he could see how men of sawdust and solder could make a democratic-republican government a corruption and an absurdity. Yet, like Whitman, he never lost faith in the ideas and the ideals of democracy. Chivalry and feudalism he never understood as necessities for their time — which is strange since he grew up within touching distance of their last stand in the English-speaking world, the old South. Colonel Grangerford, that champion of feudist honor, he could admire, yet only because his absurdity as a sentimental fire eater made him too pathetic to be dangerous. King Arthur, I should say (Mark says he has seen him on the Mississippi), is studied from a *good* slaveholder. Arthur is lovable and truly noble on his own plane, but roaring in astonishment when his privileges are denied. Then he becomes a kind of stupid dinosaur heedlessly trampling common men into the mud. And in Mark's book the Knights of the Round Table and the filthy, superstitious monks become offensive obstacles to progress. No wonder his British readers were shocked, and wished that he had not written the book.

Mark had no idea whasoever of the inner ideals or the outer responsibilities of feudalism, as, for example, his fellow American Henry Adams was to describe them twenty years later in *Mont St. Michel and Chartres.* His contrast is between a purely literary and romantic version of certain ideas and actions described in the *Morte d' Arthur* and what he himself decided, and not always wrongly, the resulting society must have been like. In this society (say of the twelfth to thirteenth century, not, of course, Arthur's sub-Roman sixth century) only two elements are reasonably accurate: the state of the peasant (the French, however, rather than the English, peasant) and the predatory greed and bloodiness of the knights. The Church is false, except in its baser aspects. The simplehearted rulers, such as Arthur, are, historically, nonsense. The contrast, therefore, is between a burlesque of feudal institutions and democratic-republicanism as one found it in Connecticut. The book belongs with *Gulliver's Travels* and Butler's *Erewhon* and should so be read. Nevertheless, its philosophy is at least fifty per cent right — and one hundred per cent in its emphasis upon the importance of soap and the absurdity of fighting except as a sport.

And yet my generation of young Americans read the *Yankee* with passionate delight. And not merely because we thought some of the episodes the funniest ever written. Perhaps they were and we have just got a little too sophisticated for the horseplay of a fireworks show pretending to be a miracle, while Huck's subtler unconscious humor that goes so much deeper still makes us laugh. And yet even though lassoing a panoplied knight made even us squirm a little, there was something in the story that warmed our heart and flattered us to the depths of our being. That is what I wish to try to explain.

4. THE BOSS AND THE G.I.

Mark did not intend to write this kind of book. He planned merely to illustrate his own ideas of Progress, with no sneering, no absurd burlesque of great figures of the imagination. Here is what he said while the book was just begun to "Mother Fairbanks," his friend of *The Quaker City*, a journalist like himself. Dixon Wecter published his letters to her in 1949:

Hartford, Nov. 16, 1886

The story isn't a satire peculiarly, it is more especially a *contrast*. It merely exhibits under high lights, the daily life of the time & that of today; & necessarily the bringing them into this immediate juxtaposition emphasizes the salients of both. . . . Of course in my story I shall leave unsmirched and unbelittled the great & beautiful *characters* drawn by the master hand of old Malory (if he drew them — at any rate he gave them to *us*) — I am only after the *life* of that day, that is all; to picture it; to try to get into it; to see how it feels & seems. I shall hope that under my hand Sir Galahad will still remain the divinest spectre that one glimpses among the mists & twilights of Dreamland across the wastes of the centuries; & Arthur keeps his sweetness & his purity, and Launcelot abide and continue "the kindest man that ever strake the sword," yet "the sternest knight to his mortal foe that ever put spear in the rest"; & I shall grieve indeed if the final disruption of the Round Table & the extinction of its old tender & gracious friendships, & that last battle — the Battle of the Broken Hearts, it might be called — should lose their pathos & their tears through my handling.

Well, he could not write it that way, and, if he had been Henry James, he would have known it. In *The Prince and the Pauper,* which was a preliminary workout for the archaisms of the *Yankee,* and so kept sweet and calm for Olivia and the children for whom he wrote it, the shrewd Howells detected a "bottom of fury." After the first few chapters in the *Yankee* of which he wrote Mrs. Fairbanks, the fury began to break the crust of humorous contrast. Arthur stays at least noble, Launcelot devoted and courageous, the humor of modern man trying to wear armor, and science *vs.* magic, remain. But the opportunity to see the "damned human race" in one of its noblest fancies, slaughtering, exploiting, in the name of courtesy and for the benefit of a stupid élite, is too tempting. He strikes at the present by destroying as far as he can the illusions of the past. Does it by a furious humor rather than by a furious satire. For he wanted to be read.

If this were all, there would be little more to say of this once so famous story except in praise and criticism of this outburst of economic humanitarianism. On the contrary, there is another and entirely unexpected element in this story, new for Mark, new in literature, prophetic in history, ominous in its philosophy. And it is this which far transcends in interest a mere contrast of new and old. A new man appears in the *Yankee,* called by everyone the Boss, for it was as a boss that he worked in an arms factory in Hartford until in a fight one of his workmen banged his head — and he woke up in the Middle Ages. The Boss as a workman had learned to make anything a body wanted, and if there wasn't any quick newfangled way to make a thing, he could invent one, and do it as easy as rolling off a log. His father was a blacksmith, his uncle was a horse doctor, and he was a mixture of both. The Boss is, of course, Tom Sawyer grown up part way and thoroughly satisfying his desire to show off. Note the kingdom he proposed to make when he got round to it, precisely in the Tom Sawyer manner. He is Huck in his ingenuity only, with the technique of a machinist substituted for the skills of the river. It is the Yankee himself that explained much of our passionate interest in the book.

He had fallen through the Time Machine by a device common to many writers of fantasy into a world familiar to him only by legendary literature. There he was at first regarded only as another product of some wizard's enchantment. Actually, however, this skilled mechanic from a mechanized world and a materialistic society of infinite toolmaking skill, is a far stranger creature in these Middle Ages than would be a devil or angel, and more powerful. Soon they are calling him the Boss and rightly. For every problem, every danger, in this naïve age of Europe, except morals, he had one only, but sufficient answer — applied science. To the simplicities of the Age of Faith, he offered his rather naïve, but how powerful simplicity. Give the poor peasants, exploited like cattle, the tools they need. Give them self-respect and the idea of equality. Do it by a decent currency and machines to increase production, by laws to secure their gains, by weapons to defend themselves against tyrants, by knowledge of science to defeat superstition. Give them everything that the American workman had in Connecticut and presto! dark ages become light. Destroy the prestige of the clergy by a few scientific miracles, break up the charges of those human tanks, the knights, by precision gunfire and a defense by electricity, train peasants technologically until they can make anything for anyone, meet any emergency whether a broken bridge, an unpenetrable jungle, or a pestilence, by a know-how that only they possess — and the world is made safe for democracy, Europe reorganized, and all by a few workers and an executive out of Hartford. Afterward — well, that was not Mark's business.

The Boss's great plan was wrecked by a moral breakdown at home. He did not know what to do about Launcelot and Guinevere. Morals and morale which are at least as important as know-how, he had neglected in his idea of progress, with other things quite as important. It was typical of the Tom Sawyer in Mark. And Mark himself was really a humanitarian not a reformer — and most of all a novelist. His job was to create what Walt Whitman called an eidólon, an imaginative type which men could imitate, and make it true and prophetic. He had created in the Boss an eidólon a half-century before this machine-age man became triumphant in history in two great wars. Once a slave, the common man is armed with the terrible by-products of science. He is irresistible — yet still the common man!

I have kept in mind in this description the phraseology of the correspondents of the last war as they wrote of the extraordinary ingenuity, the know-how of the American G.I., wondered at throughout all the armies — and have not forgotten the failures of the same type of mind in handling the greater

complications of peace. I have no intentions, however, of push-
ing the analogy too far. It is enough to say that Mark, who was
neither a sociologist nor a philosopher, was writing propheti-
cally, nevertheless, of obvious aspects of what proved to be the
near future, and particularly of Americans. This is why we
youngsters brought up in the American tradition of success read
the *Yankee* like a dime novel of whites and Indians, except that
here the kind of fellow we saw every day became the Boss by
using just the kind of science we were being taught at school,
chose our most familiar weapons, and proceeded to enforce
civilization. It was as powerful a medicine as the warm hearts
of Dickens' characters, and much more timely. For Mark, without knowing it, had found a hero (the Great Know-How) for
the Industrial Revolution. And the Boss's imitators are studying applied science in millions of high schools and colleges
today — to the alarm of humanists, philosophers, and historians.

5

A Connecticut Yankee in King Arthur's Court is in some ways
the most American of Mark Twain's books. Yet it makes a
cartoon of both Jeffersonian democracy and the Age of Chivalry,
a cartoon with the deadly truth of a comic strip. For the
Yankee of the Industrial Revolution has somehow lost his sense
of the dignity of man on the way up through the great New
World experiment. He has kept pity and courage and a passion
for human rights. But his formula for making a perfect democracy has shifted to the centers of the brain which control only
the hands and the eyes. He proposes to make democracy safe
by gadgets. As a result he is brash, if not quite so brash now as
in Mark's time; and he has brought with him to the manifesta-

tions of history a sense of superiority which is curious because
it is neither arrogant, nor predatory, but sprung from his technical efficiency, and based on extreme self-confidence with not
much self-knowledge. The reader feels sympathy with Henry
James and his passion for "refinement," when Mark hangs
signboards of consumers' goods on the towers of Camelot and
the spires of the cathedrals.

This is no fantasy. The Soviet dictatorship, with far greater
political and scientific efficiency than the Boss possessed, is quite
as brash, and in a much more dangerous fashion. It is providing
the common man not only with the tools and a political idea,
but with their own brand of pseudo religion and their carefully
controlled culture. The police state is a gadget state also, and in
its mechanical ideology is closer to the Industrial Revolution
than is old-fashioned agrarian democracy.

But if the Boss was politically naïve, so, on a long term and
in all probability, is the Politburo, which expects to build a
thousand years on a harsh dogmatism. The Boss is far more
human than the present leaders of the Russians, in the sense
that our ancestors of the West have given the word for so many
centuries. He is more humorous, more humanitarian, more
conscious of the rights and needs of the individual. It is en-
couraging to know that for many decades *Huckleberry Finn*
has been a widely read book, if not by Stalin, then by the masses
in Russia. And certainly the Boss is a far more engaging figure
than any that Russian literature has produced since the overthrow of Russian feudalism. He is the prototype of the skilled
laborer with brains as hands, the applier of science who has
made his country for the time being the most powerful in the
world, although not necessarily, or probably, the wisest.

I will go to any length to set up Mark Twain as that rare
phenomenon — an unquestionable genius, as lovable as he was
neurotic, as powerful in imagination as he was uncontrolled in
art. But I do not for an instant propose him in this chapter as

another Jefferson or Marx. Yet he could make a man (not a
woman) into what Shakespeare called an epitome, and make
him a living document that both proves and in a real sense
shapes history. I shall be accused by some of taking the humor
out of a humorist. Well, Mark himself often wished in later
years that he was not so irresistibly funny. He wanted to be
regarded as a serious person, which at bottom he certainly was,
and forgot that humor is one of the best ways of describing a
society without analyzing the life out of it. We young readers
had the damosel Sandy to amuse us — Sandy who was so bemused by what she had been told was true that she could see an
enchanted princess in what the Boss knew was a pig, who once
she began a story could not be stopped except when she had to
slosh out her knight errant's helmet with cool spring water to
keep his brains from frying. But we did not miss the triumphant Yankee with a gadget in his hand (and a bulldozer in
his mind) that warmed us to a country so inventive, so successful as ours, and so easily understood by a boy.

Chapter VIII

VARIETIES OF FEMININE EXPERIENCE

HENRY JAMES returned once more to his native land for the materials of a wholly American novel. As it happened, he came back for other reasons than literary composition. He was in Boston, New York, and Washington (which interested him most) in 1882, and returned from England again when his aging father died in December of that year in Cambridge, spending the month there on business of the estate. As one result he wrote his novel, *The Bostonians,* serialized in *The Century* in 1885–86. "The whole thing," he wrote the publisher Osgood, was to be "as local, as American, as possible, and as full of Boston; an attempt to show that I *can* write an American story. . . . A very *American* tale, a tale very characteristic of our social conditions . . . the most salient and peculiar point in our social life . . . the situation of women, the decline of the sentiment of sex, the agitation on their behalf." It is clear that Henry had a view of women's rights very different from the ideas of believers in short hair and the vote.

And *The Bostonians* failed with the American public, failed calamitously. Gilder, the editor of *The Century,* told him that he never published a novel that so little interested his readers. Not a ripple came to him from America, except that William James complained that he had inexcusably made fun of Elizabeth Peabody, last of the great abolitionists. There was a "deathly" silence, and Henry was persuaded that not only was *The Bostonians* a fiasco, but also that its flop had so collapsed his American reputation that the *Princess Casamassima,* pub-

173

lished in *The Atlantic Monthly,* was caught in the wreckage.
He now saw himself retired from American popularity, which
had outrun his British (and paid better too), and forced to
return to his specialty of international society.

This is the brief introduction to a literary tragedy. Henry
would have by no possibility devoted himself to American
social history. "I had the sense of knowing terribly little about
the kind of life I had to describe, having seen so little of the
whole business treated," he wrote his brother of *The Bostonians,* and that was much more true of the country in general. But it was a misfortune that his book failed so dismally.
To borrow from a favorite comic strip, he seemed to have been
born fifty years too soon for this kind of book about Boston,
which has been very successful since. The experience sank deep
within his sensitive spirit.

After his father's death his income was chiefly limited to
"certain houses in Syracuse," on James Street, named for his
grandfather. For this or other reasons, he decided about this
time that he had to make more money, and so the drying up of
his American fees and royalties sent him to the stage with unhappy results. What was even worse I should say, he gave up,
except in some short stories, and for a long while, his American
portraits, took England for his major scene, chose English characters too intelligent for their own welfare and for his own or
anyone's sympathy, and did not emerge for nearly fifteen years.
More of this later.

And finally, discouraged and dismayed, he came to under-
value *The Bostonians,* a book which in 1886 he told William
was the best fiction he had written, and later called it too long
and dawdling, which the ill-natured *could* have said of any of
his novels. He never revised it, nor included it in his *New
York Edition.* The omission was unfortunate for, if not one
of his major works, it is certainly one of the wittiest, and contains satiric passages not excelled elsewhere. It has never been

set where it belongs in the portrait gallery of America.

This humorous but deadly story is resharpened from the memories of Henry's earliest years. Two women hold the stage and their relation is intensely dramatic. Olive, an aristocrat of the Boston type, is a woman with no figure whatsoever and eyes of ice, who seems to be cold herself, yet with a devouring will to make the cause of women's rights prevail, the most important of which seems to be to hate men safely. Verena Tarrant, her opposite, is one of those American women of almost burning charm and beauty which James liked to do, and did well. She was the child of a slippery faith healer and an ambitious mother. Olive was rich and inarticulate. Verena, simple and quite ignorant of herself, had a genius for acting, although no one called it that, which made her irresistible on the lecture platform where women's rights was a favorite theme. She was an actress like Henry's famous Mrs. Kemble, who used to burst into tears when her part was over out of sheer momentum of the emotion. Olive had captured her; the warm girl was to become her Voice. "It was," said James, "one of those friendships between women so common in New England." It was indeed much more than that, and James I am sure guessed it, although having happily been born before Freud he was able to keep to the surface relationship, which was sufficiently tense. But a novelist often tells a truth of which he may be unaware. The word, as the story develops, is always a constantly repeated "jealousy," which is torture to the older woman and wrecks her life at the end.

The two meet and strive and struggle in a milieu of reformers, fakers, honest seekers, would-be martyrs, saints looking for converts, and starved emotionalists seeking a Cause. It is the dacadence of the great days of Concord and Boston, the health gone out of them, and much of the moral and civic fervor replaced by strident "movements" and self-advertisement. Through this satiric story move vividly "characters" both symbolic and intensely human. The best of these is Miss Birdseye, who had outlived her heroic period but not her virtues. Shaped like a hay pole, her cap and spectacles always falling off her head, she had never in a long life had a thought for herself. She is a saint of old Boston who in any other religion would have had a shrine. There was even a faint odor of sanctity about her. And there was Mrs. Farrinder, the famous lecturess, who at "any time had the air of being introduced by a few remarks. . . . The ends she labored for were to give the ballot to every woman in the country and to take the flowing bowl from every man. . . . She had a husband, and his name was Amariah."

One at least of this fantastic coterie, it was evident to Boston, was a caricature of Elizabeth Peabody, the sister of Haw-thorne's wife, who did indeed carry Boston's humanitarianism in her reticule, and was notorious for extracting money from the most hard-boiled sources, to benefit anyone but herself. But James was right in denying that he had copied his char-acter, except for the tumbling spectacles, from Miss Peabody. That lady appears in a recent biography so different from Miss Birdseye as to assure the latter's essential originality. Miss Birdseye is one of Henry's best creations in any novel, the re-duction to absurdity indeed of Henry's father's ruling principle of life that for self-consciousness should be substituted social consciousness and so the world could be saved. And in describ-ing her pitiful ineffectiveness in great causes, Henry may have had an *arrière-pensée* of his own lovable and intensely intel-lectual father, who could neither stop writing nor make anyone read his books.

It is probable that Henry did not know enough about Boston the multifarious city to write a book about it, but he did know enough about reformers, seekers, idealists, perfectionists, ascetics, and Transcendentalists. They crowded about the Jamesian circle of his youth and frequently found their way inside. Even in his youth he was allergic to seekers and improvers of human society, as his brother William, who belonged in such categories, was very well aware. Henry did not know much about their causes, but he knew their behavior as well as Sam Clemens knew his rivermen and his pilots — well enough to satirize them with deadly effectiveness. And he knew in this book why he disliked them. The Olives, the Mrs. Farrinders, even Miss Birdseye, in their zeal for women's rights were destroying "the sentiment of sex." They were destroying the essential relationship between men and women by which civilized societies (and all of James' novels) were involved, if not always constructed. If it seems unusual to say that Henry James wrote a book in defense of sex, he said so himself, and he wrote it in just that way. Verena is the very incarnation of the feminine sex. It is from her warm affections that her triumphs on the platform come. It is her passionate sex that ends her career. For she falls in love in a scene in Central Park with a somewhat improbable Southerner who has come North to retrieve his broken fortunes. He was fond of beer and variety actresses, intensely reactionary in social life, an intellectual of the legal variety (quite different from the other kind) capable of demolishing Verena's arguments, and very, very male. In the really magnificent scene of what was to be The Great Address where Verena deserts Olive for her lover, James' last line is almost brutal in its lack of sympathy for his broken heroine. Ransom, as he hurries her away from the angry crowds, "presently discovered that underneath her hood she was in tears. . . . It is to be feared . . . that these were not the last she was destined to shed." Well, this is what she got for fighting with a non-sensical fanaticism against the sentiment of sex!

It may be difficult, it *is* difficult, to explain why this novel, so brilliant and dramatic at its best, so rich in characters rich from the still vivid memories of New England's great period of militant ethics, should have been a failure with James' American readers. That it would be too special for Europe one

might understand. But after all, his American readers were
what publishers call a quality group, beyond the average
in taste and intelligence. It was surely not because the
Bostonians felt themselves misrepresented. The circulation of
The Century was not even centered on Boston. I can offer two
reasons, which supplement each other. James' ruthless analysis
of the pride of Olive and the innocent vanity of Verena was not
in the mood of the day. Still less was his almost contemptuous
exchange of a tough reactionary for the romantic Southerner
who by current literary convention Ransom should have been
in order to play his part. And, even though subtly expressed,
the mixture of underlying sexual emotions with social ideas in
this book was something Americans were not yet ready to
accept. There was, in his novel as so often in James, a twentieth-
century quality, at least a quarter of a century ahead of its
time. It is too bad. We might have had *The New Yorkers* or
The Newporters (I doubt if he could have gone further), books
that might have revealed his powers and purpose to the reluct-
ant American readers. Instead he was frightened off America
until he had found years later a new formula.

2. "PINKS" AND "REDS"

Mark had contemplated in the *Yankee* reform by technology,
and was quite willing to sacrifice an ancient culture in behalf
of the common man. Henry James would have hated the idea.
It was throwing out a beautiful baby with an admittedly dirty
bath. In Boston, he saw reform unsexing the women (as he
saw it) and did not like that either. Therefore he attacked
characteristically not reform as such but the validity of the
reformers. A social conservative in an ethically radical family,

he saw more loss than gain in this kind of woman's rights. The proper study of womankind was the individual woman, so he felt; "with all her organs balanced as nature intended them." The future of society was his brother's affair and his father's. He did not much change his opinion, and never for women, until the great calamity of 1914.

Strange and curious then that James' next, and in publication contemporary, novel, *The Princess Casamassima*, 1886, had for apparent theme not so much reform as revolution. It was no revolt in an imagined past, but a modern revolution, whose right wing proposed the reorganization of a society, and whose left wing was already organized for violence, and practising it, with spies, an underground, a potential dictator, and agents, of whom his hero became one, with the job of liquidating a leader of the opposition. The right wing in James' novel is drama-tized in a British workman of the union-leader type, very politi-cal, and determined to socialize England, as good a prototype as can be found in literature, before H. G. Wells, of the men of the orignial British Labor Party. Also by a more Jamesian figure, whom we have met before, the beautiful Christina Light of *Roderick Hudson*, half American, and now the Princess Casamassima. Frustrated in her private life, craving dangerous excitement, loving power over men, and with an intellectual interest in radical ideas sprung from an overdose of the Italian aristocracy, there was no name for her type at the time — now she would be called a "pink," or more accurately a fellow traveler. She is a right who would like to be a left, if the lefts would take her.

It is curious again that the Princess (and therefore Henry James) may have· been the first to use the phrase "the New Deal" in exactly Roosevelt's connotations of the word. Roose-velt said that he believed he found it in Twain's *Yankee* where indeed it appears in the Boss's conversation in Roosevelt's meaning and associations. But before that the Princess, talking

to the Lady Aurora, whose idea of revolution was social service
to the poor, made a little speech that Mark might have para-
phrased: "Possibly you don't know," she said, "that I am one
of those who believe that a great new deal is destined to take
place and that it can't make things worse than they are. I believe, in a word, in the action of the people for themselves —
the others will never act for them; and I'm ready to act *with*
them — in any intelligent or intelligible way." These words
were published in the *Atlantic*, in early 1886; the *Yankee* was
begun in the same year and finished in 1888. Mark took the
Atlantic and it would be surprising if their common friend and
conservative socialist, Howells, the editor, should not have
pointed out Henry's experiment in human rights to Mark just
beginning a novel on the same theme. Of course, only a recom-
mendation from Howells would have made Twain read even as
much as a chapter of a James novel! I believe this time he did,
and if so the phrase "new deal" would certainly have caught in
his memory. All this is unprovable and unimportant, irrelevant but interesting.

Yet the Princess in the story is no New Deal character. She is
far more a feminine woman than a revolutionary. Her desire
is not to be left out of the excitement; her hope, if the revolution succeeds, is to become one of the new élite. In fact, she is
more Nazi than Communist, more Communist than Socialist.
Phrase after phrase of James' analysis of this brilliant, "perverse" woman fits easily into the literature of the nineteen-
twenties to nineteen-fifties.

Finally, there is Hyacinth, the little bookbinder, who is
chosen by the Princess to show her the "lower orders." He is a
possible phase of James himself, a youthful James, lacking his
good common sense. Sensitive, excellent in taste, disgruntled
with the vulgarity around him, he is an improbable figure for
whom James had to arrange an aristocratic father, murdered
by his French mistress, Hyacinth's mother. Hyacinth is the

Observer of the story, as far as there is one. It is Hyacinth whose restless curiosity leads him into the Terrorist underground, Hyacinth who is chosen as assassin, Hyacinth who, like James, does not belong in this *galère* at all. He kills himself in order to escape his task, the Princess aiding by deserting him first.

Henry James, of course, was not deeply interested in the French and German radical ideas he had picked up by association abroad. If he is prophetic it is in his characters, his British laboring man, the masses of the London streets where he walked so much among human evidences of poverty, the Lady Auroras, the half-American, wholly cosmopolitan Princess. He had, in fact, and says so, a *"disponible"* woman on his hands, and he was a great economizer of literary material. Now there was a situation into which she beautifully fitted. She herself was in revolt against her dull but loving husband, and everything he came from. She was intelligent, she divined, as her kind were to do later, that what we call Nazism or Communism, was already approaching its power stage. There was a chance outside the tight class circles for beautiful women. Her socially climbing American mother had taught her that. Powerful over men, she guessed that this new equalitarianism would have its new leaders, a new stage, a new opportunity. In Henry's imagination, she was a woman looking for a story to be told. And London, where Earl's daughters were talking reform, where a Princess could mix with the masses and not be remarked, and where Muniment, a future Parliamentary leader of a new labor party (not to speak of Hyacinth), was already in love with her, was a scene for which Henry was entirely competent. Her tragedy was that no one would trust her. The beautiful "wings" of Christina had lifted little Hyacinth far above his powers (or interest). Then collapsed. He dies. Muniment no longer believes in her. She will go back to her infatuated husband who has cut off her allowance. She is again *disponible*. But she gave James a good book.

It is a good book, but not because James, for once, dips into the lower classes. He had watched them acutely on his strolls through London, when for a while at least, he made a practice of walking home after every evening out through streets of all kinds in that endlessly various city. What really troubled him, however, was not the poverty and debasement of the proletariat, of which he was well aware. It was the moral decay of the aristocracy, that "ruling class," which had created a life and a scene in which a *laudator tempores acti* like Henry could move with comfort and esthetic and intellectual delight. They seemed to him now to be fouling their own nest. In this same year of 1886, he wrote Charles Eliot Norton from Milan of "the damaged prestige of the English upper class. The condition of that body seems to me to be in many ways the same rotten and *collapsible* one as that of the French aristocracy before the revolution . . . like the heavy, congested, and depraved Roman world upon which the barbarians came down." In such a comparison Hyacinth might serve as the intelligent Greek slave, Muniment as the Christian reformer, and the Princess as a perverse and beautiful aristocrat, embracing both men and a new religion, and finally the barbarians themselves.

My point is that James' observation (keen as always) of the underprivileged, and the talk he heard about them, gave him not so much sympathy as alarm. What resulted, as he says in the Preface to his book, was the "suggested nearness (to all our apparently ordered life) of some sinister anarchic underworld, heaving in its pain, its power and its hate." Something which goes on, "irreconcilably, subversively, beneath the vast smug surface." This menace and the new types of men and women which it was producing, fascinated him — as the novels of H. G. Wells fascinated him later. He could not understand that to them his own fine conservative spirit was in itself a menace; and never forgave Wells when that prophetic but coarse-grained genius parodied Henry's too delicate handling of life.

The Princess Casamassima seems to have bored the readers
of *The Atlantic Monthly*. And naturally. To them the con-
spiratorial technique of an underground seemed as melodramatic as it is familiar to us today — cloak and dagger stuff.
To them, the British socialism of Muniment must have then
seemed, in a land of easy free enterprise, a little absurd. As
for their own somewhat equalitarian and more definitely humanitarian ideas, such rather alarming people as Hyacinth and
Muniment, and the vaguely American but clearly immoral
Princess, were not the best critics to represent an England undoubtedly too class-conscious and overprivileged. If they were
to read a story of democratic America rebuking the aristocracy,
they had one already this very year in Frances Hodgson
Burnett's *Little Lord Fauntleroy*. There was more to please
Americans (as well as more current sentimentality) in that story
of a boy defending his American mother because she had been
born in the middle class, than in a thousand Princess Casamas-
simas and their "new deals!"

It is hard to be just to Henry James' two ventures into the
social conscience, for in each irony is close to the surface when
not above it — an irony in themes, one of which we accept
today, and the other take with extreme seriousness. *The
Bostonians* is the more powerful book because James himself felt so deeply, not the Cause itself, but the injuries
done, and to be done, by feminism to "the sentiment of
sex." *The Princess Casamassima* is a more controlled, a
more Jamesian story. Here it is not a somewhat historical Boston, but people of his own contemporary life in
England which stir him — the tragedy of the artist-intellectual
Hyacinth; the pathos of Lady Aurora; most of all the end-
product of a flippant or corrupt expatriate society, which had
always repelled as well as fascinated James, now dramatized in
the person of the Princess eager for new sensations even if they
should destroy. With such characters he was, like Twain with

the Mississippi, familiar. As for the "lower orders," I am sure that Hyacinth is a feeble attempt (I do not mean that Hyacinth is feeble) on James' part to put himself in their place. If *The Princess Casamassima* is ever staged, and I feel sure that a play could be made from it, I should recommend La Farge's portrait of Henry at eighteen, somewhat vulgarized, as the model for the actor who takes the part of Hyacinth.

Chapter IX

MARK TWAIN WATCHES TOO
MANY BASKETS

IF IN THE stirring years of the eighties both Twain and James seemed to follow the same line of the social conscience in their novels, the contrast in what they did on that line is much sharper than any comparison. In the next decade "parallel lives" begins to seem a strained term for men whose energies went into such different activities, whose books were read by such different people, and whose personal histories are as different as the King of England's and the Pope's. Yet in this new decade both men were to suffer the greatest disasters of their careers, both were to decline in creative powers. Henry James was to see the little popular reputation he had shrink until his audience would scarcely take off an edition; Mark's fame billowed round the world, but his powers as a really creative writer could not follow it. Henry recovered, more than recovered; Mark, except for a few bright flashes and the baleful glow of *The Mysterious Stranger,* never did. Yet his great depression is more dramatic than Henry's success. Both are instructive to a high degree.

2. MARK TWAIN—WORLD HUMORIST

In the eighteen-nineties Mark Twain was undoubtedly the most popular name among American writers, and probably the best read among contemporary authors of literary pretentions in the English-speaking world. The extent of his circulation and very real influence upon readers whose language was not English is only now being realized. Before him, only one American, James Fenimore Cooper, had as wide and enthusiastic a reception abroad. Mark himself had turned his half-century in 1885, yet age should not have staled him; whatever may be true of poets, the years after fifty are notably fruitful for novelists, and with increasing longevity this Indian Summer for the fictionist may well be further extended. With Mark, who had shown only one flash of his essential genius before his early thirties, this should have been especially true. Yet the years after he published *A Yankee* in 1889, no matter how full of powerful energy, are singularly barren. He wrote one notable *nouvelle, Pudd'nhead Wilson,* the background for which came out of his Mississippi past. He published what was intended to be a major work, *Joan of Arc,* which rather dismayed his readers, who had been conditioned to laugh when they read him. It was a book much better than later criticism has allowed, a fictionized biography, in both subject and field not beyond his talents, but unsuited to his genius. There were good reasons for this extensive speculation in history, which will later appear. He began work on the strange fantasies of disillusionment, which were in his consciousness at least as early as the eighteen-sixties, and for whose explanation we shall have to plunge into Mark's inner life as deep as we can go. And through all these years he kept returning to the boys, who still were most himself, often under their names. There was *Huck and Tom Among the Indians,* left unfinished in 1889; *Tom Sawyer Abroad,* published in 1894, with glimpses of great talent; *Tom Sawyer, Detective,* in 1896; in 1897 *Tom and Huck,* unfinished. In 1896 and 1897, bankrupt and determined to pay his creditors, he returned to the travel-book type where he made his first reputation, writing *Following the Equator,* a work which brought him great publicity, enough money, and a sensible decrease in literary fame.

What does all this mean? It sounds like the declining years of a skillful writer of best sellers, revamping his old successes after vitality is gone, or striking vainly into new fields. The truthful answer is far more complex, and much more interesting. James had failed on the stage in these same years because he had miscalculated his own talents. Twain had failed to sustain his genius, though his talents had not failed. The lack was in that essential for the imagination of a writer — self-sustenance. And if James had lost his popularity, Twain, to put it cryptically, had become uncomfortably conscious of his soul.

3. INFLATION AND DEFLATION

The tale of Mark Twain's financial disasters has often been told, and I should not retell it here if, on reflection, it did not prove to be related to the decline of his literary talent — related, not caused by it. The more money Twain made and lost, the less effectively he wrote. For both Mark's business speculations and Mark's best books were products of his dreaming. In finance, Mark himself was both the father and the child of Colonel Sellers who dreamt only of millions. He was not all of Colonel Sellers and Colonel Sellers was even less of him. Sellers lived in a dream of rivers, cities, railroads, and millions in each. Mark, like a half-analyzed patient of a psychiatrist, had reduced his dreams of money to possible realization in present reality. He had got thoroughly rid of the illusory wealth of the Tennessee land which his father had bred in his children, though Orion, whom no psychiatrist could have coped with, never escaped. But the tendency to dream in millions was like a tropical germ in Mark that, suppressed in one part of the body, breaks out in another. His cure came late, and, for a dreamer, was heroic. Admitting his own incompetence in financial judgment, he turned over all his affairs, including his valuable copyrights, to H. H. Rogers, his friend the Standard Oil magnate. As a result, he died relatively rich instead of poor.

Mark was never as wildly extravagant in his dreaming as his brain child, Colonel Sellers. When "feet" in mines, newspaper ownership, stocks of extraordinary variety began to run out his very large income through a bunghole, he at least had sense enough, or so he thought, to concentrate his hopes for millions on something he really knew a little about. His money came from books, therefore he understood publishing. Also he had been bred a printer. He could understand the needs of the printing trade. These proved to be fatal ideas.

An author like Mark should never become a publisher. His success had come from a series of best sellers. No publishers live long that way. When, with an assist from Orion, he formed a company to sell books himself; when, with an audacious but highly successful scheme of selling books by subscriptions, the Charles L. Webster & Co., with Mark behind it, made a killing with the autobiography of General Grant, his fate (being Mark) was sealed. He was a tough businessman with his associates, but it never seemed to dawn upon him that a publisher depending upon successive coups of best sellers was no more secure than a gambler in stocks. After Grant, Twain looked for another man in the million class, and chose the Pope! Publishers, like banks, must have reserves, modest books on a back list that return steadily their annual increment. The history of Webster & Co. was a series of successes and failures on a large scale. It was roulette rather than publishing, with Mark putting up new stakes from his pockets which had many another hole in them. And so eventually he went bankrupt, the only essential difference between the Colonel and himself being that Sellers had no room in his imagination for creditors, whereas Mark's literary talent could always make him more money.

Even more interesting psychologically was Mark's calamitous

adventures with the Paige typesetting machine. Young Sam Clemens had worn out his fingers setting type from Hannibal to New York. The mere idea of a typesetting machine was enough to set his mind afire. Millions! — there were tens of millions in it! — and he was right. Paige was a temperamental inventor, a perfectionist who met each difficulty with a new complexity in his machine. In every test the machine proved its tremendous value — and broke down halfway! Paige was never ready when a contract was offered. The Mergenthaler, a clumsier, solider, more practical machine, came up from behind. At one time Twain was offered a merger, which would certainly have brought him his millions at last, but he refused contemptuously. He had dreamt of tens of millions and would not share with a rival. When it was all over, he had lost $300,000-odd, the profits of his books and some of Olivia's holdings also.

The man was incurable. In the early eighties a patent steam generator used up his bank surplus, followed by a steam pulley ($32,000 in sixteen months); next a watch company, succeeded by an accident insurance company, and a chalk-plate process with which to make illustrations ($40,000 to 50,000). The money for the insurance company had been guaranteed, and came back, which was an excellent opportunity to buy stock from a young inventor called Graham Bell, who had an electric contrivance for carrying the voice:

"I declined. I said I didn't want anything more to do with wildcat speculation. Then he offered the stock to me at twenty-five. . . . I said I didn't want it at any price. . . . He said he would sell me as much as I wanted for five hundred dollars. . . . But I was the burnt child . . . . [I] went off with my check intact, and the next day lent five thousand of it, on an unendorsed note, to a friend who was going to go bankrupt three days later."

You can believe as much of this as you please, for Mark was as inflationary in statements as in literature. Yet the context

of his life experience makes the essential facts of his mania un-
deniable. Perhaps he did lose potential millions in telephone
stock; at least he was the first man in Hartford to install a telephone.

This may seem irrelevant. It is far from it. Mark was not a
gambler in any true sense. A professional gambler knows when
to stop. Mark was a speculator, philosophically, temperament-
ally, like Alcott or Joseph Smith, like Mussolini or Hitler.
They never stop. They are stopped, usually, if they are hateful
men, by sudden death. Mark was stopped because, after he had
repaid his creditors, and knew that his creative powers had
failed him, a rare moment of self-knowledge led him to throw
down his cards. Rogers picked up the cards and made a new
and stable fortune for him out of the copyrights in the discard.
Money seemed in these years so easy to make, and was. Real
writing grew harder and harder, as the masses of speculative
manuscripts he left behind him proved; as the ventures in old
successes that did not come off proved; as the experiments on
new lines that were no longer triumphant proved. Somehow
he had to satisfy his restless dreaming. While there was an endless stream of money, publishing, type machines, steam gener-
ators diverted what must have sometimes been a distraught
mind. Note that it was inventions — other men's inventions,
other men's books, into which he poured the energizing flood
of his money. And in the meantime, did his own invention
flag? I do not believe that the answer is as simple as that.

One feels like placing a colon at this period in Mark's career,
which, without too much respect for chronology, can be called
the early nineties — a colon, not a period. After a period comes
something new. After a colon comes an expansion, a recasting,
often a weakening of statement. Mark's best writings always
express his self, but what was new in Mark was a slowly emerging, only half-realized, adult self which he never had the art or
the courage to express powerfully. Nor did he have the

discipline, of which James was a master, to cut out the flounderings, the self-imitations, and half-worked out fantasies, and find out what was the new thing he wanted to write, and write it.

I doubt whether discipline would have helped him. Mark had only one discipline to which he had rigorously and successfully submitted himself — language. Mark's English is superb, his taste in diction impeccable. He boasted of it, and was right. His terse, simple, effective style, his words chosen with a lively sense of values, his accuracy and his force, never fail except in an occasional purple passage when he strains after an artificial beauty which was not his forte. He writes, as I have asserted before, better English than Henry James, both by word and by rhythm, though with far less assistance from a flowing vocabulary. He would, I think, have been incapable of using *aggravated* where he means *irritated,* as James does too often. His cello is a better instrument than James' violin, though realms of expression were admittedly closed to it.

Mark had art enough when his theme was right. But his theme had to be Mark the Innocent; the Innocent for whom he invented the term, the American Innocent as Henry James again and again used the word, with only a shift of emphasis in the meaning. The Innocent was the shrewd, warmhearted, self-confident American, who was also unsophisticated, uncorrupted in faith in humanity, in hope, and in charity, though tough enough in other respects. James drew him best in his novel *The American,* much less sympathetically in his vulgar, vulgar American tourists. Mark filled *The Quaker City* with such compatriots, of whom he was the best critic and observer because he was an Innocent himself. James made him (or her) a dramatic center for the best of his novels, choosing his subtlest manifestations for leading parts, his crudest for comic relief. Mark described but did not analyze. His books were really self-revelations.

But Mark in the nineties was no longer an Innocent, not any more except in his memories, and they were growing distant. It is questionable whether he could be called an Innocent in the years when he wrote his great books, *Tom Sawyer* and *Huckleberry Finn*. Already he was nostalgic. He was self-expressive of this age of confidence only in memories of his youth. Even then the growing disillusion, which James' best Innocents, Isabel and Maggie, endured, had reached Mark's consciousness, but it was to express itself only in hints, and later in one fine book and in unpublished manuscripts. It required a fully adult mind, which he never really got. It required that he should objectify himself, and that Mark never did for long. He said in the nineties that he could not write of his own times. He meant that he could not write of his new self — and so clung — so had to cling — to his youth. He was afraid to objectify himself in his relative maturity for the public eye. I doubt whether he could have done it even in an adult *Huckleberry Finn,* where a living person completely self-revelatory should bcome part of the history of his times.

All this is partly prefatory, and rather abstract. Let us leave theory, and begin with a book in which the old-time Mark, Mark of the Mississippi, struggled with difficulties that would be laughable if they were not tragic, in order to write another nostalgic masterpiece, and did reveal part of his new mind, and also for the first, and only time, created a real woman.

4 . PUDD' NHEAD WILSON

I would much rather reread *Pudd'nhead Wilson* (1892) than analyze its tangle of absurdities and genius. Nevertheless, it is Exhibit A for anyone who wishes to see close and clear how

Mark made literature when, for such reasons as I have set down above, the going became difficult. For here is his really desperate attempt (in spite of his fooling) to make use of the rich imagination of his youth on the Mississippi frontier before it sank muddied into his subconsciousness. Helpfully, he left a preface, which is quite as wise and very much briefer than James' essays on fiction in general — those prefaces which stand before his novels like Harvard examiners for a Ph.D., saying, you have to understand my criticism first, or you must not read.

Mark got the idea for this story from his own imagination. Suppose a man should arrive in a small, primitive town, and do or say something so original that he was instantly labeled a fool, a pudd'nhead, by the not too bright populace. Could he ever outlive it? Mark thought not, yet it would be interesting to invent a story in which, after a decade or so, he succeeded. Mark, of course, was thinking of his own sensitive fears and remorses. It was fear that he would be called an atheist and denied entrance to respectable magazines that kept "Captain Stormfield's Visit to Heaven" in manuscript for many years, *What is Man?* a mild agnostic tract, confined to private printing, and the admirable *The Mysterious Stranger* unprinted until after his death.

A river town on the Mississippi was an obvious scene for this story, but an unhappy suggestion of a pair of Siamese twins to lighten the narrative gets tangled with the plot. Every novelist, Mark says, begins with a group of people, a familiar locality, and an incident or two (James calls it a situation), and usually plans to write (how true this is of James!) a short story. The story grows and with a "jack-leg," as Mark frankly calls himself, complications tie knots in the narrative. In this one there are an unsolved murder, a mulatto woman who changes her almost white son with the offspring of the local judge, and also (just like the Boss in a jam) applied science in the form of fingerprinting, to solve the plot. But by this time, the Siamese twins have become impossible. Mark cuts them apart, and gives the two a romantic-comic role as mysterious noblemen set down from the steamboat, of whom one is drunk when the other is sober, one a romantic hero, one a scalawag. He was to have one married, one unmarried to the same woman, until Olivia (I am sure it was she) insisted that they should be separated. By this time, Pudd'nhead and Roxana, the Negress, have run away with the story, so Mark in a new version gets rid of most of the original cast, keeping only the more interesting characters with something invented for them to do in the new plot, and thus you get *Pudd'nhead Wilson*, a farce become tragi-comedy, with burlesque and melodrama left like remains of yesterday's stew in a fresh concoction.

This is about the way the "jack-leg" describes his own story, which indicates that at least Mark is beginning dimly to realize the differences between his good and his bad. Though even here in reshaping his exciting courtroom scene, he threw out one of his best passages of Southwest humor while keeping some of his worst episodes. With amazement he seems to have looked at the results of his own invention run wild.

It is easy to explain it all rhetorically. Mark was neither a dramatist nor a novelist in the ordinary sense. He was an actor, a show-off, after effects, and did not care much how he got them. When Roxana began to dominate the story, he could not bear to throw away his original absurdities. He was not adult enough to do that. He was not adult enough to see his real climax. The worthless moral degenerate who was Roxy's colored son had, when he was supposed to be white, tried to sell his mother down the river. He, thanks to the fingerprinting of the changelings, was reduced to slavery, and was sold himself. But the real climax would have been the impossible situation of the white boy reared as black, and now grown up to try hopelessly, unhappily, to adjust himself to the life of the whites.

Yet genius should never he underestimated. *Pudd'nhead Wilson* as written is still one of the treasures of American literature. Roxana is a bitter, frustrated heroine who makes Uncle Tom seem the synthetic fiction of a sentimental moralist that he is. She is the somber foredoomed contrast to Huck's childish, lovable Jim, whose racial loss of physical freedom is far less terrible than her racial fate. She is a great actress playing a great part in the enduring drama of the black and the white in America.

So far Mark had matured, yet at the cost of his unparalleled expressiveness for youth. Pudd'nhead, it must be obvious, was cast for the role of a grown-up Tom Sawyer, an undiscovered genius triumphing as Tom did in his boyish fashion over the town. But Pudd'nhead Wilson, the thwarted, melancholy lawyer, cannot play the part through, because Mark was unable to create an adult Tom. Before the story ends the life has gone out of him. He disintegrates under the strain of the makeshift plot. It results from the same incoherence of mind reported by those who have read the more ambitious of Twain's unpublished manuscripts.

There were too many conflicting lines of force in Mark Twain's mind, too many eggs and some of them close to addling in the basket which he worked and watched over with such endless endeavor. For the chapter heads of this brief novel Mark wrote a series of aphorisms (and added to them later) which are evidence to any reader that a new realism, often a definite cynicism, had bred in his kindly, tolerant nature, quite incongruous with the Mississippi farce-romance which he had set out to write. He was out of tone with youth, but could express his native genius in no other way.

From Pudd'nhead Wilson's Calendar (with additions)

There is no character, howsoever good and fine, but it can be destroyed by ridicule, howsoever poor and witless. Observe the ass, for instance: his character is about perfect, he is the choicest spirit among all the humbler animals, yet see what ridicule has brought him to. Instead of feeling complimented when we are called an ass we are left in doubt.

Whoever has lived long enough to find out what life is, knows how deep a debt of gratitude we owe to Adam, the first great benefactor of our race. He brought death into the world.

Everything human is pathetic. The secret source of Humor itself is not joy but sorrow. There is no humor in heaven.

Put all your eggs in the one basket and — WATCH THAT BASKET.

This is the last of the old, perennially young Mark Twain we shall see, except for certain short stories, like "The Man That Corrupted Hadleyburg," written on a more conventional level, but excellent of their moral kind. The real short or shortish writer of these parallel lives is Henry James, who sometimes put more of his deepest self in a *nouvelle* than in a novel. By the nineties, exuberant burlesque has become only a lingering bad habit for Mark; and the thoughts of youth, though long, long thoughts, as his *Autobiography* shows, are losing their magic for his disillusioned soul.

Chapter X

CASUALTY IN FICTION; DISASTER
ON THE STAGE

IN THE LATER EIGHTIES and early nineties up to 1898 of which I am writing, Henry James must be thought of as a resident London author, which is very different from being a resident tourist which Mark was for lengthy sojourns. Henry was there to live and work, Mark to work, and escape from the distractions of his popularity at home. The difference was fundamental. By 1889, when James was writing *The Tragic Muse*, "the longest and most careful novel I have ever written," as he said to Robert Louis Stevenson, he felt that he had come to know English life better than American, and to understand the English character and mind "as well as if I had invented it — which indeed I think I could have done without any extraordinary expenditure of ingenuity." This egregious remark was made to William James, and is by no means meant to be merely humorous. Mark abroad, however, was just about as absorptive of the Old World as a clam of a grain of sand. He was still from Missouri and, except for eccentricities like German grammar and incidents of travel, took little notice of either place or people.

Henry James, as in so many other ways, resembled the modern author. His center was in the city, with week-ends in the country, and vacations abroad. His exercise was long walks and bicycling. At home he was still the diner-out, though getting a little weary of it, and more enjoying the long English week-ends in the gregarious but selective societies of great country houses whose gardens gave privacy and great dinners

brilliance. He had numerous, too numerous friends, yet few
intimates, and these were still chiefly Americans, rich, cultivated expatriates. The Boston Curtises opened their Venetian
palace to him for his work, the Boston Sturgises, where Santayana was a connection, and banking and the sea in their
background, were truly intimate. Howard Curtis conversed
with him endlessly in his English place with the delightful
name of "Qu'Acre," where he knitted by the fireside (a nauti-
cal, down-East knitting, though Edith Wharton says that he
embroidered also). His literary friends were only in an intellectual sense more intimate than his less articulate hosts at
country houses and dinners-out. In pure literature he opened
his mind and heart occasionally to Stevenson, to Howells with
whom he was frankest, though describing him as "so remote,"
by which he did not refer to geography.

In letters of this decade (and in memoirs about him) are
passages of estimate and criticism which show that, for a man
who read little in the literature of the past, he had a keen interest in his contemporaries. His comments were as independent
as they were subtle. *Tess of the D'Urbervilles*, he said, lacked
sensuality, but Hardy's language was vile (!). Nothing had
really happened to Zola except the writing of his novels. Ibsen's
"pressure of life" was intolerable boredom. He admires the
man's skill but would not care to associate with his characters.
Meredith, the touchstone for the academic *literati* of my youth,
was a master of verbiage — "not one difficulty met in his
novels." Stevenson had suffered from being Meredith's too apt
pupil. "Faint, pale, embarrassed Pater, the mask without the
face," was "nevertheless destined for permanence." We do not
now agree, but I suspect we may be wrong. Rudyard Kipling
he at first greeted with enthusiasm yet later discovered how
little use of life as a whole he could make (a favorite criticism
now of H.J.), "almost nothing of the female form, or of any
question of shades."

Biographers of these years have found surprisingly little to record directly of a man who lived so much in his manuscripts and in his "impressions" of people and places. The temptation is to fill out an account of his life from a minute study of his novels, especially the later ones; and from these an excellent study of James the Observer can be made. It may be that the most significant story of his life is in his fiction; as the best story of Whitman is in his poetry. Not that James' contacts were narrow — it is rather that these contacts were usually in the interchange of ideas, not in action. A mere list of names of his more notable correspondents drawn from Lubbock's excellent if rather too literary selection of his letters, is indicative. I choose from 1889 to 1898: Robert Louis Stevenson, William James, W. D. Howells, Alice James, Edmund Gosse, Charles Eliot Norton, Mrs. Humphry Ward, The Countess of Jersey, George du Maurier, Sir Sidney Colvin, Sir George Henschel, The Viscountess Wolseley, Paul Bourget, H. G. Wells, F. W. H. Myers, A. F. de Navarro (husband of the actress Mary Anderson).

2. THE DRAMA

From these same letters (and from other sources) it is easy to outline Henry James' setback (for so he regarded it), which set him on a new course, and what can better be called his disaster, into which he ran head on in the early nineties. The setback, of course, was his loss of popularity, especially at home. Let him speak for himself when he writes of the prospects of *The Tragic Muse* which, as he feared, shared the fate of *The Princess Casamassima*. William, who liked it immensely, had said that it was for the select few. Henry replied, "I have

no illusions of any kind about its . . . 'popularity.' From these
things I am quite divorced. . . . One must go one's own way and
. . . have . . . a private religion — in short have made up one's
mind as to *ce qui en est* with a public the draggling after which
simply leads one to the gutter. One has always a 'public' enough
if one has an audible vibration. . . . I shall never make my
fortune . . . but I know what I shall do, and it won't be bad."
How Jamesian! — the perfect description of the effect of his art
as "an audible vibration," the ill-concealed crush of what had
been his lingering hopes, even the characteristic mention of
money, and most of all the courage, which was not whistling in
the dark but readiness to meet a challenge. And then to Stevenson a little later in gay despair, "Tell it not in Samoa — or at
least not in Tahiti, but I don't sell ten copies! — and neither
editors nor publishers will have anything whatever to say to me.
But I never mention it — nearer home." And finally to
Howells, in 1895, his literary confidant always: "Periodical publication is practically closed to me . . . the money-difference will
be great." And indeed in America it was only *The Atlantic
Monthly* that was serializing his books, with its notoriously
poor pay, which Twain could not afford to accept.

All this led to Henry James' one great speculation — the
stage. Mark was sure that he understood publishing and let his
free-flowing cash run in that direction. Henry was sure that
he understood drama, and invested his pride and his most
valuable asset, time for writing, in that phase of the drama
which we call the art of the stage. This he was sure he could
master. Mark wanted money, much more money, for complete
security, which he had never so much as glimpsed in the West.
Henry wanted a little more money, as he makes perfectly clear,
also security, at least in his old age, which his inherited income
now seemed insufficient to guarantee, and to leave something
behind to his relatives. The failure of his novels sharpened his
desire to write acting plays before he died. Coolly and reso-

lutely he set himself to study the theatrical art, like a Ph.D. preparing for a thesis. He chose the skillful and very successful plays of the contemporary French stage, which were technically as superior to the contemporary British (and American) productions as French to English cooking. He labored over Sardou and his kind until he was sure that he knew every device that made a stage play different from what he now called the "pale little art" of fiction. He learned with utmost pains what the English in the days of Pinero and Henry Arthur Jones were to call the well-made play. What he offered to actors and producers was a drama that he was certain would be successful — and was sensationally wrong for reasons he never fully understood.

I call this theatrical interlude a speculation in finance, but this, as I have said, is not exclusively true. Henry had wanted to write plays even when his "pale art" of fiction was doing well. He had been repelled by the "grossness" of the English stage, the vulgarity of the theatrical life — by, I should say a snobbishness which is apparent in *The Tragic Muse* of 1890, his one novel of the theater. That book is certainly the most complete and penetrating study of *acting* in English fiction, perhaps in the English language. It is the fruit of innumerable hours at the Théâtre Français, where the art of acting had reached its prime for the nineteenth century. I say acting, for the French contemporary plays, by comparison with the classics performed at the Théâtre Français, though infinitely skillful in design and also in acting, have taken no great place in literary history.

The plot of *The Tragic Muse* might have been drawn from James' own entrails. Miriam, an aspirant and perhaps a genius in the histrionic art, is precisely the kind of woman that fascinated Victorian England, yet repelled her English admirers also by the dubious moral atmosphere in which stage life was lived. James set in her orbit an Englishman with a "secret vice" for

Paris and his own painting, but who also belonged to the ruling political class in England, with a famous political father, and already a political success of his own. He gave him a rich English widow, a "political hostess," in love with him, and made him not so much in love with Miriam Rooth as with the life of art and well aware of its importance in civilization. Thus, the choice was between two aspects of society, two aspects of national societies, two aspects of culture, with all the wealth and influence (and a splendid wife) on one side, and such a life for art as James himself lived (but a good deal more picturesque than his) on the other. It was certainly a dramatic situation, and certainly (though this was unfortunate) a wonderful opportunity for a novelist with a passion for criticism to indulge it while he told a story.

Why *The Tragic Muse* failed to get a public is not so relevant at the moment, though I shall explain it later, as is the state of Henry's imagination in 1890, which was clearly surcharged with the problems of the theater. He also had been fascinated but repelled by the grossness, not only of the life of the theater, but of the English stage itself, then at one of the low points of its history. Yet he had failed, and with this new novel was to fail again, with fiction. And gold flowed from the theater. Even Henry's culminating play when he became a playwright, and his final failure, *Guy Domville*, which ran only thirty days, and ran badly, in London, brought him in a little over $1000, probably as much as all of his recent novels, at least in book form. No wonder he was tempted. Here are his own words. To Stevenson in 1888: "I have no money, but I have a little work." In 1890, to William, when he was about to begin his new career: "It [the dramatic career] is not to depend upon a single attempt, but on half a dozen of the most resolute and scientific character. . . . It is late [he means for his success]. . . . But . . . now it's an absolute necessity, imposing itself without choice if I wish a loaf on the shelf for my old age." Nothing, indeed, is so amazing as the certainties of an author when he first gets a new idea or a new course! That excellent early novel of Henry's, *The American,* was dramatized and accepted (but never produced) in 1890. He was positive of its success and told his sister why: "There is not, in its felicitous form, the ghost of a 'fluke' or a mere chance: it is all 'art' [he means technique] and an absolute address of means to end — the end, viz., of meeting exactly the immediate, actual, intense, British conditions, both subjective and objective." As anyone with the least experience with the theater must say, this from an untried playwright is not only speculation, it is brash speculation. And if one adds that James believed, and may have been right, that only a "happy ending" could succeed on the British stage, and so proposed to streamline all his stories to such a destination, this exact reversal of his lifelong practice and belief in writing fiction made all this a dim speculation at best. For once Henry as a writer is clearly in reverse gear, with a gully behind him. Yet the golden lure was bright, the lifelong desire to be a playwright strong. His new line should mean "profit indeed, an income to my descendants."

Alas, there was neither profit nor fame. In January of 1895 it was really all over with the collapse on the London stage of *Guy Domville.* Poor James had gone to a nearby performance of Oscar Wilde's *An Ideal Husband,* to keep his mind off the first night in his own theater. He returned deeply pessimistic — if so bad a play as Wilde's was succeeding, his own was doomed. And it was. He arrived just in time to be thrust upon the stage to the call of "Author, author." Downstairs was a typical first-nighter group of the social and the intellectual. They were applauding heartily. But the unsophisticated galleries were "roaring" their disappointment, "like . . . a cage of beasts at some infernal 'Zoo,' " catcalling, abusing the play. It was a horrid experience for "a nervous, sensitive, exhausted writer to face," he wrote William. His decency was insulted,

his dignity, his art. He did not give up. With the characteristic appeal of the literary dramatist to his peers, "the
'papers,' " he wrote, "have been on the whole quite awful — but
the audiences are altogether different." He was "sickened" to
death by the ordeal. After all he had been working "from
motives as 'pure' as pecuniary motives *can* be." When it was all
settled, wit lightened his resignation. In his Notebooks he
wrote that the long vain study to meet the vulgar need and to
violate his intrinsic conditions, was only to try "to make a
sow's ear out of a silk purse." That was true, but not all the
truth.

Whitman stopped being a Quaker because he found he
could not live inside a fence. James spent infinite pains to crib
and confine his expansive imagination in the limits of the
stage play. He accepted, as an artist must, the restrictions, the
rules of the game, but as with dehydrated vegetables the vita-
mins did not always survive the process. And something important which was clearly absent from his supposed mastery of
dramatic technique, did not get into his performance at all —
"theater." It was not, I believe, merely that his plays were too
delicate, or his dialogue too Jamesian, pearls cast before swine,
as he too evidently thought. I am sure that his plays would
not "go" before the much more sophisticated audiences of
today. I doubt if his lines carried at all except to the most educated and attentive ears. That was probably why the galleries
"roared." Plot and characters did not get over the footlights,
probably because he did not really believe in plots, nor was
much interested in pure personality apart from its place in
intricate situations. Most of his plays have now been published,
yet there seems no temptation to present them, nor to rank
them as narrative with his stories. But already plays made from
his novels and stories by playwrights with a sense for "theater"
have been very successful, both on the stage and the screen.
Many more will be added. For James was a great dramatist, at

least in fiction; if not a playwright, a perceptive student of fine acting, who did not sufficiently appreciate the hard task which a representative audience forces upon the literary art. I may add that, if he had appreciated it, if he had understood what was required for good "theater," I doubt if he could have acquired it. It was too far removed from his own self-involving genius, and from his own excessive "refinement." He summed it all up himself in a letter to his friend, Miss Reubell, in 1895, "I may have been meant for the Drama — God knows! — but I certainly wasn't meant for the Theatre."

3 . THE TRAGIC MUSE

In the last chapter I have tried, from a single long short story, to begin the difficult diagnosis of Mark Twain's troubles at what should have been the peak of his career. Mark was the most lovable, most outwardly successful, least integrated. and in art and finance the least dependable man of letters of his English-speaking generation. Plutarch himself would have needed the help of a modern psychiatrist in order to explain what happened to him in the next stages of his career. As for Henry James, a man simpler of soul if far more complex in his art, what happened to him in what he himself regarded as his great collapse is quite possible to interpret, even though the task will require some oversimplification. The reasons for his final recovery and triumph are not so obvious. To put it in outline, he plunged from one technique into another — playwriting — which he failed to capture, and back to his own "pale" art with a reaction into an overspecialization where he defied his readers. This will occupy a later chapter of this book. He was not unlike a tennis player who tries to play golf, and failing returns to his own game with a show-off of fancy quirks.

The Tragic Muse, however, which succeeds his unhappy failure both in America and England to write a "popular" novel, needs more consideration. Its failure to be widely read made him determine to write for a long while, aside from his plays, no more novels but only short stories; and to this failure we may owe some of his finest stories into which his dammed-up energy, reserved for the novel, now flowed. It is the only full-length novel for a six-year period from 1890 onward, and marks, I should say, the low point of his career as a novelist, and is followed by definite signs of an overcomplex art which like an overmixed chemical compound shows signs of breaking down.

All his life James was a critic, sometimes a fussy one, sometimes a great one. In his youth he had been trained to search everywhere for qualities, values — sometimes merely technical, usually relative to a universe which in his view got its human significance by an artist's molding toward an ethical order. His joy, which was sometimes ecstasy, in an Italian hillside, before a cathedral, or in the presence of great acting, was always a sense of deep values realized in art. And when the Observer was deeply charged, and found a situation outside of his own personal experience into which currents could flow, he wrote a book. The difference from Twain, who was a lover of life as such, not for quality, not even for values except the value of being intensely alive, is too obvious to need pointing. When mere living turned distressing or disgusting for that great Innocent, he reacted into cynicism. James never did — in part because only such life as spoke his own restricted language interested him, in part because distress he had always expected to encounter with the common man, and disgust he avoided.

Mrs. Humphry Ward gave him his first idea for The Tragic Muse. She told him of a young actress, crude but determined to succeed, and a young amateur of the stage who helps her to rise, and then falls in love with her. But the actress becomes a celebrity and "soars away and is lost to him." Too simple this for James. The drama is elementary. Thinking it over he sees that the really interesting struggle is between the shocking philistinism of the young English amateur and his English friends and the temperament, the mores, of the creative artist. James is an English writer now, and has already suffered from this philistinism, which was a passion for respectability. He is thoroughly competent to handle both the actress and her art, and if he is completely ignorant of what he regards as the dirty politics of his own country, he has not been a week-ender in great houses without learning how British politics of the ruling class are conducted among constituencies, and what it costs to get a seat in the House, and how to hold it, and of the major influence of rich and attractive women. A perfect story, one would say, for James who can dramatize both ends, since both are involved. Why then did the book as a novel fail, except, I should say, with moderns who are essentially more interested in criticism than in action. Because the two halves of the story, one in England and one in Paris, are really two stories with two centers, loosely hung, with far more tension in each than in the drama between them. With (James being James) the inevitable result that brilliant lectures on the art of acting take the opportunities offered by the story, distract the plot, impede the action, and give the reader the impression, which is just, that the real concern of the novel is with esthetics, not with the personal fortunes of the lovers. Here is an often brilliant book which is just not a good novel. The great craftsman for once has forgotten which of several possible audiences he is addressing, like a lecturer who has brought the wrong speech to the hall. What James called the tragedy of his loss of a popular audience was having intellectual effects more serious than he realized. Perhaps he was doing that very dangerous thing for any author, writing just to please himself. In spite of a popular opinion that this is what all writers should do, it never works — not even (is Pepys an exception?) in a diary.

Henry's battery was overcharged with criticism and the evaluation of the life and meaning of the artist. His extraordinary essays on the drama and acting included in his novel are ethical as well as esthetic, for Henry is writing irresistibly and *con amore* of how a man whose spirit is sensitive to beauty ought to live — what he should hold to, what he should sacrifice. Gabriel Nash, the perfect esthete, is his spokesman in the story, a man whose purpose in life is to acquire a style which expresses it esthetically. Gabriel, like Gilbert Osmond in *The Portrait of a Lady,* is a dilettante. Henry could have been Gabriel, but he is no dilettante. In *The Tragic Muse* he creates superb criticism. Unfortunately it is (much of it) in the wrong place — like a nest for bird's eggs, built and filled, as sometimes happens, in an automobile.

I hope the reader will not accuse me of the old-maidish trick of complaining that Henry has not obeyed the rules. Some of the best books in the world do not obey the rules. The real criticism here is that his book as such suffers and the reader with it. For nearly two hundred of its early pages the reader of this novel (any reader I should say) does not warm to it — and this in a book which by any standards is intolerably long for its story. Henry was well aware of the fault. He had begun publishing in the *Atlantic* before he had completed his novel, and made strenuous attempts (like Mark Twain) to keep it down to a short story. It was too late, and for the reasons I have stated. He had packed too many articles in his bag, and soon the straps began to burst. Or to change the figure, he was like Mark Twain in *Puddn'head Wilson* with his Siamese Twins. Mark split the twins. But Henry's twins, or rather triplets, a political story, an actor's story, plus criticism, were not so easy to reform, unless he threw out the criticism. Hard as he worked he could not make his narrative into an exhibition of his too extensive talents. Mark, as we shall see, had no remedy, for the trouble was not with his talents but his mind itself.

It may be added as a footnote that James' failure himself on that stage about which he wrote too much in *The Tragic Muse* may have been due in part to his too minute studies of what he called the *"art"* (the italics are his) of the stage, with emphasis upon the intricacy and necessity of what I should call, and think he meant, its artifice. Acting, however, is an interpretation of a play, whether a good or a bad one. Therefore to make his own plays also consciously artificial art, both by imitating successful models, and by adding his own refinements, was dangerous. This is precisely what he said he proposed to do, and thus risked a double complexity, a double artifice. For success, he needed a superb "art" of acting a play, which was itself to be a synthetic contrivance. I do not of course say that this is impossible — Shaw succeeded in doing it. Yet it requires a sense of "theatre," by which the playwright knows what the actor, any actor, can do with a given scene and what he cannot, which James simply did not possess. Hamlet's remarks on acting are still quoted, and sometimes observed. Shakespeare's play however will act well without superb acting; we all know that. James' plays would not. Even with good acting, which he got in his London performance, the audience "roared" like beasts!

Chapter XI

HENRY JAMES: IN LOVE WITH
TECHNIQUE

I TURN with some relief from a discussion of the difficulties of
Henry James the playwright into the main stream of my book.
A study of the technique of a literary artist is dreary unless it
is an explanation of success; it can be annoying if the artist
gets more interested in his technique than in his subject. James
at this stage of his career did just this. He implies it in his
Prefaces which say in so many words: this is how I did it; was
I not clever to analyze my characters into their last elements
so that you can almost forget that they are people and judge
them abstractly and therefore with truth!

If this were more than a phase of James it would be impossible to support a contention that James was a very great
novelist, whose aid in understanding the peculiar qualities of
the nineteenth century in contrast to our own is likely to be of
the first importance. Of course it is not all, except in a few
novels and a number of short and long short stories in which
Jamesian specialists have taken great delight because they are
particularly difficult, and sometimes just short of being unreadable. The next three novels I wish to present are of this category. They are frankly rhetoric, brilliant rhetoric; only in a
secondary sense literature. And I label them here horrid examples (to the indignation I fear of some), in order to distinguish between brilliant rhetoric and admirable fiction, which
anyone who wishes to promote the intelligent reading of Henry
James must first of all do. By the admirable fiction of Henry
James, I definitely do not mean the cleverest, the most difficult,

not even the most characteristic of his stories, but rather the most readable because, thanks to their art, they best reveal to us a past which we now know was the end of an epoch.

2. JAMES GOES FIN DE SIECLE

Fortunately James himself, and for reasons already suggested, supplied a laboratory test, controlled by experiment, in just these *fin de siècle* days which we have reached in this book. He had lost his American audience as a pay-as-you-enter group. The stage had failed him in every way — no money for him there; or any new audience in sight except the very sophisticated, who were mostly English, and whose extent could be perhaps measured by the rather esoteric circulation of *The Yellow Book* to which he had begun to contribute. Really short stories he could with difficulty sell — there was little market for them in England. And he could not begin with the longer *nouvelle* without being dragged after its space-hungry developments into a small book published with difficulty, or, worse still, into a long and unsuccessful novel. When there was a unifying mystery, as in "The Turn of the Screw," he could keep his task in hand, but where the situations involved many characters only a triumph of technique could keep the story short of two volumes. It was a ticklish moment for a writer like James who reacted to a difficulty, not by discouragement, but by a flow of words. No wonder that he was discouraged.

If he had been a different man and as English as he thought he was, the moment might have been propitious. A new society was forming in England which it is more accurate to call Edwardian after the Prince of Wales than *fin de siècle*. Before the old queen's death a new and brittle morality had become

notoriously evident in upper-class London. James was well
aware that the moral code in which he had stepped so firmly
was beginning to disintegrate; he was aware but not yet clearly
so that new sets of moral values were beginning to crystallize.
The child Maisie, in the best of these "clever" novels which I
am about to describe, was, so he says definitely, "1897" — in the
modern fashion of dating a hero or heroine in a given year. On
reading one sees that it is not so much Maisie as the environment she had to live in which is dated. As a result of the new
society he is representing, adultery, sexual irregularity, passion
as an overt motive, decadence, all aspects of life which did not
interest the earlier James because they did not much concern
his characters except in their results, now enter the immediate
action. He describes his treatment of these fragile Edwardian
morals as "ironic," but that is not true. It is flippant. Henry
is not at home in these stories, even when he is an Observer.
He strains, like a serious man telling a dirty story, and justifies
his labor upon their thin and sometimes trashy material by
his wit — and his technique.

It happened that in these years James, for various reasons,
was furthest in his imagination from America, most focused
upon England, and entirely domesticated there — least conscious that he was still an outsider looking in. In 1897 he
notes that it has been nearly four years since he has crossed
even the Channel. A shrinking income, and by 1898 his stiffening fingers which made him depend upon a typewriter and a
secretary, had made his continental visits, which were working
times as much as vacations, difficult to manage, if not impossible. But there was more than this. In one sense he had
become British, and insular. Europe no longer drew him as
strongly as in the past. Even when he did get back to Rome,
the effect was only to sharpen his memories. He was no longer,
as his fiction shows, an expatriate American, sensitive to his
compatriots' reactions to Old World society. His intimacy was

now with London behavior. Americans ceased to appear in his novels. And yet he is clearly not really intimate with this society. His best stories are those with a touch of mysticism or allegory. When he wrote directly of the Edwardians it is difficult to remember any name but Maisie, which was in the title.

Henry, in fact, temporarily ceased being the American turning East. He became, or thought he became, all English. He was out of sympathy, and he believed for good, with his own country. Barbarism was destroying what civilization had once been there. He hated its jingoism as in the Venezuelan incident, its "bloody billionaires" of the McKinley régime, and later the raucous Teddy Roosevelt. He hated the "split" that was coming between European East and American West (familiar terms now with a different implication). His "sky was darkened," so he wrote to them at home. "How long I have lived away from my native land, how long I shall (D.V.!) live away from it and how little I understand it today." In brief, he had become a British novelist, and proposed to write as an Englishman, and about the English.

One of the closest of his English friends was Mrs. W. K. Clifford, who was constantly familiar with him until his death. She was the widow of a famous philosopher, a friend of Browning, and herself a successful novelist. Kipling and James were both her intimates. "How thoroughly English Henry believed himself to be," she said to me once just after his death, "and yet, poor dear, he was always *so* American." Yes, in the sequel it will appear that he was in his subconscious still deeply American, and Mrs. Clifford and her friends were shrewd enough to feel it, and value it for the special quality it had given his work. But to Henry's own considering, he was no longer at the moment an expatriate in any sense. He had suffered acutely from the loss of his public, by which in other references he meant his American public. Now, however, he is a free man, to write of the British as a Britisher.

It did not work. He was not happy either in his 'ife or in his books. "I do not go out any more," he says at this time, "but I *am* out — and wonder why." He groans over the dinners and the "long visits," from which the immediate impressions for at least two of these new novels must have come. Preoccupied with all the work that even "*my* technical temper can desire," he can only hope that "something not irremediably nauseating will not improbably spring." In 1902, Howells is his confidant. *The Sacred Fount* (the cleverest and most technical of the group of novels) he fears has proved to be "chaff in the mouth." "The *faculty of attention* has utterly vanished from the general Anglo-Saxon mind." (A deeply true criticism this last, but it must be admitted that *The Sacred Fount* required attention to an almost unbearable degree!) Here (and in dozens more of possible quotations) is a creative writer in deep distress. He is suffering from what his father, I think, would have called "dryness," a slackening of the spirit, a want of emotion. He was not so English as he thought; he did not know the English as intimately as he had boasted; he did not like the new society into which he had been thrust. And he had rashly severed the umbilical cord which had kept his inner consciousness for all these years vitally American.

This defeat of pride and confidence, of which this group of novels is the climax, I take far more seriously in explaining Henry's career than any psychological disturbance due to expatriation, or the failure to love women, or to fight in the Civil War (!) which various critics have tried to build into James' psychiatric background.

These clever British novels lacked pregnancy, and when one comes to read them, the results are obvious. Henry in each case had little more to write about of deeply personal interest than would have filled a short story. He is like a powerful engine spinning without a load. And even more interesting is what I suppose a psychologist would call a transference of emotions —

such as happens when a woman disappointed in her husband
shifts her emotions to her child — or, since this figure is a little
dramatic for the occasion, a rich man who finds his new wife
less interesting than his last, and goes in for connoisseurship
in art.

3. THE "CLEVER NOVELS"

The three books which have suggested all this preface are *What
Maisie Knew,* 1897, *The Awkward Age,* 1899, and *The Sacred
Fount,* 1901. Maisie is an affectionate, gentle, and articulate
child of twelve, set in the midst of a highly immoral situation
in which divorced parents, step-parents, and lovers actual or
would-be, are sexually involved with each other in a complex
about a child of whom someone must take care. Maisie is
neither embittered nor corrupted, as with the still more articulate boy of "The Turn of the Screw," a more brilliant Jamesian
creation. She simply develops a set of values which provides
for the good in the worst, the best in the good. Henry's problem in her would have warmed any literary artist's heart and
have challenged his every subtlety. The child must intuitively
apprehend all that is happening about her without experiencing anything; it is impression without understanding. If only
this had been a *nouvelle* in a less contemporary British world!
But the novel (he wanted it that way) is a series of balanced
scenes, in which Maisie is passed rhythmically among divorcées
and amorists as in a ballet, with her support in stiff Mrs. Wix
the governess, who acts the part of Victorian morals which she,
but not Maisie, believes to be morality. The effort is too great.
Even Maisie seems a prodigy rather than a real child, and the
victims of sexual passion, vanity, and jealousy seem to have

been called in for the occasion from a cold and somewhat scabrous society, with the effect of "chaff in the mouth" and somewhat soiled chaff for both author and reader. If there is emotion on James' part it is roused by the difficulty of his task.

A few paragraphs in James' Notebooks describe the inception and development of most of his best novels. *What Maisie Knew* occupies pages of packed description over which he broods happily, "Ah, this divine conception of one's little masses and periods in the scenic light — as rounded ACTS; the patient, pious, nobly 'vindictive' ["vindicating" was James' note] application of the scenic philosophy and method — I feel as if it still . . . might carry me as far as I dream!" This is no novelist stirred by the plight of a child who is involved in passionate, selfish, or corrupt adult life, without taint herself and without real comprehension. It is the technician enamored of a "scenic philosophy" which he and no one else can turn and twist as the parents or guardians grasp or repel little Maisie for their own purposes. The child is lost in wordage, though her spiritual reactions are true and tender. Henry was trying to follow a "scenic philosophy"; in other words, he was trying to write a stage play but in the form of a novel. Maisie as a human being has little chance, and the unsympathetic though often sharply drawn adults still less, except as character parts well acted. James really cared little for this society (which was, of course, Oscar Wilde's, who did). It was possible stage effects, not character and personality he was after — "masses and periods."

What we have here is a great artist and an even greater technician momentarily discouraged, and driving his indomitable energy in new paths leading toward no heartwarming destination. And therefore he gives a display of architectonics which satisfies even *"my* technical temper," but nothing else. Soon he will be calling it a waste of words. I am reminded of a great artist, at least his equal in technique, who encountered a *really* decadent and inferior society, did not like it (as his portraits show), but memorialized in great painting precisely the aspects he did not like until his pictures became the types of such a period. I refer to Goya, who painted Spain at her lowest moment, instead of England in the merely frothy *fin de siècle*. But Goya was not brought up in the Jamesian circle where a high morality was in the air they breathed.

Actually, of course, Henry knew he was in a depression. He had determined to write for a while only short tales, and was afraid to invest the enormous labor of a full-length novel into what would, he was sure, not sell, nor as one sees from his own comments, seem likely to satisfy him. But when he writes the short tale he proliferates until he loses sight of the warm rich soil in a chase for the subtlety of a "clever" society of week-enders as different as might be from the far more worthwhile group the friends to whom he wrote his self-revealing letters.

The second of his "clever" novels was *The Awkward Age* in 1899. Only a simple note records its inception. The theme is Nanda, an innocent young girl, naïve at first, but not pre-cocious like his American girls. She is, if you please, a grown-up version of Maisie, but simpler than Maisie had been at twelve. Nanda has failed to marry after her début — a Victorian tragedy — partly because she was abnormally tall, and so she has to be admitted, still virginal, to the "free" society of her brilliant (and sordid and corrupt) mother's drawing room. It is a society in which only three things are valued: wit, money, and only half-hidden sexual relationships, some of them so decadent as to seem almost incestuous. And Nanda inevitably learns about it all, without being allowed to act. The man who would have married her thinks she must have been corrupted; and at the end she is unfitted for marriage, as for companion-ship, except with an old man who had been in love with her grandmother, a member of a less neurotic generation! Ibsen could have made a play of the story, says James in his Preface, but it would have been as "simple and superficial" as *A Doll's House!* And so James takes this morally disintegrating society not for the significance, like Ibsen, but, as with Oscar Wilde, for the brilliance of wit which needs such a "free" society in which to coruscate. The result is what might be expected. James was as witty as Wilde — I think his wit has never been fully appreciated, buried perhaps too often in words — but not so "smart" as an American might say, and determined to write his book like the stage play of which he was incapable. Nanda is real in her talk, the others all rattle, and require expert acting to realize them; and one gets 482 pages of difficult, allusive, and expert writing which is like a show of intricate fireworks far above the heads of the spectators. It is not surprising that his publisher should have told him that no one of his books had ever been treated with such general disrespect.

The Sacred Fount in 1901 was the last of these "clever" novels, and should have been the best, since scene and personnel are perfect for a James who was in his Oscar Wilde period. It did not satisfy, certainly not James, who admitted to his brother that in expanding this tenuous story to interminable lengths he would have stopped in mid-course except that he just could not afford to "waste" so many written words. Nevertheless, for me, it has the rather horrid charm of a slightly intoxicated bishop in a night club.

The scene is Newmarch, a great week-end house in the country, a house and gardens ideal from Henry's point of view, since a "free" society of five or six intimates can wander, meet, and separate unobserved by the multitude of guests and servants, who screen the intrigues of the principals while never entering their story. The gardens, the corridors are there for assignations. There is a stage set, where faces of the intimates are unveiled, or masked, along a vast dinner table. Included is a final touch of the exotic, after the women retire. Then the men can meet in a special smoking room to smoke (including the Observer who, if he is Henry, has once smoked a cigarette). For this occasion they wear extraordinarily fantastic costumes — with a strong Oriental tinge. The idea is that they should be out of their dress clothes and at ease.

This, like the gardens, is an admirable arrangement for a piece of intellectual detective work, which is precisely the theme of the story. Now sex comes out into the open, and is recorded by the Observer who is a new phase of James assimilated to this unstable society. The supposition is that pretty much everyone concerned may be presumed to have, or have had, a lover, probably present. The Sacred Fount is love, drained by the Sacred Terror, which is passion. James' original notes reveal the plot, which is simply to discover what has made a dull man brilliant, and who has made an old wife young. And the answer is in terms of passion, which has drained the tragic Mrs. Server dry and transferred her sparkle to another, and stolen youth from a husband to transfer it to a wife. Of course this is highly artificial, nor in itself especially important, except for poor lovely Mrs. Server. The real emotion is in Henry's rapturous working out of the problem of who and what in incredibly intricate dialogues with his friends. It is the most closely knit novel in the language, I think, and naturally so since every character except a lost, naïve woman is James himself in a mirror. Naturally again, as Mrs. Briss says, he talks too much. Yet it is a cruel novel, nor is it even dignified. The Observer, like a nasty brilliant old woman, risks the destruction of poignant relationships by his infatuate curiosity and indefatigable gossip. It is a game played with a pack of male and female gossips and philanderers, with no solidity of character except for the unhappy Mrs. Server. She was the theme for the intended short story, and a good one, but is talked to death before their tongues have ceased twittering. No wonder this novel has fascinated some literary critics with the scenic skill of its involutions. No wonder it best represents

what repels many good readers in too many novels of James.
The subject is good, as the man said who wrote the Lord's
Prayer on a postage stamp, but it was the difficulty which led
him to attempt it.

A great man trotting from one scene to another in search of
variety, and showering words behind him, is a sorry spectacle.
And yet there is magic in these dream gardens and halls of Newmarch. No excellent writer can ever be judged entirely by his
wholes. He may be at his best even in his worst. Nor by
"periods" either. Two years before he began to think about
this last novel, James had considered another novel, briefish
to be sure, but of a different type entirely — and a triumph of
characterization. In *The Spoils of Poynton,* long a favorite
with readers, character and theme unite in happy harmony in
a story where a fatal passion for "things" means more to the
obsessed than the sacred fount or the sacred terror of life. The
"things" are the adornments of a house, and the narrative is as
concentrated as one of Voltaire's. In scene and characters the
"clever" books are all essentially English. Note that Mrs. Poynton's self-defeating yet magnificent selfishness, and a young
companion's failure to "let herself go," either in sexual passion
or in *her* love for "things," might readily have been written in
New England and is far more closely related to Hawthorne than
to the world of Oscar Wilde.

4. REVIVAL

The turn of this depression and of the "dryness" of Henry
James began in 1897, the same year, indeed, as the publication
of *The Spoils of Poynton* and *What Maisie Knew.* Quite a
psychological moment, James called it, but did not realize the

full significance of the fact that the conversation which gave him new heart was with an American, Howells. His acknowledgment of its importance for him to Howells a month later in 1898 is so Jamesian that I must quote it entire.

> It all comes from that wonderful (and still-in-my-ear reverberating) little talk we had that morning here [in London] in the soft lap, and under the motherly apron, of the dear old muffling fog — which will have kept anyone else from hearing *ever* — and only let me hear, and have been heard! I mean that the effect of your admirable counsel and comfort was from that moment to give me the sense of being, somehow, suddenly, preposterously, renewingly and refreshingly, at a kind of practical high pressure which has — well, which has simply, my dear Howells, made all the difference! There it is. It is the absurd, dizzy consciousness of this difference that has constituted (failing other things!) an exciting, absorbing feeling of occupation and preoccupation — and thereby paralyzed the mere personal activity of my pen. . . .

This talk, as we learn from an earlier letter to Mrs. William James, was "professional" (i.e., commercial), or at least did him a lot of good "that way." We can safely guess that what happened was a renewal of faith that there was for James both appreciation and subject matter in his homeland — specifically, still possibilities for publication. Certainly, as any reader of his letters for the next years can see, the references to America become interested not bitter, nostalgic even. America, he says, is now for him almost as romantic as Europe had been in his youth. It is of the greatest interest to find him in 1898, in a review of Whitman's letters to James Doyle, writing with the most sensitive appreciation of the simple sincerity of Walt. And to know that by 1905 at Edith Wharton's house in Lenox, he was chanting Whitman's greater poems with such enthusiasm that his stammer disappeared. And this was the James who once had regarded Whitman as "brash" and unrefined, with a complete misapprehension of the new America in the ex-

pansive nineteenth century whose voices were Whitman and
Mark Twain.

Even though painfully and slowly, James began the resolve
to go back home, at least for a long visit, and this was coincident with what I shall call the American revival in his books.
By 1904, Howells had been speaking to him of an American
novel. In 1903, James speaks guardedly of a project which
proved to be the *New York Edition*. I note that even in 1899
he has begun to speak to his friend Henrietta Reubell in defense of *The Awkward Age*, that it was a study of a special
London and an "actual" group, written for clever people. And
describes his own cleverness by remarking that all explanations
are reduced to the explanation of everything by all the other
things *in* the picture. But it appears that people aren't clever
enough to follow him and "J'en suis pour mes frais," which
have been considerable. It would seem that a little fresh air,
and fresh subject matter was badly needed.

Howells at the least gave him the impulse to save himself
from this "dryness" by an injection of American confidence. In
1896 he was rowing hard with creaking oars, proposing still to
win his little battle of technique. The simile is his. When
Howells left him his "pressure" of ambition had been renewed
into a "dizzy consciousness." If James in the letter quoted
above had followed Mark Twain's advice to strike out the
Adjective when in doubt — he would have been more specific,
but his state of mind could not be clearer.

Chapter XII

THE AMERICAN WAY

I⟶ is a curious fact and noticed by many literary historians that the American imagination releases itself very easily in the short story — and has done so since the beginning of our national literature. We have been a country of tall-tale tellers, and swoppers of anecdotes, certainly since the frontier began to move westward. And when Grandpa at the fireplace corner took to a desk and pen and ink he found a new literary medium ready to publish his yarns, or more literary efforts, if he was good. Americans did not invent the magazine, but they soon made the American magazine the most vigorous and best liked in the world. Now it is almost an American monopoly. Ambitious American novelists of the first half of the nineteenth century found it difficult to sustain competition in the absence of copyright with the powerful English novel sold at a cut-rate price. For obvious reasons this was not true of a local periodic product. The succession of famous American short-story writers quickly began to crowd our magazines — Irving, Hawthorne, Poe, Melville, Bret Harte, Sarah Orne Jewett, Henry James, O. Henry, Hemingway and others in our own times.

The short story (well, the *rather* short story) was always close to Henry's heart. "With God's help," he wrote to Stevenson in 1888, "I propose, for a longish period, to do nothing but short lengths, I want to leave . . . a multitude of pictures of my time, projecting my small circular frame upon as many spots as possible" — a perfect description of the short-story writer. Of course, this was in reaction from the failure of his novels, which were always spilling out of their frames. But there is much more than self-criticism in this resolve, and he did write toward a hundred short and shortish stories, some of them among his masterpieces. Like those other Americans mentioned above, his intention was frequently toward the small, sharp, clear picture — an impression, an effect, or a powerful suggestion. He usually failed to be small and sometimes to be sharp and clear, though he never missed his impression and especially his suggestion. This was natural in the most elaborative of writers. "I shall never again write a *long* novel," he wrote to Howells in 1895, "but I hope to write six immortal short ones — and some tales of the same quality." There were only three "immortal" novels, but they ran to two volumes apiece! And the like expansiveness was true of his tales, yet the best have as fair a chance as any literature of the period for survival.

It is impossible to know Henry James without reading his short stories and *nouvelles,* and in some respects it is easiest to learn to know him there. Their difficulties and triumphs deserve much more than a cursory opinion. Mark can be discussed with more brevity. He wrote only a few notable short stories, though numerous anecdotes! Yet he was as American as they bred them. Why did he not follow the American way, and write short, sharp, impressionistic stories, which were not so much the small change as the legal tender of his compatriots? The literary short story, a feat in elaborated suspense with a sharp climax, the whole a product of rhetoric as much as literature, was not his favorite form, probably because he found a better medium for his genius, the nostalgic, highly personalized biography. That made his fame. And yet if we take the whole American tradition, and not just its most "literary" part, Mark is the type product of a short-narrative school. He is our greatest anecdotist. However, the yarn, the tall tale, the quips and quiddities of the anecdote, belong to a different area of writing from the circular frame with its picture of life included that James praised. It lies in the border between folklore and literature, and is usually the source of literature (and of wisdom), rather than the thing itself. As anecdotist Twain belongs with *Uncle Remus* rather than in the line of Hawthorne and Poe.

And yet, what anthology of American short stories is complete without "The Man That Corrupted Hadleyburg" (1899), without (to my taste) "Captain Stormfield's Visit to Heaven" (published 1907), without (more doubtfully) "The £1,000,000 Banknote" (1893). This writer *could* do almost anything except poetry or a sustained novel of manners. The conditions, however, had to be right. Anyone clever enough could have written "The £1,000,000 Banknote," which is the best story I know on credit, though otherwise mediocre enough. The other two stories mentioned above were conditioned by strong personal factors in Mark himself, and can wait for the next chapter.

2. THE MAN WRITING

Henry James in no way took to the short or shortish story, which I have called the American Way, just because he could sell it more easily than a novel. With him it was a central effort, the result of a mind congenitally elaborative and his conditions for writing. It has been said and justly that no one can understand the social history of America without constantly remembering that after the pre-history of the Republic we became a race of races, intensely mobile, fluid as to classes, anarchic in our freedoms. We had, as James constantly repeats in his Turn Eastward fashion, no unified traditions, no continuity of culture, no general continuity even of residence. He oversimplifies in his comparisons with Europe, yet in contrast with the Old

World tradition this was true enough. And our history explains
why the anecdote, but still more the short story, which is a snap-
shot, a circular frame, an impression, limited in time and space,
has been so effective in our literature. It has indeed been surprisingly effective, for no one can doubt that the short-story
snapshots of these diversely descended Americans give a convincing picture of a new and highly individual race. These
Americans may be too fluid, too mobile to analyze, as peoples
in old societies can be analyzed to the roots of social experience, yet they vividly impress the onlooker by their originality
and so make good short stories.

Henry found the native aptitude for quick effects from a
society rapidly changing of the greatest value when he became
an international specialist, where different cultures came into
brief but dramatic contrast. He was handicapped, however,
from the beginning. He *could not* write short (he could not
talk short). His genius was expansive, analytical. He never
wrote an anecdote, except in his Notebooks where he deposited
them, like a squirrel burying acorns. He could not write a
really short story (except once or twice). He could not write a
nouvelle, without vast and often successful endeavors of the
genii of inspiration to escape from the bottle. The craftsman's
history of Henry James was of a never relaxing and often failing attempt to "keep it short."

Mr. Leon Edel, one of the most productive of modern writers
on James, and others before him, has chosen Henry's own fantasies to illustrate the man himself. He selects the charming
story "The Private Life," whose idea can be found in James'
Preface. In this Preface James discusses a problem we all recognize, that so many great writers present a public life which
seems to have little relation to the private life that lives only in
their books. Browning, whom James knew well in his later years,
serves as one of his studies for this story. Clare Vawdrey, a
great literary figure, has alternate personalities, one of which

(as he suggests was true of Browning) is the true Vawdrey, vital
for literature, always retired (as behind a door) writing at a
desk in the dark. He seems to have little relation to the other
Vawdrey known familiarly to all the rest of the party. The dark
shadow writing is surely a symbol of James himself. So he
describes himself in many a letter, a man writing whenever he
can escape from his social life, to write. But I should carry the
parallel with James further, since this obscure and absorbed
figure is evidently wrestling (as all the story implies) with a
never-ending task, whatever his courteous, talkative, sociable
self may be like in society.

James' whole writing life in creative fiction, once the Observer had done his work, was, I suggest, an attempt to control
the long short story of a situation, which last was the form in
which the ideas that caught his imagination settled themselves
in his mind. To keep his story from a damaging compression;
to keep it from expanding under his hands into a long amor-
phous novel like *The Tragic Muse,* or into an expedition
among unfamiliar peoples and theories of living like *The
Princess Casamassima,* this was the job of the man writing.
Only by reading his numerous shortish stories can one see how
often he failed, one way or another, though often brilliantly
succeeding when his material came from his deep consciousness
where suggestion could do much of the work of analysis; how
often he failed (according to his high standards) by dry digest-
ing, or by an escape into what was neither sharp as a short story
nor ample as a novel. It is probable that the three writers of the
nineteenth century who worked hardest per day in their fruitful periods were Balzac, Twain, and James. Twain's almost
desperate reason will be discussed later. James, with a far
better understanding than Twain of what he had to do, may
have worked fewer hours, but his wrestle for a "form" (how
often he says it) was certainly as arduous. And particularly because this "form" was incredibly difficult for a critical mind,

incurably desirous to squeeze the last articulate drop out of the English language. His *nouvelles* (and the *nouvelle was* his favorite form) he said once were "space-hungry." And yet if one fed them too much, there would be another two-volume and probably unsuccessful novel, too little and he botched the job! The dark figure hesitated, and worked on.

3. THE SHORTER STORIES

Henry James' "front" in the years between the late eighties and the turn of the century, when he gave so much of his time to short or shorter stories, is well known, and with some still in vivid memory. By the late nineties, the man writing had become the man dictating, since as much as he hated the typewriter, his stiffening hand could be used for no more than his more intimate correspondence. Away from home he was still the man of meticulous and sociable courtesy to all and sundry, a good listener, a talker in his hesitant fashion in lengthy monologues, never visibly bored or irritable, even when the pull back toward his desk could hardly be resisted. I was fortunate enough to know his amanuensis in the early part of the new century, Miss Theodora Bosanquet, and shall not forget her descriptions of his pacing to and fro, dictating a mass of what was a description of the work which engaged him, longer by far than the telling of the story itself that succeeded when he had digested his own experimental approaches. This was his private life. The slow-spoken, yet voluble Henry, questioning his lady friends, who delighted in his warm curiosity, responding in such circles as Edith Wharton describes in *A Backward Glance* with excitement to any discussion of art or technique, was the familiar public figure, now marked by fame, if not success. A James loving luxury but often appalled by it, dependent upon comfort and privacy, the shadowy man at his desk was still more real in his emotions than the literary figure — and remained so at least until the great breakup of his world in 1914. His task was the fabled hag riding invisible on the shoulders of the social man.

With some of his shorter fictions it is more possible than in his novels to sit at the other side of the darkened desk (or beside his amanuensis) and with the aid of his recorded comments see the memories, the inventions, the difficulties, and the consistent purpose of this author at work. I choose for an example, a long short story, *The Reverberator* of 1888, little read though worth reading. The memory this time was his own of "a grand old city of the south of Europe," into whose pleasant society came a pretty, confident American girl, well introduced and "taken to twenty social bosoms." Intensely attractive, she was utterly unaware of the vital difference between her own country, free to the edge of vulgarity, and the "consciously critical retreats" of an old society. Unhappily she is an amateur journalist who writes up her new friends in a sensational American paper called *The Reverberator*. For them it was enough to be written about at all to spread consternation. The story is too light for a novel, too slender for even a short story. But James' invention quickly takes care of that. What happened to the girl was trivial. Her importance was in her type — one of those innocent Americans for whom Europe was a "vast painted and holiday-toy," for whom there was no responsibility except to describe it for those at home. Such Americans were passionless pilgrims unaware of the depths of experience through which they trod so lightly. And Henry remembers (though he does not say so) an earlier experiment with a like situation, the novel *The American,* in which an honest and admirable compatriot entangled himself so deeply in a society he did not understand that the young James had been forced

to invent a melodramatic badness among his enemies in order
to work out the story. Why not in *The Reverberator* try it
again with *good* people in this Old World society where the
"innocent" is to flutter like a web-caught butterfly? He does
so, this shadowy worker, with the speedy result, later described
in his Preface. The story has now become "space-hungry." It
is already too long for the six or seven thousand words, which is
all, as he wrote to Howells in 1901, that he is allowed by his
magazine people in England. It begins to spill over into a
nouvelle, threatens to become a novel. His "good people" are
too insignificant for that, the situation not importantly dramatic
for such length. How then to save it, and escape the waste of
vast labor on an elaboration? But what, says the man working,
is the story? It is precisely the "comparative *state of innocence
of the spirit of my countryfolk.*" That is the coiled spring
which released makes the story go, and in brief space. To put
it in his own subtle language, "Conscious of so few things in
the world, these unprecedented creatures [the travelling Ameri-
cans] . . . were least of all conscious of deficiencies and dangers;
so that, the grace of youth and innocence and freshness aiding,
their negatives were converted and became in certain relations
lively positives and values. I might give a considerable list of
those of my fictions, longer and shorter, in which this curious
conversion is noted." This "left me with all I could manage
on my hands." No writer, no critic, will dispute this statement.
Here is the task of the man writing — to find a "form" which
will enable him to compose without disaster from either the
Scylla of compression or the Charybdis of length.

Sometimes the labor was easier, if one can judge by the off-
hand way of which he speaks of a story which has now become
famous. If it was easier, it must have been because the tale he
had to tell was what the colloquial today calls a "natural" —
a story naturally limited in time and space where a sharp suspense resolves into a climax that needs no explanation beyond

the effect on the reader. This happened — one can guess — when some dream of his sensitive youth rose from his subconscious to give intensity to an anecdote told him by a friend. For this his formula of accretion by which a situation gained in significance was well suited, and the need to concentrate upon an impression which must be vividly felt, kept him from elaboration. The Archbishop of Canterbury tells him as they sit talking by the fire a half-remembered ghostly tale of two children corrupted by the spirits of vicious servants. In the story which James made of this anecdote in 1898, the horror is not in the children, nor indeed in the ghostly visitors who remain always in the margin of possible hallucinations. It is in the mind of the frightened but courageous governess, who saves one child but loses the other. It is in the turn of the screw of terror which the reader experiences with her which makes the effect as sharp as one of Poe's parallel stories. There is a past at which we are only permitted to guess, and a possible future for the governess with the children's neurotic uncle which James nips off like a branch from a plant in order to secure a brilliant flowering. This, says James in comment, is the way to write a ghost story, and his success with this one, which has extended to the drama made from it, shows how right he was.

He invents another story, "Louisa Pallant" which carries his favorite theme of the aware and the unaware in dramatic contrast. This situation was not space-hungry, and too quick in its action to drag him into a novel. It happened at Homburg where vagrant Americans pass and meet like ships in a channel. There is a beautiful American girl with a pure and candid smile, and a battered and worldly mother who proves to be a one-time predatory sweetheart of the observing bachelor who tells the story. And here they are, the mother and daughter, wandering in Europe on next to nothing a year, an ancient pirate craft with a gilded transport in tow, looking for a sale — and the Observer's rich and innocent nephew just coming over the horizon for his first splash in Europe. It is not the teller of the tale, but Mrs. Pallant who is aware of the situation. She has paid the price of worldliness, and now her moral life has improved while her lovely daughter, Linda, has degenerated. She has taught her daughter to be worldly. "I'm horrified at my work. . . . I say I'm horrified because she is horrible." So Mrs. Pallant saves the innocent nephew from the treacherous beauty of Linda as reparation for her own past. Here the man writing easily steered between brevity and elaboration.

I must not fall into Henry's cherished vice of expansion. These accounts of his short stories, which would have made him notable in our literature even if he had written no novels, are an illustration rather than an analysis. But even the illustration is incomplete without an instance where the writer was confused by the pull of his theme for more space, and has to sacrifice his climax because there was not room enough to prepare for it, or to allow it the human tragedy that cries for expansion at the end.

James was told a story of Jane Clairmont, half-sister of Mary Godwin, Shelley's second wife, and the mother of Byron's daughter Allegra, who was living on at a great age in Florence with a younger female relative. A Boston devotee of Shelley, sure that she had documents from the past, took lodgings with her, hoping that he might become the residuary by purchase. James' imagination took fire. For Florence he substituted Venice with which his memory was charged, for Shelley an invented American man-of-letters, for the devotee of Shelley, an editor with an ambition to complete the record of the dead American genius. It is he who takes rooms in the old palace to be near Juliana, the new name for Jane Clairmont, and he nearly succeeds. The price of the manuscripts is to be marriage to the companion, now Juliana's niece, and not young. The plot fails. The proposed marriage is seen to have contemptible motives, the papers are burnt. Four things Henry proposed to accomplish in "The Aspern Papers." He wished to recreate a contemporary Venice of back canals and mouldered little palaces that tourists did not know, and succeeded so well that his little book is a good guide to Venice. He delighted also in the opportunity Juliana offered to come close to a "palpable" imaginable past where her original had lived and was now the last of a famous coterie. And in the complicated intrigue by which the journalist hoped to gain his ends, he had a story to tell which required skill. This was enough to engage all the energies of the man writing, but what happened was what he might have expected but did not. Tina, the credulous niece, fascinated by the guileful stranger, and under the powerful domination of her aunt, who will sacrifice her letters to give the girl a future, becomes the heroine of the story. Her tragedy, not the loss of the papers, is, or should be, its climax. Alas, James had not so cast her. She is not a dramatic, scarcely a very human figure, certainly in her flurried emotions she lacked the fiber of a heroine. The man writing may have realized this; certainly he must have known that only another fifty pages of narrative would have done justice to the emergence of a new center for the story. That meant a slide toward the novel which he could not afford, and he left this most attractive story with a weak ending. He had tried to do too much, even for a long short story. The "visitable past" was realized, and so was Venice, and so was the drama of the papers, but the final emotional climax of the narrative was compressed into a sketch, where Tina, who had become a figure of great interest, was left unrealized.

Yet the shadowy private life of James was not all hard work in the attempt to find a "form" for his too fruitful invention. Many of his stories came easily, with a humor less emphatic than Twain's, but also less forced. American journalists were

always comic figures to Henry. Their impudent poking of
fingers into the most delicate or complex of situations seemed
to him to call for satire or irony, according to the moral
worth. They were living insults to the noble art of literature,
like monkeys trying to imitate men. What he would have made
of a press photographer is beyond my imagination! Retired
American businessmen adrift in Europe were also comic
figures, though often with a hint of tragedy. They stroll in a
wondering boredom while their wives excitedly shop. Mark
did them too, but with a full understanding which Henry
lacked of what they had done and been at home. But Henry
knew what was the matter with them. They were Innocents,
wise as to practical affairs, naïve except as to the simplest of
human relations, innocent in any society not organized by the
most elementary of moral codes. They were kind, and Edward
Sackville, an English critic, in his *Inclinations,* thinks that
James shows not his tolerant humor but the breakdown of his
own moral judgment when he depicts such a millionaire as
Adam Verver in *The Golden Bowl* as being tenderhearted,
innocent, and trusting in his old age. But this is simply to mis-
understand the American capitalist type, as James did not.
Lewis Galantière, in a recent essay, has explained the difference
between the typical European amasser of great wealth, who has
always been essentially a miser, and that American phenomenon,
so common, the rich philanthropist, who, however "hard-
boiled" in his money-making, turns enlightened philanthropist
at the end. He is innocent in Henry's sense of the ideas of a
society which cannot conceive of this lack of self-aggrandize-
ment. Such softening, not of the brains but the heart, has
Henry's sympathy. The worn-out men, whose occupations are
gone, looking with vacant eyes at a culture whose origin they
do not understand, and whose activities seem to them trivial if
not immoral, or collecting its relics, are to him humor of a

deep and revealing kind. They are like bees who have blundered into a parquette of artificial flowers. The most humorous, if not the most deeply studied, of these men and women are in James' shorter stories.

Again, it is in the short story or the *nouvelle* that James came nearest to at least symbolic autobiography. In the novels he is always the Observer. Here he can take his own private life and dramatize it as a self-knower, who this time is the man aware of himself. Among those short or shorter stories, "The Figure in the Carpet" and "The Death of the Lion" are often cited as contributions to biography. What caused the death of the literary lion in the latter was simply too much adulation for the wrong reasons and in the wrong way. There were too many visits at country houses, too many self-seeking disciples. James was vulnerable here, and his protests are a little on the defensive, but wrathful when the "lion" is cornered, kept from his work, and driven to despair. All this comes out best in "The Figure in the Carpet," in which some rather absurd hangers-on of greatness try to find the hidden pattern of a novelist's work. The secret pattern, the novelist says cryptically, is "the organ of life," and his explanation is cryptic also. He complains that their curiosity is badly directed, should concern itself with spirit and form, and that marriage and love may help these chatterers to understand him. May it not be true that in this much discussed story James is uttering a personal complaint which I believe has not been much heeded? His own practice, as he says elsewhere more than once, was an unwrapping fold by fold of a situation until an inner intensity of emotion has been bared. The technique of unwrapping is what he himself talks most about in his Prefaces, but who can doubt that the inner core of passion must have meant most to him — as for example when in *The Portrait of a Lady,* Ralph Touchett bares his heart. That is the organ of life — even for the most obsessed technician of his day. And James would have more readers if attention were more often drawn to this inner pattern of his greatest novels and stories.

This is notably true of one of the most successful short stories he ever wrote, "The Beast in the Jungle." This is the narrative of the almost insane egotism of a man persuaded that some terrible unknown fate hangs over him, and who finds a loving heart to give him sympathy. It has that emotion which Henry says in a note to another superb story "The Altar of the Dead," can alone justify such jeweler's work, for in "The Beast in the Jungle" there are only a few external facts of setting, and the story is told almost entirely by figures. James himself, so far as we know, had missed passion for women, but by no such simple cause as egotism. Here is an old tragedy of misunderstanding reduced to an Egyptian simplicity, with a reversal quietly inevitable at the end. For we learn that the beast that did spring at the hero was only his selfish fear striking down at last the woman who had always loved him.

It would seem to be probable that, because James was born and early bred in an American society, he was accustomed, like many of his literary countrymen, to carry from experience sharp impressions which had more depth than length and breadth in space or time. This was natural, as has been said, in a society so little homogeneous, so relatively unstratified. This habit of viewing by impression and effect was a godsend when he became an expatriate. Throughout his writing career he knew instinctively neither the long past of Europe nor the active present of America. His strongest impressions were naturally of dramatic contrasts between national types and national cultures among the reasonably educated and well-to-do like himself. In the novels it was the contrasts between the mores of America and of Europe, especially England, that gave him his best drama, with the American expatriate as a symbol of a third hybrid civilization. But the short story and particularly the *nouvelle* gave him his best instrument, since there his inevitable lack of familiarity with any one nation as a whole was not a handicap. I find some lack of homely blood in the most carefully analyzed of his English characters. They are superb surfaces, but not vivid personalities. It is hard to remember them. This makes far less difference in a short story than in a long novel. The reader of James may instantly reply, "But Brooksmith, the perfect butler spoiled by good company, a name with a reputation worthy of Dickens, and as indigenous to England as Mr. Pickwick." To which I answer that the effect of that admirable story is not of Brooksmith, who, on his retirement, proves himself to be a cipher, but of the richness of English manners as James, a lover of the visible past, encountered them in his day, the good talk, the most supple and muscular, if not the most brilliant, in the world, which Brooksmith reflects like a deep mirror — talk with which James was as familiar as with his own thoughts.

4. THE AMERICAN WAY

Twain also had his difficulties with writing *nouvelles* as we have seen in *Pudd'nhead Wilson*, where a plot that deals with a social discrimination that can make the moral immoral, and vice versa, gets tangled with a study of the unpopularity of wisdom. Yet he had the natural, fluent, and often shameless talent of the professional yarner, one of the oldest of the professions. Anything for a laugh, anything for a sensation, which is quite different from what James called an impression or an effect. His anecdotes shine through his loosely woven travel books like brilliant pebbles in a stream. He dealt with surfaces. The Surface, Henry called it often, saying that the Surface should tell all. And indeed Mark's surface description does tell all that is needed since he can create personalities and so convey his imagination. That was hard for Henry who had to unwrap his figures before you could understand their full significance — and then there was always the danger of remembering the significance and forgetting the person. He had to work harder than Mark or, rather, work more intelligently. His *level* of achievement is much higher for just that reason. And it is especially well represented in the short story.

Chapter XIII

DECLINE AND FALL: MARK TWAIN

IN USING Gibbon's famous title I am giving to it a meaning much more limited than the crash of a civilization. It is the decline and fall of Mark Twain's creative power which is interesting for this book. His business failure was only a harsh incentive to his industrious pen, the death of his beloved Susy was a disaster from which emotionally he never recovered; but the last ten years of his life, to 1910, were triumphant, if by triumph one means world-wide acclaim and a long-sought-for financial security. Yet I agree with Mr. DeVoto that the *Yankee* in 1889 was the last display of his creative powers in full strength, adding that *Pudd'nhead Wilson* in 1894 and *Joan of Arc* in 1896 were steps in the decline of one of the most characteristic of geniuses, while the brilliant *The Mysterious Stranger* left unpublished in probably 1905 gives some explanation of his fall. And yet these last three books are only a sparse salvage from a mass of writing, finished and unfinished, which belongs to this period. Something happened to Mark Twain in later middle age more serious for the creative writer than his bankruptcy or the death of a beloved daughter.

2. THE DREAM GIRL

Mark Twain had a recurrent dream which came to him at intervals of about two years from 1854 when he was nineteen to about 1898 when he finally described it in writing. It came

239

in brief moments of sleep, and even in daytime when he was
crossing a street, where the actual duration could have been
only a few seconds. It was a serial, like a soap opera, and while
the place differed, the girl was always the same. He had a
dream sweetheart. She was always fifteen, he was always nineteen. Their minds and their wills always ran together. They
were intimate, they kissed and caressed, but there was nothing
like the passion of adult love between them. They saw strange
sights and places, more vivid to Mark than the reality of such
experiences. And once she was killed by a chance arrow, and
he suffered as he did later after Susy's death. She was not only
lovely in his eyes, she felt instinctively all that he wanted, and
was utterly content with what he was. She was wise and witty.
The current of her life ran always with his, never against it,
never deflecting it.

It is not necessary to call in Freud to explain this dream. "My
Platonic Sweetheart," 1912 (Paine's title, I suspect, not Mark's)
is clearly a persistent vision of the kind of woman Mark's
imagination required, even though in the dreams she never
got beyond early youth. She is Betty Thatcher of *Tom Sawyer*,
a little older. She is also in *Joan of Arc* when his aging imagination built up from secondary sources a biography of an utterly
unselfish, utterly good, and also a shrewd and courageous
woman. She is not, of course, Roxy, the only completely real
woman in his books. She is not Olivia, whom he loved passionately and deeply respected, for Olivia's currents from the beginning ran sometimes against but more often deflecting here and
there his own.

There is a close parallel, however, between the dream girl of
Mark Twain and the dream world of Mark Twain in his youth.
The environment of the Mississippi had its dark colorings of
slavery, rascality, and violence like the arrow which killed his
sweetheart, but its core, so he passionately believed, was goodness — Aunt Polly's goodness, the goodness of Jim the slave.

Its life ran with his, and he could turn its faults into a deep and humorous sympathy, even if their lack of reason tormented poor Huck Finn. But by the time of *Pudd'nhead Wilson* these colorings had become almost too dark for sympathy. He took refuge in burlesque, and by 1905 he was making his Mysterious Stranger say to the boy who was his friend that there was only one weapon left against the organized self-deception of the miserable human race — laughter. When Mark's dream girl and the dream world disappeared at last in an adult world of disillusion, he remained a jester, an "evoker of the horse-laugh," but like the human race, as the mysterious visitor described it, he had no longer the "sense and courage" to face the "high-grade comicalities" of a world that under the pretense of being good seemed to do nothing but evil.

Now it must be remembered that the hideous happenings in the world and the human race with which Satan's nephew, the Mysterious Visitor, frightened the boys he chose to befriend, were dreams; and the new blackness for Mark's world was also a dream — a bad but not necessarily an untrue one — for Mark. There was very little real personal experience in it, though much in the good dream world of youthful life on the Mississippi. He had sunk deep in personal troubles and financial disaster, but not too deep for recovery. This bad dream, which seems to have sapped his creative faculties, was clearly psychological.

His long adolescence was coming to an end. When he looks back into his memories for another woman as a heroine, he gives us Roxy — a combination of fury and devotion, of easy wickedness and unbreakable strength, an aspect of Negro (and feminine) experience which he had the power but not the will to go on with. So he turns from his own mind to history, and chooses an ideal of womanhood made of salt and wisdom, and undeflatable goodness and bravery able to combat a world

which Mark now thinks has always been mean and treacherous.
Joan of Arc becomes his heroine, and while he can no longer
use his own boy's memory where his genius lay, he takes a
youth to be her secretary and devoted friend, who sees her and
all she does through a youth's eyes. Joan is his last argument
against pessimism.

His *Joan of Arc* is a magnificent piece of well organized
writing, not original except for Mark's fervor for the Maid, but
excellent in the trial where the emphasis is all upon her invio-
lable code of ethics (the Voices), and upon the intelligent
shrewdness of her answers, where she could not have been more
skillful if she had been a criminal lawyer on trial for his own
life. This is authentic history of course, but Mark felt its significance for personality more than have his rival historians.
There is an almost desperate emphasis upon the power of such
good to resist the vilest evil. Otherwise the book makes no contribution to history. He does not understand, as Anatole France
writing later did so well, the acute dilemma of the Church,
whose very existence was imperiled if it admitted divine inspiration except in a saint. The politics, the people, are all black
or white. It is in no sense a novel, but rather a testimony and
a tribute. It is Mark rewriting history because he feels he no
longer has a subject that he can write out of his own imagination into a work of creative art.

3. MARK FEARS THE LOSS
OF HIS POPULARITY

It would have been more accurate to say that he could not write
a *popular* work out of his creative imagination — or so at least he
thought and may have been right. Henry James, a sensitive man

but far less sensitive internally than the wild jackass of the lecture platform, destroyed, rewrote, revised, but he tried to publish everything he finished except for some plays. And this although he prophesied that several of his novels would be failures — and they were. But Mark, in this new and later mood, left unfinished or unpublished many manuscripts not only because some of them were weak, but also because others were or threatened to be too strong. To break down in the midst of a story was his characteristic in this period — and that I shall take up later. But of the most promising of these later manuscripts which were finished, he seems to have been afraid. Like a moving-picture star he was morbidly afraid of failure. He was in no great danger of shocking his public by being "too coarse," or "too rough" — Olivia could take care of that. But to shock them morally, to disturb the religious-ethical code of America — the old-time religion in which he grew up with daily doses from his mother — was, to put it mildly, incompatible with popularity. Even the brilliant Ingersoll had to fight his way. The audience that Twain had gathered he was sure would not stand it — not for a single book.

And it is clear from numerous and often quoted references in later life that if he were to write from his heart, this was the kind of book he would have written — a book shocking in its ideas, not in any sense in its sexual morality. In that direction — in spite of the bawdy *1601*, privately circulated and offending none of its readers — he was not drawn.

One story which carried him close to the tabus which protected the religious mythology of the nineteenth century, he did write and it was among his best. He wrote it in about 1868, and did not dare (or he was not allowed) to publish it until forty years later. Heaven, even in my youthful time, was as concrete in the imagination as the massed towers of New York for untraveled barbarians today. The biblical imagery had been stylized into symbols of which the crystal sea, the sapphire thrones, the golden harp, the robes of white, were so far from reality as to escape criticism. It was not necessary, as one passed childhood, to accept this Heaven literally, but in advance of further revelation it was unnecessary and unwise to question its substantial truth. This was the biblical version of Heaven, and one part of the Good Book was as sanctified as any other. Mark was happily inspired and consciously daring when he first wrote "Captain Stormfield's Visit to Heaven."

Toward this Heaven, the old navigator, thirty years dead and getting restless, sailed at about a million miles a minute, caught up with a comet and would have beat her if the captain had not been carrying a cargo of brimstone for Hell, came to the fiery walls of Heaven (he was sure they were Hell), and began his search for friends from his planet which was so small that they called it the Wart. It is all good innocent fun, too funny to be offensive — the rather stuffy old prophets and patriarchs, the magnificent if stupid angels, the billions of souls with nothing to do but chant (and most could not sing), all in contrast with the busy, hopeful, hazardous America the Captain had left behind him. If Mark lets the satire peep out of the picture, it is only when the Captain discovers that Heaven is no republic but a totalitarian state, all classes and hierarchies with active race prejudice and an irresponsible dictator at the head. Even so he suppressed it for forty years.

4. MARK SPEAKS OUT—PRIVATELY

But fear of a loss of popularity was scarcely his reason for printing privately a selection of dialogues called *What Is Man?* in 1906, and allowing it to be reviewed. It was a deterministic

argument intended to prove that man was responsible neither
for his seeming goodness nor for his evident evil — not really
responsible for his acts at all. If anyone was to blame it was
God. But this attack was too long delayed to disturb his regular
readers. It was old stuff to everyone — if they read it, and few
did. The really brilliant bits of case history were not enough
to float the stale thesis.

The Mysterious Stranger, dating from 1904 or 1905, according to DeVoto who has examined the variant manuscripts,
is in quite a different category. Paine published it in 1922,
after Twain's death in 1910. This bitter fantasy must be regarded as one of Twain's major works, although it lacks that
power over creative personality which most of all distinguishes
his greatest books.

In the still unpublished manuscripts of these last years,
Twain becomes almost inarticulate in the attempt to express
by figures and symbols the neurotic morbidity which had un-
balanced what Santayana might have called his "animal faith."
He could not even finish what he had to say. Yet when he drew
his evidence not from his own experience but from history at
one remove, he could be beautifully articulate. *The Mysterious
Stranger* is an eloquent, smooth-flowing picture of human history, digested and illustrated by magic for the naïve minds of
three boys. It is highly significant that for this last effort of his
genius, he returned to youth and the youthful mind to record
a philosophy of which in his own youth he would have been
incapable.

The three boys of whom one tells the story of what happened
in sixteenth-century Eseldorf are Tom and Huck on their best
behavior. But such terrible things are to be seen by them that
it was safer to put them far in the past. The town itself is
donkey town in fact where all the inhabitants are either good
fools or bad fools, or their victims. It strongly resembles

Pudd'nhead Wilson's Mississippi town, but the camouflage of
the late Middle Ages makes it easy to introduce more cruelty,
more prejudice, more of the fantastic than would have been
probable on the Mississippi, and the blasphemies Mark proposes will be easier to get away with if he ever decides to publish. The Mysterious Stranger himself is such a dark angel as
Milton conceived of in *Paradise Lost,* who comes as a youth
whose very presence makes experience more lively and whose
charm captures at sight even without the aid of his casual
miracles. For he is Satan's nephew whose purpose on earth, it
would seem, is to bring happiness even if he does not leave it
behind. He is like the Greek gods who had never experienced
morality, and were free in any way to win the worship of mankind. So it seems, but actually he is a seducer of faith, the faith
of love and loyalty in a boyhood such as Mark's — that boyhood which was always at the heart of his dreams, where his
imagination had been most beautifully stirred.

We have to go back to Tom and Becky in the cave, or to
Huck playing the part of a little girl, to find a more enchanting
episode than the little men made of clay by the Stranger for the
boys, who come to life and build a towering toy castle swarming
over it as they work, until two fall to quarreling. Then the
idyll breaks. The angel squashes them like bugs, for like ants
or flies he makes no distinction between good and evil. Only
slowly do Mark's boys realize that their friend can be amused
by mortals but is incapable of love. So within the shimmering
net of the story Mark's thesis develops, which is that man's sole
distinction is the knowledge of good and evil — which has
enabled him prevailingly to choose the evil deed! And the
boys, transported by more magic, are allowed to see in the wide
world, and to learn in their own fates, how inescapable is the
determined wickedness of the universe for which God must be
responsible. Yet for Mark there is an escape from self-torture

in Satan's final devastating statement, "There is no God, no universe, no human race, no earthly life, no heaven, no hell. It is all a dream — a grotesque and foolish dream. Nothing exists but you and you are but a *thought* — a vagrant thought, a useless thought, a homeless thought, wandering forlorn among the empty eternities!" The humorist of the Mississippi Valley comes to the same final conclusion as Prospero:

> *These cloud-clapp'd towers, the gorgeous palaces,*
> *The solemn temples, the great globe itself,*
> *Yea, all which it inherit, shall dissolve. . . .*
> *We are such stuff as dreams are made on. . . .*

And both magicians break their wands. Although not, it should be noted, until both had left behind them examples in their creative work of pure love and successful virtue.

Mark had forgotten that once before he had written an attack upon depravity and the uselessness of man as revealed in history. The King and the Duke in Huck's raft and ashore are brief epitomes of such history as the Mysterious Stranger taught it to the boys at Eseldorf. These two scamps are parodies of privilege and prejudice, of greed, cruelty, and the stupid conventions from which so much misery has flowed. Yet here Mark attacked with the only human weapon which Satan's nephew respects — laughter. His creative, satiric laughter is more effective than his somewhat adolescent metaphysics.

It was apparently too late with Mark by the nineteen-hundreds for this kind of laughter. Once again, in 1909, he let himself go, in an unpublished manuscript, a transcript of which I owe to Mr. DeVoto. In a series of letters written from the deplorable earth which God had created, Satan himself, still the great archangel, though temporarily banished for talking too much, sends words of his discoveries to his fellow archangels. These letters, unfinished, but to be edited in a popular

edition for circulation in Heaven, are the most violent of all
Twain's writing. There is burning sarcasm in them, but no
possible room for laughter. They are all unrestrained wrath,
against that God which the old-fashioned biblical religion had
led men to create, and so make themselves cruel, stupid, and
vile in his image. The horrors and absurdities Satan finds on
earth almost choke his expression. Of these absurdities he finds
the worst to be, the suppression, hypocrisy, stupidity which
man since the Garden of Eden has inflicted on the rich gift
which, possessed as we possess it, makes all other possessions
trivial, sexual intercourse. These benighted worldlings have
even denied that it exists in Heaven. Women are the chief victims of these tabus, and he proceeds to prove it by an elaborate
analysis of biological function which, if Olivia had been alive
to read it, would have had effects on that admirable woman
which I cannot dare to try to imagine.

Now this often brilliant, sometimes merely vituperative
manuscript is a new and original Western version of such ideas
and philosophy as Voltaire and Anatole France expounded
less crudely, and written as Mark doubtless would have liked to
present them for the confusion of some Presbyterian confer-
ence. It is too violent, too indiscriminating to have literary
value. There is not much humor in it. And its satire too
much resembles a drunk in a barroom throwing bottles at the
crowd.

Psychologically it is important. If such violence, such ideas
as these had been raging beneath the public life of the great
humorist, it becomes more obvious why in the creation of
personality he could satisfy himself only with youth, and highly
probable that we have here outbursts which must have been
long familiar to his friends, and may well, according to a
familiar psychological principle, have acted as an outlet for his
neuroticism which relieved the pressures of adult disillusion

while he was at work upon his idylls of youthful biography. It may help to explain also the wild breakdown into parodies and burlesques of a great artist who seems to have been unable even to finish the majority of his later works — which in bulk apparently almost equal his published books.

5. WHAT WAS WRONG?

Something was wrong with Mark, and it is not enough to say that his shift from a confident optimism to bitter cynicism merely reflects a changed mood in his overconfident country. It is true that, superficially, he was as representative of that country as a tough, sweet maple tree whose sap flows from cold nights and sunny days, and whose roots are deep in the soil. Yet his responses are too violent to be satisfactorily explained by external history. What reversed his faith in human nature? What caused his still overflowing energy to beat and break against a wall when he tried to create? Why did his old vein of tender boyish imagination lead only to baleful fire and ashes? And why, in those remarkable frustrated fantasies which DeVoto in his *Mark Twain at Work* has published from his unfinished manuscripts, does the inner life depicted there explode into diatribe, or come near to insanity?

He had undoubtedly shifted with his times from the extravagant optimism of Walt Whitman and his own Colonel Sellers and Manifest Destiny to the social criticism of the eighties and nineties and the Henry and Brooks Adamses who, like Henry James, believed that America, having overrun a continent, had failed to make a civilization. Thoughtful Americans by the latter decades of the century had come to believe that the Amer-

ican dream of a brotherhood of equality had been sold in the
market place and was indeed only a dream. Yet Walt Whitman
(another printer's apprentice and journalist) who experienced
at firsthand the debauching of the democratic processes, died
in these same nineties still confident of the democratic pro-
gram, still confident of the ultimate victory of a democracy
based on faith in the common man. And Mark himself was too
comfortably at home in the market place to be philosophical
about its effects. He did not give up speculating because he
thought it was wrong for the business of America to be business, but because he was a bad speculator and found someone
wiser than himself to handle his profits for him. More than a
change from a land of hope to a land (for the sensitive few)
of disillusion is needed to explain the morbid pessimists of
genius who have from time to time since the mid-century ap-
peared in our literature. Mark, an *émigré* from optimism, in
his last important book is as bitter as Swift, without the great
Dean's evident reasons for cynicism.

Something ailed Mark himself, and was more important than
anything in current history. He had never been much concerned with current history. Looked at it, yes, the stupidities
of Congress, the venalities of politicians, at stupidity anywhere.
But when his imagination was warm he had always rejected the
contemporary and gone back to the past, his own past, or much
earlier centuries. He seems to have had from youth a horrid
fascination, like a boy's for gangster pictures, for the deprav-
ities of early history. Suetonius was his bedside book, and he
reveled in his debauched tyrants who stood for civilization in
their day. See him in *The Innocents Abroad,* telling horror
stories or examples of injustice to man at each old tomb or
monument, explaining to his fellow Innocents the cruelty of
man to man. But a faculty of self-protection kept all this from
youth and his beloved country while his adolescence lasted. We

were tough, but at least we were humanitarians at heart. It was in fact a boy's version of history that he made for himself while he expanded his idylls of the river and his adventures in the Middle Ages. Such history was uncomplicated by too much knowledge, which may have helped him in his youth from passing a judgment on humanity that has turned many an artist into a preacher. But when the creative memories of this youth dimmed and dulled, a brooding over a human race which simply did not, and would not, behave like a boy's dream but was stupid when it was not vicious, mean in its pretentions, hopeless in its future, captured a mind which under its gay fictions must have been sensitive to disillusion from the start. Mark grew up in a young civilization, and stayed young himself when that society about him was becoming adult. Only the vivid boy in him enabled him to carry on with his nostalgic realism of youthful experience so long. But he was born neurotic, which accounts for the brilliant sensitivity which makes his two finest books masterpieces. Yet in the end neuroticism destroyed him as a creative artist.

6. A NEUROTIC GENIUS

In calling Mark a neurotic genius I am taking the simplest and most indisputable meaning of a term which has been generalized into vagueness. A neurotic is simply a mind of too great sensitivity, too much sensibility as the eighteenth century would have called it. His sensitiveness easily escapes controls. Hamlet of course was a neurotic of genius, and Horatio's chastening of his excesses is the best example I know of intellectual neuroticism. "Alas," Hamlet says, "poor Yorick! . . . a fellow of infinite jest, of most excellent fancy" — whose flashes of merriment were wont to set the table in a roar. And now only a stinking skull — "To what base uses we may return, Horatio." And Horatio replies, " 'Twere to consider too curiously, to consider so."

A certain neuroticism, of course, is invaluable, perhaps indispensable to a writer, and in calling Twain a neurotic we are comparing him with the curiously long list of great American writers who in the most successful country of the nineteenth century have built triumph as well as some failures upon their morbid excess of sensibility — Hawthorne, Poe, Melville, Thoreau perhaps — and in our day Robinson Jeffers and William Faulkner. Neuroticism becomes dangerous only when it defeats its own ends by an excess which denies the validity of the creative artist's own genius. What had given Mark such vivid delight, and led him to create with such sympathy a boy's pageant of America in its youth, was followed by a disillusion almost to be expected. He considered it "too curiously" in his maturity and this very sensitivity betrayed him.

Even in his creative period of the Hartford-Quarry Farm days, I am told by Dr. Booth of Elmira, who knew him, that he was subject to depressions and wild outbursts against "the human race."

There is another aspect of neuroticism in Twain, which cannot be charged to intensity of happy experience, and is more irrational than a reaction from happiness. When Mark was twenty-two and a pilot on the river, his young brother died of his burns in the explosion of a steamship where Mark had got him a job. This job entailed no more dangers than thousands of travelers risked on the Mississippi, and were such as Mark never counted for himself. His brother's ship had an accident, his did not, that was the extent of his responsibility. But his letter home is of such self-torture and exaggerated remorse as can be interpreted only by saying that if he was not guilty of his brother's death, then he personally must be guilty of something else. And this neuroticism of considering too curiously runs as a guilt complex through his life. If his daughter dies of disease, he personally is guilty. Appearing in his letters, and with special reference to his beloved ones such as Olivia, one can see a coiling spring of remorse and guilt which apparently explains the final relief when after listening to Satan's nephew he decides first that an immoral God is to blame, and finally that all evil and good are no more than a thought.

Perhaps a psychiatrist will find some new explanation for such neuroticism as this. The present efforts of psychiatric critics to find a cause are not persuasive. He did not have an unhappy childhood, nor a brutal father, nor a dominating mother. That his mother jilted the man she said she wanted to marry, and took another (Mark's father) whom she respected but did not love, is scarcely material for a guilt complex. It is only fair to say that Mr. DeVoto's knowledge of psychiatric conditions, which is superior to mine, leads him to differ with me here. He feels that Sam's father exercised some compulsion upon him, especially in regard to women, which marked him for life. But at best this is not proven. The late Dixon Wecter also was without a final solution. If some secret sin was hidden in his past more serious than "cussing" and the kind of wild oats cultivated in mining camps, it had plenty of opportunities to reveal itself when Mark asked for an exposure of his sins and vices in his attempt to win Olivia honestly. His earlier life as a roving reporter was about as private as a traffic policeman's, and in any case Mark was never one to hide his light under a bushel, even if it were a red one. As for his family, his father's family and his own, he is always accusing himself of some injustice, some neglect, some failure of care, a concern almost unique in the none too good records of literary genius.

Neither Freud nor the behaviorists seem to help us here. I suggest a possible course in heredity, whatever else may have contributed to the result. The gnawing remorse from beginning to end of his personal confessions may be over trivial things, but the revelations of the subconscious in the fantasies published by Mr. DeVoto are not trivial. Indeed for every outburst against the damned human race in his later years you can find somewhere in his personal confessions a *mea culpa*. No, the *results* of this neurotic guilt and excessive sensitivity are easy to point out; the cause is not. Some later psychologists may discover a hitherto undetected paranoia, coming from a conformation of the brain, and pin it on Mark. I prefer to say that Mark's neurotic tendencies (for good as well as ill) were both due to oversensibility, and were congenital. The complex, if that is the right word, was born in him — a tendency like genius or meanness.

7. ''SUCH STUFF AS DREAMS
ARE MADE ON''

A reference to Henry James, and a summary of Mark, useful even if repetitious, may conclude this chapter. James' sensitivity was of course also extra, but it was to places, and especially to the dramatic situations in which complicated people involve themselves. It was not primarily to personalities. These he could understand more intricately than any of his contemporaries; but as with the highly intellectualized novelist today, he lacked that curious interpenetration of self and created character when the sensitivity of the artist transfers his own life to his creature, who becomes, not a study, but a human being realized not merely described. This lack explains the disappointment felt in many of our most skillful modern novels after an intellectual curiosity is satisfied, and the ease with which they have been forgotten except by literary specialists. Henry James by his extraordinary talent could compensate with a parallel but different achievement. He could observe with the scrutiny of genius, the innocent American in Europe, naïve, confident, kind, and generous, deeply moral in a simple code, who in the decaying society of a semi-feudal Europe was frustrated, corrupted, and sterilized — and his power increased with age.

But Mark was an Innocent himself, born in a region and a time when everything, it seemed, could be explained by the future. He had been a boy then and happy, and had only to transfer his boy's sensitiveness to his imagination. When he brought his simple, but how vital, enthusiasm East, he kept his impressions fresh because they were already beyond comparison or competition with current living. They remained true and idyllic so long as he could reconstruct them in terms of a boy's imagination. He had been that boy. He was still a boy at his own creative depth. Even the Boss is still a boy proposing to overthrow superstition and economic slavery with the lightheartedness of a Tom Sawyer. But this feat of nostalgic realism was made possible by a memory so intense in its sensitivity as to threaten reaction. He had made a pattern for self-expression into which the modern world, which he now begins to experience violently, will not fit. It is viable neither for idyll nor for laughter except on the shallow upper levels. Once again he turns to the past, and at second hand this time, depicts a woman whom every evil smites. Yet she keeps her faith. These are the same old evils that he once shrugged off by laughter because he believed that the heart of the world was good. But they are beyond laughter now. And so the boys find it when Satan's nephew begins to speak for adult Mark.

And so one begins to see his vulnerability. The evil of the

world strikes at him personally, as a man, not as a boy. Hitherto it has been struggle and adventure, now it is an assault by history. Pap Finn was a poor-white, but there was still an aura of the epic pioneer about him. Give him his rights and he could still, so he says, get to the top of the New World. But the wretched squatter left behind a half-century later in a lost valley of the Appalachians, living in squalor and decay, has no more hopes, nor dignity. Mark's reaction is very different, but his drop was great. He loses his fortune and most of his wife's, and goes bankrupt. He loses by a brain tumor his beloved Susy. All the intensity of his joy in living turns inward and finds nothing but disillusion. He must be guilty. The Lord giveth, and the Lord taketh away. Blessed be the name of the Lord. He will not accept the third proposition. The Lord is guilty, the human race is guilty for having believed in such a God. But this strikes at the foundations of his faith in life, and what was as serious for his creative powers, the confidence upon which his work was based. His New World faith is shattered, and with it faith in the people of his imagination. He cannot write any longer about the only thing that interested him, human personality in a world fit for it, because he no longer believes in personality. It is a scum of iridescence on a foul pool. By the stern necessity of a man writing who must always write because this is his condition, he drives on. He fails when he imitates his earlier self, succeeds only with trivia, and as his persistent neuroticism deepens, makes almost inarticulate symbolic pictures for himself of the distress of his uncontrolled imagination. Only once again does the artist take control, and then, with a boy as spokesman, he writes *The Mysterious Stranger,* where Tom and Huck grown up, are told that good and evil and happiness and misery are all illusions, the products of a cheating, vagrant thought, and so wiped out of literature.

This, of course, is not the end of the career of the world-famous Mark, the elder statesman of wise epigram, the beloved humorist to whom degrees are given, at whose appearance hats rise with affectionate cheers, a man whose life seemed by his death in 1910 to have summed up the achievement of the American who turned Westward, and created the happiest memories of the American Dream. But it is the end of the biography of a great creative writer.

Chapter XIV

HENRY JAMES: THE CLIMAX

THE DECLINE AND FALL of Mark Twain's creative genius was in his early sixties. Henry James' long depression, and what might be called the wandering of his talent, was in his fifties. By the end of that decade he had recovered, and in three brilliant years from about 1901 through 1904, wrote three of his four finest books. He was eight years younger than Twain and was to live six years longer. For both men, the turn of the century, called then the *fin de siècle* with a significance now beginning to be forgotten, was a period of crisis. As an artist, Henry emerged triumphantly. As an artist, and as a great creative imagination, Mark did not.

In these years both men were living abroad, Henry continuously, Mark for most of the time. Both were, in different ways and degrees, alienated from America, Henry politically, Mark perhaps chiefly by geography and his inner self-centered conflicts. Yet three times in this period did Twain try to carry his imagination back to the Mississippi and his two boys — and with some success. For the children who read the *St. Nicholas* in 1892, he had restored the immortal two with the Negro Jim in *Tom Sawyer Abroad*. The old charm, the old loving humor is almost as good as ever. But the story of a balloon trip part way round the world has little substance except adventure, and what it does have comes from Mark's new role as an amateur metaphysician. His deeper interest now is in the irrationality of the human race. The trio are all Innocents, and it is easy

fooling to make fun out of the surprise of Jim, the most innocent, when Indiana, as they cross it, is not yellow as on the map,
or to tie up Huck's too literal mind with the imaginary line of
the equator and changes in time. Yet the romantic Tom cannot persuade the Negro and the river rat that it is right to
attack "paynims" or other outlanders in order to make them
Christian and civilized. Mark is still the great humorist of
humanitarianism. His magic has gone.

Both men were troubled by the nascent imperialism of the
Spanish War in 1898. For Mark it was disillusion, a decline
into greed, jingoism, and later cruelty, from the American
Dream. James had never believed in the American Dream.
His reaction was disgust. It was the result of the crude vulgar
strength of an uncultured continent turning aggressive and
breeding billionaires and leaving us the jingo Theodore Roosevelt crowned as heir apparent, and the country delivered over
to vulgar newspapers. When he had time to think, he decided
that it was imperialism which had given the British he so much
admired the solid responsibility for civilization he felt his own
country lacked. Perhaps a dose of the same would be good for
our vulgar materialism. That grabbed-up empire had provided
great issues for the British, where our concerns had been small
by comparison and often vulgar. This is a curious bit of thinking, which once again illustrates that great novelists are not
necessarily consistent philosophers. Henry himself admits that
all this is not "decent morality." Of the Boer War that follows
he was content to say that probably such messy areas had to be
cleaned up, presumably for the benefit of the "grabbed-up" empire. In the Dreyfus case he could not even work up an interest.
These compromises with what his father would have certainly
called "decent morality" were to trouble him later when imperialism blew the world up in 1914. At present, they meant
only that Henry James was far more interested in his new

novels than in politics. Nevertheless it was in the early years of
this crisis that he broke away from his obsession with English
fin de siècle cleverness, turned back to his old international
theme, chose for his leading characters Americans who were
still "innocents," but by no means naïve, and reached his full
stature as a novelist who could create personalities that would
stir emotions as well as titillate the intellect.

2. "LARGE AND CONFIDENT ACTION"

Many men of talent and ambition ride upon waves of increasing or decreasing energy, until one slow and concluding swell
carries them under. Yet out of the trough they may, on the
contrary, rise into new and more vigorous rhythms. This latter
is unmistakably true of Henry James, and in an earlier chapter
I have described how the waves began to rise long before *The
Ambassadors* which was the first (and probably the best)
written of his new series of novels. In 1898 he was apologizing
to Paul Bourget for his fatal technical passion that kept him at
work upon stories which were after all only the "exercises" of a
virtuoso — potboilers he called the shorter ones, studies (not
achievements) in the scenic art, the novels. Yet as early as
1895 there is a separate paragraph in his Notebook which is
worthy of close reading and remembering. It is very Jamesian:

> February 14, 1895
>
> I have my head, thank God, full of visions. One has never too
> many — one had never enough. Ah, just to let one's self go — at last:
> to surrender one's self to what through all the long years one has
> (quite heroically, I think) hoped for and waited for — the mere
> potential, and relative, increase of *quantity* in the material act —

act of application and production. One has prayed and hoped and
waited, in a word, to be able to work *more*. And now, toward the
end it seems, within its limits, to have come. That is all I ask.
Nothing else in the world. I bow down to Fate, equally in sub-
mission and in gratitude. This time it's gratitude; but the form of
the gratitude, to be real and adequate, must be large and confident
action — splendid and supreme creation. *Basta.* . . .

Evidently when Henry speaks of "confident action" and
"supreme creation" he is not thinking of governments and nations, nor, in literature, of such characteristic products of the
fin de siècle as his own "clever novels" or the plays of Oscar
Wilde. I cannot find any dominant explanation in the *fin de
siècle*, or the rise of imperialism, for the so-called "great period"
which James entered at this time. If he had a great period, it
was chiefly because he had more to say and said it better. And
the more to say was, in spite of what he called the vulgarity of
their current history, more to say about Americans.

By the actual end of the century his projects were so numerous that he determined to disregard the financial perils of
space and "let himself go." When in 1898 Arthur Christopher
Benson urged him to write a sequel to *The Portrait of a Lady*,
he answered that his past production now inspired him with
terror. "The *P. of an L.* — admire my emphatic article — it's
all too faint and faraway." "I have bloodier things *en tête*. I
can do better than that!" He had certainly not done so in the
intervening years. Now he had *en tête*, if not on paper, two
American women, and an American man — the women young,
beautiful, and rich, as Henry liked them, the man an aspect of
James' own spiritual history. They were all "innocents" in
James' phrase, "moral" — in his sense — not vulgar, not naïve.
All were set in a complex of European immoralities — in both
Henry's and the public's sense of the word. These Americans
were to dominate the international scenes of the novels, calling

forth James' most consistently satisfactory talent. But this time
the travel book was finally to transform itself into a novel of personality, where the scenery and contrasting customs merely
supplied the action for dramas in which Americans took the
main parts.

3. JAMES TURNS TOWARD HOME

There had been something wrong with Henry James in the
eighteen-nineties, as there had been something wrong with
Mark Twain — and it was not psychological. The easiest explanation is his own, which is good enough as far as it goes.
I need not repeat the struggles of the man writing, whose manuscripts, except for some fortunate short stories, kept proliferat-
ing into *nouvelles* or novels too verbose for their subject matter
and too long for successful publication. He thought he saw the
cure. If he could not do a successful acting play, he at least,
through sweat and agony, had learned how to make a drama.
He knew how to write, and boasted of his mastery of, the
scenario. Now a scenario is only a series of interlocking scenes
held together by a rigid development of plot moving toward a
climax. Transferred from a play to a novel, it becomes a scenic
art by which the dialogue a novel requires — and for James life
always expresses itself in dialogue — is ordered in a series of
carefully articulated scenes. The Prefaces to the books of this
period plus the comments of his notebooks together constitute
a magnificent essay on The Scenic Art, as he calls it. And
looked at technically, both the "clever" novels of the *fin de
siècle* period, and the three great books with which he finished
his career, are illustrations of the triumph of a new technique
over the unruly proliferations of Henry's too fertile mind. (I
say "triumph" with qualifications. If the triumph had been

complete then *The Wings of the Dove* and *The Golden Bowl* would not have still remained the wordiest of super-analyses among great novels in English — but then they would not have been Henry James.)

James felt that he had solved this problem, which was to give his long story, which was meant to be read, the beautiful efficiency of a good play which is meant to be seen. He had not done so in his first experiments for there was something else wrong with Henry in this period. A great novel requires an emotional focus, which, since it is a study of manners, must be personal. He had achieved this in shorter stories such as *Daisy Miller*, where emotion carries narrative as he said into poetry.

He had come near it in *The American* long before, but fumbled at the end. He had come nearest to it in *The Portrait of a Lady*, which, perhaps because he had not yet mastered the scenic art, breaks into too many scenes, so that the deep personal emotions we feel in the unhappy Isabel betrayed by the ruthless selfishness of her husband, gets transferred somehow or other to the dying Ralph Touchett who takes the final last scene of the novel. But the purely English novels, from *The Tragic Muse* to *The Sacred Fount*, have no focus of this kind, because these *fin de siècle* English do not move James, it is he who moves them in their pattern of scenes. The conclusion seems inescapable, that, in general and admitting minor exceptions, it is only an American who can provide the objectively analytic James with a central character whom he deeply feels as well as thoroughly understands. Hence the spiritual drift back toward his home land, which is evident in the latter nineties, is of the utmost interest. Was the cause in some unconscious craving in his imagination? I think so. Certainly by the time he planned his trip home which resulted in the book *The American Scene* in 1907, he had resolved to write a purely American novel or novels as a result, and began one in *The Ivory Tower* and never finished it. But this was much later.

This drift began clearly in the nineties, but I shall pick up
the evidence where it comes. In 1903 he confesses to William
that America has become romantic as Europe was once to him,
that he wants to travel again before he dies, and not in Europe,
of which he has nothing more to say, that he encourages an in-
fatuation for every kind of American phenomena, except bad
eggs and bad English. Nephews and nieces were beginning to
visit him frequently at his house at Rye. He thought of himself
as old, and an old man dreams more of his youth. Did they still
scuffle their feet, he asks, in the fallen autumn leaves of Fifth
Avenue? He applauds (this is in 1899) William's intention to
send his Harry and Billy into the "forest primeval" (I suppose
the Adirondacks) for "experience of a sort I too miserably
lacked. . . ." Let them "contract local saturations and attach-
ments in respect to their *own* great and glorious country, to
learn, and strike roots into, its own infinite beauty, as I suppose,
and variety. Then they won't, as I do now, have to assimilate,
but half-heartedly, the alien splendours" of Europe. "Make the
boys, none the less, stick fast and sink up to their necks in
everything their *own* countries and climates can give de pareil
et de superieurs." What he wanted when he made up his mind
to go himself, was the production of prose such as no other
adventure would give him — "supreme creation," something
"bloodier." A belated homesickness helped him to it.

Only those, and there are too many, who believe that Henry
James in his thirty-odd years of expatriation had become as
entirely Europeanized as his manners and his speech can take
this homesickness lightly in the search for the cause of the new
vitality of his work after 1900. And only those who will not
consider the thesis of this book. For the Henry James who
turned East from America left a culture small but significant
of men and women like himself, like the James family, like
the numerous Americans whose bonds with the Old World

strengthened rather than weakened in the nineteenth century. Emotionally, morally, and in some respects intellectually, Henry after his decades away was still closer akin to Eastward-looking Americans than to either the French or the English.

4. JAMES AT LAMB HOUSE

Not even the scenic art, nor the new themes of the last novels of James explain their distributed power, or the mellowness of their style — the pages of nervous fireworks disappear, the characters stop rushing in and out, the stories develop with, for James, extraordinary continuity. There is a plot always in view. More than a new technique accounted for this. There was a better opportunity to use his best. Mark had lived for months upon months in an alien continent among alien languages, and usually to escape the distractions of a celebrity at home, perhaps to keep under the restlessness of his old journalistic habits. Henry James in 1898 had run away to escape the burden of social success. Run away, I suspect, in fact from the society of the very English *fin de siècle* society which had made the fabric of his "clever" novels. He had already contracted his social habits, now he proposed to take himself where only friends would find him. The old woodchuck, if I may be allowed such an irreverent term for Henry, had come home at last after decades of nibbling in other people's gardens and hothouses, and holed in behind his own walk, with an access both to sea and cobbled streets and hills. In Lamb House, at Rye, "semi-historical" in its enclosed gardens, with a garden house pitched beside the Georgian doorway, he was for the first time for thirty years freed from *pensions,* hotels, lodgings, and clubs.

London was near if he needed to change, but he left Lamb
House only to long to be back. To say that he became a
countryman would be an absurd exaggeration. Gardening was
usually something of an adventure, and something was always
happening to his dogs. But he was content in spirit here until
the war in 1914 and increasing disabilities made residence in
London more desirable. There was a King's Room in Lamb
House, where he could entertain the kind of women he liked,
and his relatives and intellectually minded friends. And to
the garden house in the wall he could escape with his secretary
for his daily stint. The increasing success of protected work in
familiar surroundings made him happy. At first it was the last
of hothouse London that was his theme, but as he wrote "large
and confident action" emerged from his notebooks and he
wrote in gardens quiet and without sensible interruption his
best books. This is what he had always been crying for with
rows of exclamation marks. Now he had it and of course it
shows in his style. In the letters he wrote with his own hand in
his room late at night, there is a kind of wise and humorous
youthfulness.

5. VALUES

Every book worth putting on the shelves of a library is either
a value in itself or about values — value in this instance meaning a quality of living. A book about values can, of course, be
a value in itself also, but let us keep the argument as simple
as possible — as it stands, the distinction is at least more useful
than most critical stir-me-ups on the difference between
romance and realism. Now Mark Twain, it seems to me, had a
more confused sense of values than any of his peers in the art of

literature. He was "fine-fibred," which means that he was sensitive, but he was about as discriminating in the values of living as a zestful boy who lives too fast to think about what it all amounts to. He knew what he liked, and still better what he did not like, as in "classical" painting, but very honestly refused to go a step further, because very honestly he did not know how to, except in matters involving a very simple morality which was as ingrown as his digestion. That was why it was such a terrible shock for him to discover that God, as he understood God, was immoral as he understood morality. *A Connecticut Yankee in King Arthur's Court* is essentially a conflict between morality as it was understood by the best people in Hartford, and the ethics of the Middle Ages as they were largely misunderstood by Mark himself. The book has its very great values, but as a tract on values, it is a satiric burlesque. A moral history of Mark would show an almost complete confusion through life among the various sets of manners, ethics, and preconceptions in which he succeeded in tying himself in his progress from the Mississippi through the Far West and the post-war United States in its great period of business and industrial expansion.

This did not prevent him from writing great books; perhaps it helped him. For his great books are values in themselves not studies of values, and the perennial youthfulness of his mind, while it lasted in its primitive simplicity, and while he could recall that simplicity in idyllic prose, kept him pure, so to speak, as the representative artist he was born to be. The values of *Tom Sawyer* and *Huckleberry Finn* are the youthful values of pure delight in experience, indelibly registered, never analyzed into the abstract — and of course true. A book *about* values in the Mississippi Valley would for the same years give a picture of living which would attract the curious, but certainly never make an idyll.

It is scarcely necessary to emphasize that Henry James' books from first to last are *about* values. They have very great literary values of their own, but it is to analyze values that from the days of his first emergence from the James family he determined to write. Even "The Turn of the Screw," which is as close to pure value as anything he ever did, was, so he said, meant to study the values of terror which can only be apprehended in the effect on the observer. And one of the reasons why Mark's creative powers burnt out at the age when Henry's were reviving was that the creation of pure value is subject to the many hazards of disillusioning experience, and the staleness of age, whereas the criticism of values should, within reasonable limits, increase in acuteness as long as the mind continues to mature.

Henry's first problem (at an age when Mark had no literary problems at all except to survive) was how to live as a youth who very consciously and candidly wished experience that might contribute to a great art. This question deeply engaged him when he was with his superheated family, and the attempt to solve it took him abroad for half a lifetime. But what to write about was by no means so clear in James' mind except that there was a great deal he did not want to write about, and a good deal more that he simply could not. Hundreds of pages of Prefaces — and in notes — show him experimenting with this idea and that, until finally he began to confuse both the difficulty of the task and his skill in unwrapping his parcels of material with the value of the thing itself. As a process, he may have been right, but his audience did not think so. Now, in his late sixties, his technique was satisfyingly complete. And he had not a new theme — he had always been asking how or how not should his characters live — but a subject matter focused on personalities so living, so poignant that there was no danger that they would unwrap into mere psychological equations. He needed and he had what, in truth, he had seldom possessed, what Mark had possessed from the beginning of his really literary career, he had flesh and blood upon which to work — marble (pretty tough to be sure) that could be made to glow under his hands. He was an artist already, a far better one than Mark, but I cannot believe that except for brief moments he had until now been a creator of personality.

Of course James in one sense had magnificently triumphed. He had escaped, as he felt, from a gadget civilization to enrich and perfect his mind from the culture of the past. And in creation on its lower levels, the creation and enrichment of types, he had given the prime pictures of the New World man trying to purchase that culture, or careening among its masterpieces, physical and human, like a ball in a bowling alley. He had made the American expatriate famous in literature. Also he had lived intensely in a rich but narrow range of society. But not intimately, not emotionally with any of his characters, unless with the young American girls embodying charm and idealism that he sought so often as *ingenues* for his drama. Now apparently his lifelong question took another form. It became, Have I lived? It became at the second asking, Whom have I *known* as men and women most deeply know each other, those who have lived to the height of emotion? These are the subjects of the first two of his last novels.

A word of explanation, however, since the earliest-written of these books, *The Ambassadors,* is deeply concerned with the problem of morality as New England still by preference used the word. I mean sexual morality according to the prevailing nineteenth-century American code. James, as I have said, preferred the pure if "affectionate" American to what he calls the "adulterine" practice of the Old World. But true immorality for him, whether sexual or any other kind, is best defined concretely in terms of art. It is essentially a grossness, which he often calls vulgarity — it is meanness, personal treachery, greediness, unrelieved by worthy ends. It is an offense against culture in its truest sense. The expatriate esthete in *The Portrait of a Lady*

was not immoral because of his vices, it was the egoism that
made him try to kill a fine spirit which made him immoral.
The Prince in *The Golden Bowl* is not immoral because of his
adulteries, it is his deceit practised upon a courageous soul.
Adultery, or any sexual breach, is not a prime immorality.
James uses it with interested comments in his Edwardian
stories. In itself it does not shock him. Since the second and
third of these new novels, *The Wings of the Dove* and *The
Golden Bowl,* are built upon a question of morality in Henry's
own special sense, this comment is useful.

6. THE CLIMATIC STORIES

Henry James in 1901 when he wrote *The Ambassadors* had
passed the age when men, as a rule, commit themselves to emotional, especially passionate, experience. He was at the age
when many a man asks himself, In fullness of experience, have
I really lived? I believe that the warmth of *The Ambassadors,*
the intensely personal sensitiveness of Strether, its hero, may be
explained very simply by saying that Strether is a dramatization
of a possible spiritual and emotional adventure of Henry himself. One phrase in a conversation seems to have startled James
into an awareness that the time had come to ask himself the
vital question above — a question incidentally which carping
critics of his books are always asking for themselves. It was
his younger friend Jonathan Sturges talking, and the reference
was to Howells' wandering in Paris where he had scarcely ever
been: "He laid his hand on my shoulder," the Notebooks
record that Sturges said of Howells, "Oh, you are young, you
are young — be glad of it: be glad of it and *live.* Live all you
can: it's a mistake not to. It doesn't so much matter what you

do — but live. This place makes it all come over me. I see it now. I haven't done so — and now I'm old. It's too late. It has gone past me — I've lost it."

The flash of a theme from life was always like an ultra-violet ray turned upon James' imagination, but this time there was something that had crystallized there and was ready to glow. Note that there is neither plot nor situation in Howells' words — these were to come — but pure theme, and with James, I am sure, purely personal. And through all the elaborate scene-after-scene of *The Ambassadors* of which this was the genesis, the insistent question, "Have I lived?" never subsides. The character, Lambert Strether, whom James creates to answer it dramatically, is out of himself. For Strether is a stay-at-home American, an editor and an essayist, such as James would possibly, I should say probably, have become if he had remained in Boston or New York. By chance only and in middle age, Strether's rich patron, who supports the magazine which is his livelihood, implores him to rescue her son who has drunk of the poison of the charm of Old World living, is entangled with some Parisian sorceress, and must come back to marry the girl waiting for him, and save the plumbing business (or whatever it was, James could not guess) for the sake of the family. And Strether discovers when he sets about his embassy that there is some secret of living in the old European scene not yet learned by energetic America. And that there are aspects of love which the runaway youth has learned from Madame de Vionnet, his lover, which are more ennobling as well as more sweet than is provided for in the philosophy of New England. Strether must decide what compulsion to put upon this son of his patron, who is still young, who has learned to live in a richer culture than his own — whether to bring him back to plumbing or leave him with the lovely Madame de Vionnet. And what compulsion to put upon himself, for he also has been offered marriage and safety as well as a magazine at home. The problem raised for many an Eastward-turning American, looking at the golden apples of culture hung in orchards across the sea, was whether there was a taste of moral poison in them, so that as with Adam, in eating, troubles as well as joys began. And, for Strether, whether, if he refuses this finer life, it will be too late.

Yet in *The Ambassadors,* the reader's interest never chills in analysis, never is distracted by too brilliant conversation. And the reason seems to be more than the now matured technique of Henry. The focus of his story is an American problem close to his heart; the hero is an American intellectual feeling his way in an old culture — indeed his hypothetical self.

I can remember reading on publication the first to be printed (in 1902) of the new novels, *The Wings of the Dove.* It seemed then immensely difficult, and yet with a warmth that carried the reader through — though, to be sure, at a pace in that now highly elaborated style which was somewhat slow for a dove's flight. It does not seem so difficult now since so many writers have followed the Jamesian way, although even Henry admitted, not, of course, that it was too complex, but that it was too long.

And here James raised again and with far more depth, and much more poignancy, a question of values which had always fascinated him. It was the old one of the morally innocent American entangled among predatory Europeans. But this time morality was to be interpreted in Henry's sense. It was to be the clash of the confidently generous Innocent against the brilliant self-seeking of a rigid society. And again he sought not merely for an American heroine, but for a girl of the age that touched him most, this time it seems for a girl whom he had known and loved in his fashion, and who could never be merely a subject for analysis.

He found her. "Its essence," he says of the novel in his Preface, "is that of a young person conscious of a great capacity for life, but early stricken and doomed, condemned to die under short respite, while so enamored of the world; aware moreover of the condemnation and passionately desiring to 'put in' before extinction as many of the finer vibrations as possible, and so achieve, however briefly and brokenly, the sense of having lived. Long had I turned it over" — seeking for "the precious experience somehow compassed."

Of course his mind was warm with it, for the indirect reference is evidently to his cousin Minnie Temple, whom he said he never loved but whose death changed his life. Minnie's own story was tragic enough though it was of tuberculosis not a broken will to live of which she died. But it was her indomitable purpose, though she knew her fate, to "put in" as many of the finer vibrations as possible which was born into Henry's imagination in their long intimacy. Nor is it to be forgotten that James himself, and unknown to her, was suffering under what he believed was the lifelong veto of an injured back upon all future activities except those of the brain. So that the heroine, Milly, of *The Wings of the Dove* was heir of a double intimate and vital experience.

As the plot develops Milly takes the old part of the Innocent, lovely, generous, and confident in human relations. Incredibly rich, and independent, she is steered into the English society that James knew so well. She is indifferent to personal gains except as a means to savor the life her imagination grasps to the full, including love. For drama, James adds the journalist Merton Densher, a man incapable of gross money-making, and Kate Croy, intelligent, "good" as the world runs, hard. Both are in the grip of the English social code that makes a sure and ample income essential for a good life. They are secretly engaged. Why should not Densher accept the love for which Milly too evidently is waiting. If she dies, as she must soon, she will leave him a fortune, if they marry first he will inherit. It happens, but not as Kate plans. A rejected suitor tells Milly

the ugly truth. She turns her face to the wall! Melodrama! But
not as James writes it, with the colors of warm and noble
reality, recalled from the story of Minnie Temple, and a memory
in the author of what it seemed like in his own youth to expect
to lose the full flavor of living. And here in another American
is the focus of warmth which brings the long novel into a syn-
thesis that is not only a study of values but a value itself like life.

The last of James' three concluding novels to be published,
The Golden Bowl in 1904, was the first to be conceived, as early
as 1892, but in a form so spare, so concentrated in action, as to
be little more than a sketch for a scenario. Someone told him a
story of a devoted daughter whose widowed father married a
friend of her own age. Through the years this story grew into
a novel of American "innocence," until the narrative shook
itself free from all lesser purposes to be a drama of contrasting
values as direct as Jane Austen — but by no means as short.
The golden bowl itself is a *fin de siècle* symbol of beautiful
living, a present from the Roman prince of the oldest stock who
has married Maggie Verver (the daughter) for her wealth. And
it is to live beautifully, as with so many expatriate Americans,
that is Maggie's desire — as it is Adam Verver's, her millionaire
father's, to buy the best of noble beauty in art to take home to
found a gallery in raw America. But the bowl has a flaw. It
breaks. The Prince is instinctive with "finer vibrations," he
offers the life, and Maggie believes the love, that she wanted.
He is as authentic art as a Pinturicchio. But in conventional
morals of sex he is unscrupulous. Charlotte, Maggie's best
friend, an American of Continental mores, has been his mistress. It is she, too poor to marry him herself, who presents
him to Maggie. It is she and the Prince together who contrive
that she shall become a compensation prize for Adam Verver's
loss of his infinitely loved daughter, thus leaving the lovers
rich in opportunities.

Maggie is no defeated invalid to turn her face to the wall
when the revelation comes. She can keep her Prince, for he
cannot afford to run away, but can she hold him in a vital relation after the humiliations? Yet the moral price is not the
shame of taking back another woman's lover. The price is her
father's happiness, for there is a relation between father and
daughter so tender and devoted that a modern psychiatrist
might well suspect it. Her father's happiness centers upon her.
If there is a flaw in the golden bowl of beautiful living, let it
shatter. She is an Innocent no longer, but the old man shall
suspect nothing. That kind of immorality, for wealth, position,
and pleasure in a complaisant society, he could not endure.
"Nothing will come out," says the Observer of the story. "She'll
die first." Maggie is strong, as James seems to imply American
innocents in a youthful society often are. She is stronger than
her Prince and Charlotte. She keeps the Prince. She saves her
father. The *"subject"* of this book, James said in his earliest
notes upon it, "is really the pathetic simplicity and good faith
of the father and daughter in their abandonment."

If the situation seems fantastic, this is because in outline the
reader does not grasp the dramatic contrast between the two
cultures. The Ververs, simple people at heart, do not understand what power, what dangerous attraction their vast but
quickly gained wealth gives them. They do not guess how
naïve their search for a beautiful life among beautiful things
seems to the Prince and his intelligent but impoverished
Charlotte, who have everything the Americans crave but money.
Since honest emotions are not among their values, they do not
scruple to trick innocence in order to get wealth. It is their values
that Maggie discovers. She can take it. But her father's happiness is a more important value for her than the shallow success
of a decaying society. Let her bowl shatter. It was only glass.
But not his illusion of his daughter's rich life.

And the reader will note that in this long novel where all the

important characters but one are American, there is again an
emotional focus which spreads its warmth through the story —
the deep affection for each other of two Americans of the kind
that James could feel as part of his own experience. Adam
Verver is an American type which only Americans seem to
recognize and understand, the powerful accumulator of great
wealth, who is not a miser, nor a founder of dynasties, but in
his age spreads philanthropies through the world, and not in-
frequently proves to be of a simple and kindly heart. As for
Maggie, she is another Milly with the same desires for beautiful experiences. And she encounters the same trickery in
her contact with different mores, a Milly who can fight
back, who believes after disillusion in the essence of her "innocence."

And it is James' own especial moral sense which is illustrated
in all three of these stories. He may have been and probably
was an undersexed man, but it is not sexual relations which
shocked him. Kate Croy gives herself to Densher with a freedom of circumstance which Twain would have avoided, though
not of course that freedom of detail which the current novelist
indulges in, and which to the sensitive James would have
seemed merely vulgar. Nor is it the stolen adventures of the
Prince and Charlotte that trouble him. It is the trickery, not
for love, but for much grosser motives in the stories of both
young women that makes the drama of innocence. And in *The
Ambassadors,* to take another aspect, the classic scene of pure
and beautiful emotion is Strether's discovery of Chad and
Madame de Vionnet, the lovers, on the hidden reaches of the
river, tasting of the life which he had never lived until too
late and which no longer seems to him immoral. The greatness
of the book is in the moral psychology of two cultures never
so well compared. Its poignancy comes from James' own emotions. He is touched far beyond analysis.

I do not mean to state dogmatically that only by Americans

could the great objective realist be moved into a warmth of characterization that makes one forget (as with Twain at his best) the art in the life. The most delicately conceived as well as the most touching of all his women is Madame de Vionnet, she whose secret influence upon young Chad whom Strether was asked to rescue has civilized, she whose tenuous grip on an exquisite life is loosened when Strether carries the youth back with him. Here is a woman who, if France were overrun with barbarians, might still explain the incomparable values of French culture — and yet as human and as emotionally imagined as James' American girls. She is the triumph of James the Internationalist, and also the masterpiece of his method of the analyzed dream; yet so perfect in his realization that he found it unnecessary to reanalyze her in his Preface! However, it is chiefly from some area of his conscious or unconscious memories of America that James best drew these pure yet passionate young Americans who most moved him, women intelligent even in their innocence, intensely energetic (even in the intervals of their dying) from Daisy Miller to Maggie and Milly twenty years apart. It cannot be supposed that they all rested upon the vivid impressions of his cousin Minnie Temple. There must have been to his mind a basic type — limited by the restrictions that most of them were rich and all of them sensitive to the "finer vibrations," although with Daisy these vibrations were infantile. No one was vulgar, not even Daisy. All were generous and kind, all like beautiful young animals rearing, or at least longing, to go. And of course this has been an American type known round the world, clear of line, self-reliant, driven by some fire within. James chose, as his favorites, the rich variety, because no need to make a living, or as in England "place," warped them, because no crudity of cash, as with the career women, numerous among his Americans, vulgarized them, blunted their innocence into aggressiveness. Warmth, I repeat, is the quality James most lacked, except in his passion for the beauty of landscape, and for intellectual brilliance. In human nature he warms best with women like Milly, a dove with sheltering wings for her treacherous friends, who is frustrated, wrung out of life, to the patent emotion of her creator.

Nor should I fail to add for the record the rich old Americans, wise, gentle, infinitely kind, Verver and Touchett, such men as Strether himself was sure to become even with his different history. They are symbols I think of the will and the material power of America, grasping, worthily this time, what James considered its lost opportunities. I wonder if James' own father was not his source here — a man with far different values and earlier experience, belligerent, energetic, whose letters to his children in later years have a living concern not easily equaled in literature.

I am not trying to sum up even Henry James' last novels in two or three characters where he gave us men and women who can be remembered by name as well as by analysis and definition. His gallery is extraordinarily rich, and though limited to what might be called a class, is more extensive than any other American's. A book longer than this one could be written, indeed it has been done, merely upon James as a master of psychological analysis, in which Milly and Maggie would be only two of a crowd, and by no means the furthest dissected. But for this study of parallel lives, it is the American reference of the two writers that I have chosen as a central theme, with James especially because his American inspirations seem to have been least noticed, and prove to be of unsuspected importance. The writer of the entirely English *What Maisie Knew* was clearly one of the most brilliant observers in our times of a somewhat alien subject; the author of *The Ambassadors* was one of our greatest novelists.

Values have been a modern obsession and especially in America, and particularly in the twentieth century. Our maturity as a people has revealed, rather than destroyed, our "innocence," which spreads far beyond the narrow limits of this book and has become international in a new and desperately important aspect of politics, economics, and diplomacy. Here James was a pioneer in method, and now, it becomes clear also, a pioneer in insight. It is difficult to imagine a Willa Cather, or indeed a Sinclair Lewis, or faraway but not faint, an Ernest Hemingway without James in their background.

I am trying to write not so much literary history in this book as a just and rich appreciation of what men of parallel lives achieved as their best. Plutarch sometimes strains his contrasts in his conclusions as when with Dion and Brutus he argues at length whether the Greek or the Roman most shrewdly and nobly planned the murder of a tyrant. I do not think that the contrast is strained if I offer at the end of this chapter the books upon which the fame of Mark Twain and Henry James can most revealingly stand, *Adventures of Huckleberry Finn* and *The Ambassadors*. And if I am sure that neither writer could have been hired to read the other's masterpiece, that is just another, though extreme, proof of the significant qualities of West-turning and East-turning Americans, who have been a great deal more different than Democrats and Republicans.

Chapter XV

DECLINE AND DISILLUSION
OF HENRY JAMES

I HAVE LIMITED these parallel lives of writers chiefly to their history as writers of fiction, and for good reason. When they are storytellers their "awareness" of life, to use James' favorite term, becomes most effectively articulate, by which I mean closest to life itself, much closer than in criticism or description. Even James, that persistent analyzer, is far more interesting as a creative observer than as a critic.

Some exception should be made for the last of James' major books, *The American Scene* of 1907, which was the fruit of his travels in America in 1904 and 1905. It is the best of his travel books, indeed only scenes lifted out of his novels of Rome and France and England could equal it. His nephew, Harry James, so close to him in his later years, thought it was the best of his books, and might outlive his novels. I cannot agree. *The American Scene* was a preliminary not a final work — and unfinished at that — a magnificent collection of notes descriptive, notes analytical, in preparation (as he implies himself) for an American novel or novels. The new life of his imagination which had kept the elderly man soaring vigorously through the extraordinary feat of three major novels published in three years was still calling for more material, "bloodier," rich in new possibilities of superb creation. His final purpose was a work of art or works of art for which this book of American interpretations and investigations was not the real subject, but the foundations upon which he could tread as firmly as upon English ground. Actually, although Henry moved his none too easy dignity from New England to California, he got in his book only as far as Florida. And in his proposed second volume he was intending to attack the vast subject from other angles, and to have *"contributed"* much more. Though brilliant and perceptive, where James *could* be perceptive in this new America, *The American Scene* just preceded the decline of the creative powers of Henry James. Ill health and the oncoming of the Great War were responsible for the feeble outcome of all this eager preparation for new fiction. This was the unpublished, unfinished *The Ivory Tower* (1913) published in 1917 after James' death, which certainly gives no measure of what he wanted to do.

A careful reading of *The American Scene* itself shows too clearly that the great critic and elegist of beauty had already begun to outlive his gifts as a novelist, although not as a critic. America gave him a brilliant book — the inspired table talk, much of it hotel and dining-car table talk, of a great raconteur; but America was too much for the novelist. There are possible beginnings of novels which he may have been planning, but in every instance I think no probability of a continuance. James' book is a study of his own reactions, only in a limited sense is it even a useful account of America in the early nineteen-hundreds. Here are his favorite ideas given the spice of a new setting, but we learn much more of Henry than of the country in which he says that the Eastern region was dull but the people significant, whereas California was stunning but the people terrible!

2. THE OBSERVER GOES HOME

Three good reasons carried him home at last after twenty-one years. One I have already discussed — a new interest in an America which might in a renewal of experience give him a country which was still his own, and therefore could be a subject for intimate fiction. A second was the project for a collected edition of his novels, revised, and with *Prefaces*. The Preface of *The Golden Bowl*, as it appears in the edition of 1917, tells in detail why and how he expected to give his earlier books an expressiveness which he had not the power to give them in earlier years. Old war horse of the technically articulate, he sniffed an opportunity which comes to few, and proposed new perfection so far as his powers would permit. It is also clear from several letters that he hoped by means of this great edition, which was in the making from 1907 to 1917, to provide the financial security for old age that the stage had so cruelly denied him. He was disappointed again.

No readers of Henry James should criticize this attempt to gives his stories a final dress until they have read this Preface to *The Golden Bowl*, which is itself perhaps the classic essay on revision. His idea was to let alone, in general, the substance of his earlier novels, even when, as in the case of *The American*, he thought he had bungled the values and the emphasis of the story. Sometimes his corrections were meant to say more beautifully what he had intended. More often the changes were to make the expression release more clearly his ideas. This, he said, a rearranged sentence, a different word, or even a comma could sometimes accomplish. The result of course was more complexity, a denser medium of words. Any judgment of the result must be relative. If it is the story, the literal scene, the statement of situation that you want, the original, the simpler form may be more readable, with less stylistic interference. But if you read James' books for the play of his mind over life, then much is to be said for the revisions. He himself believed that he did not become fully articulate until his later style. There is no question that he regarded his revisions, not his originals, as his own authentic art.

The labor was intense. That he undertook it at all is surely an indication that after *The Wings of the Dove, The Golden Bowl,* and *The American Scene* he felt his powers declining, wished to rescue from his little popularity his early books (now beginning to go out of print), and make them perfect for his monument.

The third reason was to satisfy his unsatisfied desire for travel, a passion from youth, which close work and a tight pocketbook had later largely denied him. He wished to see "the American extension" of Anglo-Saxonism which "now most interests me." Soon he would be too old. And it was not New York, not Newport, not Cambridge and Boston he wanted to see with new eyes, but the country, *all* of it. When his secret wish to write novels of America, perhaps as an immediate result, failed, he went back in his writing, his memory refreshed, to the old regions of his youth, and wrote as his last task, those little-read autobiographies, brilliant in introspection, rich in nostalgia, *A Small Boy and Others,* 1913, *Notes of a Son and Brother,* 1914, and the unfinished *The Middle Years,* published after his death in 1917.

Yet *The American Scene* deserves great consideration for itself. In it he had proposed — a task for an old gentleman who hated hotels and bad eggs and worse vocalization — to do the country in *cadres* as complete and immeasurably more mature than those of the celebrated Taine when "he went, early in his sixties, to Italy for six weeks in order to write his big book." *The American Scene* must be regarded as one of those demifictions like *The Innocents Abroad,* where incidents and the background are factual, yet the whole united by a stream of consciousness of the perceptual observer. Again and again with James, a chapter is such a beginning of a novel or short story as he wrote of Venice, or Hamburg, or London. The best of these, and most revealing, is his account of Charleston — a perfect beginning of a novel which he not only did not but I am persuaded could not write.

He wanders over Charleston, charmed by the slumbrous
houses indifferent even to their own beauty, life dragging its
feet in the grassy streets — a sleep (this pleased James) of
"success," all that was modern ugly, all that was old a reminder
of "the great folly" that left the city menless, feminized, saved
from dowdiness only by the tragedy of its fate.

Yet when he came back to his hotel he found himself im-
mersed in a tableful of drummers, a human animal new to him,
and afterward met them more extensively in the club car of a
train heading further South. They were friendly, earnest, yet
as devoid of awareness of anything but their respective com-
modities, as hens of flowers growing in their chicken yard. They
anger him, but finally he likes them without condescension or
snobbery, and speaks of them in language with which the
American commercial traveler perhaps never was addressed
before or afterward. They were vulgar ministers to a declining economy, creatures of a "sordid and ravenous habit,"
blatant and brazen sellers each of his "special line of goods."
Here they were, "solemnly feeding" in the outward decency
and inner blank of American society, and in unchallenged pos-
session as if to deny the existence of other professions, other
interests — he might have added other values; and to oppose
them only the "shirt-waisted" young American girl, pitiably
publicized (by Mr. Gibson?) is responsible for what social
graces could be presumed to exist.

All this outdoes Taine and his six weeks for Italy, since it is
the stream of consciousness of a man whose contacts had been
with a society infinitely varied within its narrow intellectual
limits, and a traveler so avid of privacy that his only unquali-
fied joy in Charleston was its walled gardens. If in this chapter
the drama of contrast between an older America and the still
raw buds of industrialism is shaping in James' imagination, it
is already clear that he is not going ever to be able to write

these novels of a new extension of Anglo-Saxonism. At the best he will find it possible to retell such stories as his pupil Edith Wharton (with far more intimate experience) is doing of the "innocent" replicas of European society in New York or Newport.

Those who admire, as I do, Henry's intricate carving of a scene in a story into a pattern of dialogue will take sardonic pleasure in seeing how the society of America baffles him, how he wastes an unsuitable talent upon a railroad junction in the woods, a fumbling Negro porter, a "pale, carnivorous coffee-drinking hotel child," all proliferated into an argument that America is "thin" and that money only is important. He is a little humorous like Dr. Johnson grumbling in the Hebrides, and yet, as in his novels, what sudden miracles of perception, what final triumphs of the language (after much puffing and blowing) in the art of description! A fussy man, a ruthless craftsman, a master of the phrase if not of the sentence, a virtuoso in controlled sensitiveness — what he would in sheer ruthless description have written of Hollywood, of Miami, of a transcontinental highway, of the radio and television in the mid-twentieth century, defeats guessing except that it would not be in novels! He would have been hysterical, but magnificent.

There was too little that he understood for real fiction, even after such biting description. And it was too late to understand it even in the Jamesian way. It was too big in its faults as well as its virtues. It would have required an effort not so much of observation as of creation of new American character types for which he had not the energy even if, which is doubtful, he had the power. He faced the task in *The American Scene* and let the book remain as a unique observation of American life at one of our turning points from provincialism toward world magnitude.

3 . DEATH ON THE HORIZON

If I am right in thinking that America, when James had at last reseen it, required too much of a new effort for creative fiction, it was not only the (almost) impossibility of the task for a mind conditioned like his. Henry's health was failing. In 1907 he could say that no one realized the unhappy nature of his physical consciousness, even though for four years he had been better than he had ever been. In 1908 he had a "cardiac crisis." At Lamb House, working on his great edition, he had given up dining out "under any colour," and all but necessary guests. His hand shook, his teeth were going, on Christmas Eve he ate a baked apple and a biscuit all alone. In 1910 he was in a profound depression under the shadow of angina pectoris. The pain was often subdued, but never conquered. In the same year he had taken his dear brother William home to die. The change took his mind off himself and his growing hypochondria, but pain returned. He had become a fussy old man, though his sickness was of course real. Finally he moved permanently to Cheyne Walk in Chelsea, where it was easier to care for himself. His letters show how all this affected his writing. With difficulty only could he dictate the three or four hours daily he set aside for work; then he was "gone."

"Gone" by 1911 or 1912 was the happy artist, whose great moments always were his return to his desk. But not "gone" as a writer. His declining strength went into his Edition and his autobiographies — and his letters. Each evening, it would seem, from the record, he crept upstairs to his room, writing such letters both in length and excellence as would suffice to make the reputation of a lesser man. And most of these letters are from the heart, simple and vigorous in style, and not too "literary." I quote passages from a letter he sent to Howells for his seventy-fifth birthday in 1912, because it recalls early days in America, when Howells "showed me the way and opened me the door . . . when we knew together what American life *was* — or thought we did." This was the America that has smelled so sweet to him through all his chosen exile. "I seem to myself to have faltered and languished, to have missed more occasions than I have grasped, while you have piled up your monument just by remaining at your post. For you have had the advantage, after all, of breathing an air that has suited and nourished you; of sitting up to your neck, as I may say — or at least up to your waist — amid the sources of your inspiration."

It is a fine letter of the testimonial kind, perceptive, too generous perhaps to the "essential distinction" of Howells as a literary artist, a little nostalgic, and regretful for his own inability to make himself "documentary," like his friend, for American life, before the wholesale importations and so-called assimilations of this later time.

Sargent, in these years before the war, painted his robust and very British portrait of Henry, which shows no trace of his "physical consciousness" of pain. Indeed it is a portrait of the diner-out (now reduced to baked apples and biscuits), a dean of letters, yet still with the sensitive mouth of La Farge's early painting. Henry liked the mouth. He liked the portrait too. This was the way that after so many years in England he wanted to look. Reynolds would have painted him thus, he thought, to hang beside his Dr. Johnson. But Reynolds was profounder than Sargent. There was more American, more Irish, especially more sensibility in James' face than in Sargent's portrait.

Henry's nervous depression lightened after 1912 or 1913, and one hears less of his physical disabilities, probably because the shock of war and its approaches drove pitying thoughts away. Some of his finest letters were written in these years. It was in

1915 that an exchange took place between Henry and H. G. Wells which is invaluable for a book like this one. Here James, for probably the last time, and certainly in the most poignant manner, writes down the credo of his literary life. He had with grateful excitement, often acknowledged, looked through the windows of Wells' early novels upon an English life and an English thinking which was as unfamiliar to him as contemporary America. His reward was to be described by Wells in a book of parodies as a hippopotamus picking up a pea from the corner of its den. Henry was hurt in the most sensitive corner of his consciousness, his dignity. Yet he was content to reply by no more abusive return than "bad manners," far more concerned, great artist and great gentleman that he was, to defend his conception of literature. What would happen, he says in effect, if we were all H. G. Wellses, insensible to a fullness of life and of a projection of it "which seems to me most beautifully producible of interest." "I hold that interest may be, *must* be, exquisitely made and created, and that if we don't make it, we who undertake to, nobody and nothing will make it for us." To which Wells, who has said he was quite willing to have his books die as soon as their ideas were absorbed, answered that he would rather be called a journalist than an artist. "I use the word [art] for a research and attainment that is technical and special." In other words, art is merely a utility, which, if Henry accepted, would reduce his lifetime search for a form to, well, not a hunt for peas, but certainly to something merely useful for a good typist! To which James returns that it is art which *"makes* life, makes interest, makes importance," and knows "no substitute whatever for the force and beauty of its process." The ancient controversy has seldom been so well argued, and so significantly as in a world which was excluding everything but the "thing" and the "fact." The charge that Henry's mind was "futile and void" could be lethal to a writer who had made every "sacrifice of an easier way in order to pursue the difficult." "For myself," he wrote, "I live, live intensely and am fed by life, and my value, whatever it be, is in my own kind of expression of that." The diamond, he might have added, so rare and so difficult to cut, is not less important for *that* reason than the common quartz.

I wish we had a like correspondence between James and Twain. Mark, like Wells, would have made no allowances for the esoteric quality of much of James' fiction. A brilliant, cultivated society, devoting itself to contacts where, so often, action expressed itself only in talk, would have bored him to extinction. Yet Twain as a man of letters was far closer to James than to his fellow journalist. He was an artist in his use of language, and never for a moment would have regarded his style as something applicable like paint by "research" and special technique to his story. Even if he did study (or remember) the seven different dialects of Missouri English for *Huckleberry Finn,* the research is unimportant by comparison with the art that makes Huck and Negro Jim so intensely expressive in two of them.

4. CLIMAX

Henry James' career was not to end without its climax. Few men of first-rate minds have, on the whole, been less concerned with politics and social history than he. Even the Princess Casamissima interests him as a restless, egotistic woman far more than as a social revolutionary. Now in 1914 he is precipitated into a crisis of war which seemed to him (and probably was) the end of that peculiar society to which he had devoted a lifetime. His reactions to the war in general were the ordinary ones of liberal, kind, morally sensitive men. But the

particular violence of the impact upon him personally is easily
explained when one considers that this attack upon civilization, as he regarded it, seemed especially upon a culture that he
had spent a lifetime in making "interesting" and therefore
durable. Writing alone, he became a sounding board to every
implication of breakdown, a Henry Adams sniffing doom, a
patriot who fears that his horror will prevent a sane concern
with life. Yet slowly the affirmations of prodigious energies in
man, even horrid ones, arouse a fascinated interest. Soon he is
trotting hospital wards talking with satisfaction to wounded
soldiers. We have Whitman's accounts of such experiences. I
wish we had more of James', but most of all the soldiers' who
talked with him. They must have recognized his sincerity, but
I doubt whether they understood much that he said to them.
All this was but a beginning of what became a crushing disillusion, and ended with a gesture in the grand style.

That first great world crisis of modern times was to expose
the foundations of the successful and so complacent nineteenth
century to thoughtful men and women all over the Western
World, and especially in England, the leader in the Industrial
Revolution. The first effect upon a pragmatist like James —
and it was in pragmatism only that he was in complete agree-
ment with his brother William — was moral. That comfortable
society of cultivated minds, which he had spent his energies in
bringing into the representation of art, was not, he realized in
a flash, what he supposed it, the final product of "culture," and
most stable in contemporary Britain where he had taken his
stand as observer. It was resting precariously upon a substruc-
ture of balanced but predatory passions, and upon the greeds
and the suppressions of the underprivileged. He did not sink
like the neurotic Mark into a disclaimer of the human race.
Nor like the post-war modern novelists into hysterical defeat-
ism. He had never set up as a philosopher and knew his own
limitations in that field better than did Mark. His concern

was with the special society which he had created as every moral artist from the Greeks down had done as an outlet for his own genius and as a partial yet significant portrait of his own times. This society at a stroke had shown itself to be subject to aspects of itself which were as rotten as Hamlet's Denmark.

Henry's special reaction was not against Germany — he had never praised that society — it was against England, his second home, and later, when the response to moral responsibility seemed to him too slow, against his own people, the Americans. English society he felt had let him down. In the ample, generous life of the great country houses with their setting of beauty, and also in those rich experiences of European culture in general which had drawn his Americans back across the sea, he had been aware of moral corruptions which had given him situations for his books. But he had questioned the present, not the past. He had not considered that the society which seemed to him the most desirable gift of his times might only be a bubble blown across a river heavy with mud and sewage, and bound to burst. Listen to him as he writes at the eve of calamity:

To Mrs. Alfred Sutro — Lamb House on the eve — June 28, 1914.

"I hug whatever provincial privacy we may still pretend to at this hour of public uproar. . . . I cravenly avert my eyes and stop my ears — scarcely turning round even for a look at the Caillaux family. . . . may we muddle through even now, although I almost wonder if we deserve to! That doubt is why I bury my nose in my rose-trees and my inkpot."

To Sir Charles Phillips — July 31, 1914.

"The intense unthinkability of anything so blank and so infamous in an age that we have been living in and taking for our own as if it were of a high refinement of civilization . . . finding it after all carrying this abomination in its blood, finding this to have been what it *meant* all the while. . . . With it all too is indeed the terrible sense that the people of this country may well — by some awful brutal justice — be going to get something bad for the exhibition that has gone on so long of their huge materialized stupidity and vulgarity . . . without a redeeming idea of a generous passion."

To Howard Sturgis — August 4, 1914.

"The plunge of civilization into this abyss of blood and darkness by the wanton feat of those two infamous autocrats is a thing that so gives away the whole long age during which we have supposed the world to be, with whatever abatement, gradually bettering."

To Miss Rhoda Broughton — August 10, 1914.

"Black and hideous to me is the tragedy that gathers, and I'm sick beyond cure to have lived on to see it. You and I, the ornaments of our generation, should have been spared this wreck of our beliefs."

To Hugh Walpole — February 14, 1915.

"I have in a manner got back to work . . . but the conditions make it difficult, exceedingly, almost insuperably. . . . The subject-matter of one's effort has become *itself* utterly treacherous and false — its relation to reality utterly given away and smashed. Reality is a world that was to be capable of *this* — and how escape that horrific capability, *historically* latent, historically ahead of it? How on the other hand *not* represent it either — without putting into play mere fiddlesticks?"

The gesture that followed in June of 1915 was not really surprising, and too much has been made of its significance. Henry James gave several reasons for his request to be made a British subject. He was annoyed by Woodrow Wilson's messages. Writers are always annoyed by other writers who ought, they think, to be acting. In Wilson's case, he felt that he should be sending over millions of soldiers, who were, he had no doubt, immediately available. This is a little childish. The real reason he makes clear in a letter to his nephew, Harry James.

He wished to "rectify" a position that had become false by making "my civil status merely agree not only with my moral but with my material as well, in every kind of way. . . . I have spent here all the best years of my life — they practically have *been* my life." It was a simple act of recognition and gratitude.

Yet he admits that, if it were not for the war, the really simplest thing would be to stay as he was. My own guess is that a very minor incident changed a feeling into action. He was not only an American, but an Irish American — his sister violently sided with the Irish in their English troubles. He was always consciously an Observer, in England as on the Continent. But if never English, it had never been questioned for a quarter of a century that he was *of* England, honorably and famously so — as much domesticated there as his house in Rye. And suddenly he learned, as he wrote Gosse, "with horror . . . that if I go down into Sussex (for two or three months of Rye) I have at once to register myself as an Alien and place myself under the observation of the Police . . . that is only the *occasion* of my decision — it's not in the least its cause." He was an old man now, and constantly so speaks of himself, "kind of shaky and easily upset." "Alien," the word appalled him. That at least he had never been to England!

There is no more to tell. In Cheyne Walk at work again but mildly, he began his third volume of autobiography, and poured out — the term is felicitous — the last of his letters. A stroke on December 2, 1915, from which he never recovered, led to his death on February 28, 1916.

Chapter XVI

CONCLUSION

WHEN PLUTARCH wrote a Conclusion to one of his sets of parallel lives, it was usually moral. He made no attempt to analyze the generally accepted standards of the Graeco-Roman world, was content merely to point out whether his subjects lived up to them or did not. Demosthenes, for example, faced death bravely; Cicero, for all his great qualities, squirmed and evaded when it came to the final test. The stories in Plutarch's lives are more effective than his final moralizing of them.

Twain and James (in spite of what Mark hinted neurotically of his youth) would both be called by any standards moral men; and both lived up, Twain with passion, James consistently through his life, to what might be called the distinguishing characteristics of the American code. They were generous and tolerant men in their estimates of others. They hated most of all treachery, and self-seeking, and loved most of all loyalty, kindness, integrity, and intellectual courage. Coming from a country of broad opportunities, and from families (and regions) where an easy friendliness was the rule not the exception, they were both inclined to give strangers and stranger races the qualities they were proud of in themselves. And both were shocked (and Twain angered) when they did not find them. Both were Innocents, James as regards morals, Twain in culture and morals, the latter rather proud of it. The Americans, according to Twain, were crude, but honest; according to James, crude, generous-hearted, and naïve. Both men were sensitive to the affronts of moral innocence by the agelong injustices and the special privileges of the Old World. Mark was stirred to satiric wrath; James, more subtly aware and discriminating, made this innocence and its reactions the drama of his international stories. We are still "innocents," it is said, in our relations with the rest of the world when it does not accept our code. At bottom it is the result of two centuries of relative isolation from regions overseas that still surprise us by not thinking and feeling just as we do.

Between Twain and James, the contrast is more striking, if not more important, than the comparison. For example, one of the reasons that they are so valuable in American literature is that they come from two very different Americas that are contemporary. Mark's frontier culture of the Mississippi is a young civilization. The East of Poe, Emerson, Hawthorne, Melville, Thoreau, later James, is no longer a young country, though both East and West are branches from the same parent stem, and feed from the same roots. Mark's almost complete absence of an artistic conscience, except in language, his technique which is almost entirely oral, like a teller of tall tales or a balladist, are both aspects of cultural youth. Henry James even in his own youth was not young in this respect, nor were his Eastern predecessors mentioned above. Even Walt Whitman, who thought of frontiersmen but lived in Brooklyn, labored over a conscious art of which Twain seemed incapable. Our two men, so indubitably American in their conditioning environments, are as diversely representative as South Carolina and California.

The contrast is as great in the qualities of their work, both in subject and in art. For both, the survival values are, I think, very high, but not alike. Mark will live, I believe, chiefly by his best books, Henry James eventually most by his books as influence. *Huckleberry Finn,* for instance, has such validity as a unique portrait of a time and a personality that it might conceivably outlast the name of its author. "Was it Clemens, or

Twain? — what difference!" Not that Twain was without influence. He was probably more responsible than any other
author for the cult of youth that grew so strongly through the
nineteenth century. Yet this historical and psychological importance can scarcely equal the literary value of his masterpieces.

Henry James can never be like that. No one of his books has
the survival value, in and by itself, of the great masters of life
in representative portraits — Dickens, Shakespeare, and in his
limited field, Twain. But James did create a cult which gives
his books a significance outweighing sometimes even their interest. It was not, as his enemies said, a cult of difficulty and
obscurity. Difficulty was his personal choice. Obscurity is the
fault of the reader who lacks, as James complained, the faculty
of attention lost by the wayside in our modern flood of print.
(Take ten per cent off this statement for Henry's vice — every
writer has his vice — of verbosity.) The true cult that Henry
founded was the cult of awareness. We have become sensitive,
and largely through James and his followers, to depths and
complications in quite usual courses of living where earlier
novelists have been either unperceptive or blind. James has
educated his readers and imitators in *seeing,* much as the psychologists and phychiatrists have educated us in *explaining,*
new aspects of behavior. And it should be said that it was the
literary man, and especially, in our times, Henry James who saw
them first. In this his scope was broader than that of Proust.
Awareness, intense, subtle, sympathetic, and unrelenting, has
been Henry James' gift to the art of the novel.

My old teacher, Thomas Raynesford Lounsbury, one of the
great scholars of the nineteenth century, once said, with a
familiar gesture, through his gray beard, "There are two kinds
of great poets. One writes and rewrites, like Wordsworth or
Tennyson, piling up corrections; and the other seems, as Ben

Jonson said of Shakespeare, never to blot a line." "And one kind," said Lounsbury, "is just as good as the other!"

I would not be as impartial as this. Nor was Lounsbury, who when he came to teach, visibly warmed to the sculptured and carefully polished couplets of the seventeenth and eighteenth centuries. Nor can Twain and James be placed easily in such general categories as the labored and the fluent. If either man was fluent it was the infinitely plodding James, and if either man left rewritings and corrections of his works, it was the supposedly so spontaneous Twain. I would merely say that every great writer has his own values for which his methods are means of making articulate. It is for the good reader to give both the attention for which James begged, in order to search them out and make them his own.

THE END

BIBLIOGRAPHY
INDEX

A Reader's Bibliography of the Books Chiefly Used in the Preparation of this Work

FOR MARK TWAIN

Andrews, Kenneth Richmond, *Nook Farm, Mark Twain's Hartford Circle* (Cambridge, Harvard University Press, 1950).

Brooks, Van Wyck, *The Ordeal of Mark Twain* (New York, E. P. Dutton & Co., 1920, 1933).

Clemens, Clara, *My Father, Mark Twain* (New York and London, Harper and Brothers, 1931).

Clemens, Samuel Langhorne (Mark Twain), *Definitive Edition, The Writings of Mark Twain* (New York, Gabriel Wells, 1923). This edition of Mark Twain's works contains Albert Bigelow Paine's biography (listed separately below). This is a de luxe edition.

——, *The Writings of Mark Twain*, the Stormfield Edition (New York and London, Harper and Brothers, 1929). The plates for this edition are identical with the *Definitive Edition* above. In thirty-seven volumes.

——, *Mark Twain, Business Man*, edited by Samuel Charles Webster (Boston, Little, Brown and Company, 1946). Correspondence concerning an important side of Mark Twain's life.

——, *Mark Twain in Eruption*, hitherto unpublished pages about men and events, by Mark Twain, edited with an introduction by Bernard DeVoto (New York and London, Harper and Brothers, 1940).

——, *The Love Letters of Mark Twain*, edited by Dixon Wecter (New York, Harper and Brothers, 1949).

——, *Mark Twain's Notebook*, with comments by Albert Bigelow Paine (New York, Harper and Brothers, 1935).

——, *The Portable Mark Twain*, edited by Bernard DeVoto (New York, The Viking Press, 1946).

NOTE: There are, of course, many editions of separate books by Mark Twain and numerous sets in addition to the listing above.

DeVoto, Bernard, *Mark Twain at Work* (Cambridge, Harvard University Press, 1942).

——, *Mark Twain's America* (Boston, Little, Brown and Company, 1932, 1935).

Ferguson, John De Lancey, *Mark Twain: Man and Legend* (New York, Bobbs-Merrill Company, 1943).

Howells, William Dean, *My Mark Twain* (New York and London, Harper and Brothers, 1910).

Lawton, Mary, *A Lifetime with Mark Twain* (New York, Harcourt, Brace and Company, 1925).

Paine, Albert Bigelow, *Mark Twain, A Biography,* 3 vols. (New York and London, Harper and Brothers, 1912).

Paine, Albert Bigelow, *Mark Twain's Autobiography,* 2 vols. (New York and London, Harper and Brothers, 1924).

Spiller, Robert E., Willard Thorp, Thomas H. Johnson, Henry S. Canby, *Literary History of the United States* (New York, The Macmillan Company, 1948).

FOR HENRY JAMES

Bosanquet, Theodora, *Henry James at Work* (London, L. and V. Woolf, The Hogarth Press, 1924).

Brooks, Van Wyck, *The Pilgrimage of Henry James* (New York, E. P. Dutton and Co., 1925).

Dupee, Frederick W., *Henry James* (New York, W. Sloane, 1951).

——, *The Question of Henry James;* a collection of critical essays on James by various hands (New York, H. Holt and Co., 1945).

Grattan, Clinton Hartley, *The Three Jameses* (London, Longmans, Green and Company, 1932).

James, Henry, *Novels and Tales,* The New York Edition (New York, Charles Scribner's Sons, 1907–1917).

——, *Novels and Stories,* New and Complete Edition (London, Macmillan and Company, Ltd., 1921–23).

——, *The American Novels and Stories of Henry James,* edited with an introduction by F. O. Matthiessen (New York, Alfred A. Knopf, 1947).

——, *The Art of Fiction,* with an introduction by Morris Roberts (New York, Oxford University Press, 1948).

——, *The Art of the Novel; Critical Prefaces.* With an introduction by Richard P. Blackmur (New York, Charles Scribner's Sons, 1934).

——, *The Complete Plays of Henry James,* edited by Leon Edel (Philadelphia and New York, J. B. Lippincott Company, 1949).

——, *The Great Short Novels of Henry James,* edited with an introduction and comments by Philip Rahv (New York, Dial Press, 1944).

——, *The Letters of Henry James,* selected and edited by Percy Lubbock (New York, Charles Scribner's Sons, 1920).

——, *The Middle Years* (New York, Charles Scribner's Sons, 1917).

——, *The Notebooks of Henry James,* edited by F. O. Matthiessen and Kenneth B. Murdock (New York, Oxford University Press, 1947).

——, *Notes of a Son and Brother* (London, Macmillan and Company, Ltd., 1914).

——, *The Scenic Art,* notes on acting and the drama, 1872–1901, edited with an introduction and notes by Allan Wade and a foreword by Leon Edel (New Brunswick, Rutgers University Press, 1948; also, London, Hart-Davis, 1949).

——, *The Short Stories of Henry James,* selected and edited with an introduction by Clifton Fadiman (New York, Random House, 1945).

——, *A Small Boy and Others* (New York, Charles Scribner's Sons, 1913).

James, William, *The Letters of William James,* edited by his son, Henry James (Boston, The Atlantic Monthly Press, 1920; also, Little, Brown and Company, 1926).

Lubbock, Percy, *Portrait of Edith Wharton* (New York, D. Appleton-Century Company, 1947).

Matthiessen, Francis Otto, *Henry James, the Major Phase* (London, Oxford University Press, 1944).

——, *The James Family* (New York, Alfred A. Knopf, 1947).

Perry, Ralph Barton, *The Thought and Character of William James,* as revealed in unpublished correspondence and notes together with his unpublished writings (Boston, Little, Brown and Company, 1935).

Spiller, Robert E., Willard Thorp, Thomas H. Johnson, Henry S. Canby, *Literary History of the United States* (New York, The Macmillan Company, 1948).

Wharton, Edith, *A Backward Glance* (New York, London, D. Appleton-Century Company, 1934).

Index